GROUP COUNSELING

First published in 1979, *Group Counseling* has consistently been a widely used and praised text, providing both novice and experienced counselors with a framework from which to expand their group counseling skills and knowledge. This fifth edition has been thoroughly revised and updated to reflect the newest work in the field, the 2009 CACREP standards, and the Association for Specialists in Group Work practice standards. As in the previous editions, the authors draw upon their extensive experience and share their own styles of leading groups as a personal and practical way to illustrate the differences in group leadership.

Berg, Landreth, and Fall present a thorough discussion of the rationale for using group counseling with an emphasis on the group's role as a preventive environment and as a setting for self-discovery. The authors examine the group facilitator's internal frame of reference and ways to overcome initial anxiety about leading groups, and they also explore typical problems in the development, facilitation, and termination of the group process and provide suggested solutions. Application of group counseling is considered with children, adolescents, adults, and the elderly, as well as with special populations, such as abused children, juvenile offenders, and individuals with emotional difficulties. A helpful glossary of group counseling terminology provides a quick reference source for important terms.

New to this edition are

- a chapter on diversity and social justice in group work
- an expanded chapter on co-leadership, a topic often ignored in other group counseling texts
- separate chapters on group work with children and group work with adolescents so that readers can focus more easily on the unique aspects of working with each population
- a chapter on evaluating groups at the leader, group, and individual member levels.

A collection of supplemental resources are available online to benefit both instructors and students. Instructors will find PowerPoint slides and test banks to aid in conducting their courses, and students can access questions for thought and reflection to supplement their review of the chapters in the text. These materials can be accessed at www.routledgementalhealth.com/cw/Berg

Robert C. Berg, EdD, is Professor Emeritus at the University of North Texas and Adjunct Professor at Southern Methodist University.

Garry L. Landreth, EdD, is Regents Professor and founding Director of the Center for Play Therapy at the University of North Texas.

Kevin A. Fall, PhD, is Associate Professor of Counseling and Program Coordinator in the Department of Counseling, Leadership, Adult Education, and School Psychology at Texas State University—San Marcos.

GROUP COUNSELING

Concepts and Procedures

Fifth Edition

Robert C. Berg, Garry L. Landreth, and Kevin A. Fall

Routledge
Taylor & Francis Group

NEW YORK AND LONDON

Please visit the Companion Website at www.routledgementalhealth.com/cw/Berg

This edition published 2013
by Routledge
711 Third Avenue, New York, NY 10017

Simultaneously published in the UK
by Routledge
27 Church Road, Hove, East Sussex BN3 2FA

Routledge is an imprint of the Taylor & Francis Group, an informa
business

First edition published by Routledge 1979

Fourth edition published by Routledge 2006

Library of Congress Cataloging in Publication Data
Berg, Robert C., 1938–
    Group counseling: concepts and procedures/Robert C. Berg, Garry A.
    Landreth, and Kevin A. Fall—Fifth Edition.
    pages cm
    Includes bibliographical references and index.
    1. Group counseling. I. Landreth, Garry L. II. Fall, Kevin A. III. Title.
    BF637.C6B442 2013
    158′.35—dc23   2012029650

ISBN: 978-0-415-53291-4 (pbk)
ISBN: 978-0-415-95681-1 (ebk)
ISBN: 978-0-415-64482-2 (pack)

Typeset in Garamond Three
by Florence Production Ltd, Stoodleigh, Devon

Printed and bound in the United States of America
by Edwards Brothers, Inc.

CONTENTS

PREFACE

We continue to believe that groups offer a unique format for interpersonal exploration and growth and that the "success" of the group is most likely related to the skill and competency level of the group leader. Through our years of teaching, practice, supervision, joint lectures, and group demonstrations, we have attempted to discuss and evaluate group methods, theories, and procedures—always with a profound respect for and fascination with the powerful intervention that we call group. We hope that our own development as group facilitators is reflected in this present volume as we attempt to address and share some of the topics that continue to grow out of our personal observations and research.

The purpose of this book is to provide encouragement to the beginning group counselor, to furnish support for the efforts of the practicing group facilitator, and, hopefully, to contribute to the stimulation of both through the presentation of ideas and practices that we have found helpful in our work with groups in a number of different settings. The potential group leader should find this book especially helpful when initiating a counseling group as well as anticipating some of the practical group problems that can be expected throughout the working life and ending stages of the group.

Our intention is for this text to serve as a primary resource in traditional courses in group counseling. In addition, we feel that this book can be used as a method of acquainting the reader with group counseling concepts and procedures in survey courses for human service providers in the fields of counseling, psychology, social work, rehabilitation, and sociology. The social impact of group work has become increasingly apparent as we begin the twenty-first century. Professional practitioners in educational settings and the many community social agencies will need to extend and validate their knowledge, skills, and competencies as experts in the application of group dynamics in their work.

In many ways, this is a very personal book in that we have insisted upon maintaining contact with the direct clinical aspects of group work rather than simply treating it as a theoretical intervention system. We continue to do groups as well as to teach and speculate about them. As such, our intent has been to present more than a cookbook or how-to manual but rather a sharing of some of our deeply held convictions and personal experiences that have helped shape us not only as group leaders but also as persons. It is our firmly held belief that those two things are virtually inseparable.

Remarks that James Muro made about group counseling in the first edition of this text are still pertinent. Because questions he raised about the field of group counseling have been an impetus for exploration in this current text, we have chosen to include Muro's original remarks:

> While numerous authors have attempted to define group counseling in contrast to the more clearly established procedures labeled group guidance and group therapy, these attempts, though well meaning, generally have neither provided

the clarity nor delineated the competencies that are required of a professional group counselor. Certainly this gap is not because of lack of interest. Interest alone, however, does not provide the counselor/educator or practicing counselor with answers to the basic questions that are essential for complete professionalization.

Why, for example, should a process so personal and intimate as counseling be conducted in a group meeting? How does one delineate the thin line between group counseling and group therapy? How can the consumers of this process, the children and adults of our nation, have faith in what counselors profess when the counselors themselves are ill-prepared to provide evidence that the graduates of training programs are competent to deal with the sensitive issues that arise in the world of small group life? What must group counselors do? What must they know? Who should they be?

Readers of this book are provided with responses to the basic concerns of the group counseling process. The "why" of group counseling is explored and defended in understandable, humanistic terms. One can initiate a personal philosophy of group counseling from this overview. Philosophical considerations, however, represent only the tip of the group counseling iceberg.

Readers, once oriented, can follow a developmental program of skills necessary to become active group leaders. The dynamics of groups are outlined clearly and the mechanics of organizing and maintaining a group are presented.

Following, listed in concise, summary form, are what we consider to be some of the singular attributes of this book:

- a thorough discussion of the rationale for using group counseling with emphasis on the group providing a preventive environment, a setting for self-discovery, an opportunity to redefine self, and the development of interpersonal awareness;
- an insightful look into our personalities as manifested in our differing approaches to the development of a theoretical approach to working with groups;
- practical suggestions on the skills needed for effective facilitation of groups;
- an examination of the group facilitator's internal frame of reference and the overcoming of initial group leader anxiety;
- a rare look at Carl Rogers' personal feelings about group members as shared by Rogers;
- detailed guidelines for forming a counseling group and accomplishing the difficult task of facilitating the early stages of development with emphasis on encouraging interaction and member responsibility;
- an exploration of typical problems in the developing group process with suggested solutions that facilitate group cohesiveness;
- a description of frequently encountered issues in group counseling related to structuring, and an analysis of the practical application of structuring;
- a thorough exploration of potential problems related to termination of a counseling group with recommended procedures for termination, evaluation, and follow-up;
- an insightful and practical examination of the application of group counseling procedures with children, adolescents, adults, and the elderly;
- a helpful glossary of group counseling terminology that provides both beginning and advanced practitioners with a quick reference source for important terms;
- topical presentation of group counseling with abused children, juvenile offenders, and individuals with chronic diseases, emotional difficulties, and addictive behaviors.

In addition to the specific strengths listed above, this fifth edition of *Group Counseling: Concepts and Procedures* provides graduate students and practitioners meaningful material in the following significant areas, which contribute to the uniqueness of this fifth edition and help to make it a very user-friendly text:

- a new chapter on diversity and social justice in group work, which highlights the major issues of being a competent group worker in a pluralistic society;
- an expanded section of the use of theory in groups which still includes each author's approach to integrating theory into practice;
- a reworking and reorganization of the chapters on leadership to make the concepts and key elements clear;
- an in-depth focus on the planning and implementation process of beginning a group, taking the reader through the process of starting a group from the idea stage through the first session;
- an expanded chapter devoted to co-leadership, which stands out in its coverage of co-leadership—a topic that is often ignored by other group counseling texts;
- a new chapter on evaluating groups at the leader, group and individual member levels.

Group work with children and group work with adolescents each have their own chapters now, enabling the reader to focus more on the unique aspects of working with each population.

Robert C. Berg
Garry L. Landreth
Kevin A. Fall

1

RATIONALE AND HISTORY
OF GROUP COUNSELING

Things come in kinds; people come in groups.

Chinese proverb

Group procedures in counseling and psycho-education have long been considered and used by counselors as an expedient method for meeting the needs of increasing client loads. Although efficiency in terms of saving counselor time often has been considered a major attraction of group counseling, research has shown that the use of groups for various educational and counseling functions provides advantages other than expediency (Erford 2011). Group counseling programs can provide individuals with the kinds of group experiences that help them learn to function effectively, to develop tolerance to stress and anxiety, and to find satisfaction in working and living with others (Gazda et al. 2001).

What advantages within the group experience are possible for members? What are the unique features and values of the experience? Logically, a rationale for group counseling should be understood clearly before counselors attempt this approach. Counselors are unlikely to be effective if they do not understand the process they are attempting to facilitate. The following concepts and dynamics illustrate group's unique approach to the process of change.

Preventive Environment

Taxed by large client loads and faced with escalating demands on their time and talents, counselors must continually evaluate their current methods of meeting increasing demands and seek to investigate and appraise new approaches. As counseling programs expand, counselors will have to become innovators in order to cope with increasing demands. Adoption or incorporation of new approaches, however, is never justified simply on the basis of expediency.

Most counselors in an educational setting, and almost always in agency environments, concentrate on those clients who seek assistance *after* they have developed emotional or academic difficulties. For many students, emotional or adjustment problems predispose them to develop maladaptive study habits and poor attitudes toward academic work that, in turn, lead to lack of achievement, to rejection of a teacher's authority, and often to rejection of authority in society. Such students often leave school (drop out) with a psychological predisposition to be hyper-resistant; that is, they tend to react to the offerings of society with a mental set characterized by the expectation of rejection.

Counseling should be preventive and developmental with an emphasis on therapeutic prevention of emotional or adjustment problems in students. The prevention of maladaptive academic habits and attitudes that may stem from such problems would enable more students to acquire the educational experiences necessary in order for them to make positive contributions to self and society.

The trend toward the application of group-counseling procedures in meeting the needs of individuals is likely to grow, stimulated by greater acceptance of this preventive approach to problems encountered and by increased recognition of the effectiveness of group counseling. Sufficient research and experience with group-counseling procedures have accumulated to support the use of this approach as a part of the process of helping individuals to grow. As a result of extensive research and experience in group counseling, Erford (2011) commented on the empirical and anecdotal support of group effectiveness, and numerous quantitative and qualitative research articles demonstrated the effectiveness of group work with a wide variety of clientele (Baker et al. 2009; Burlingame et al. 2003; Shen and Armstrong 2008; Steen 2011).

Opportunity for Self-Discovery

> When Man is placed within the context of a group, he cannot continue to rely only upon himself for a view of himself. Through the process of group interaction he comes in contact with the group's perception of what he is or what he purports to be. Thus, it is within the context of the group that Man gains a greater self awareness. He is confronted with the perceptions of others rather than relying solely upon a subjective perception of himself. The catalytic nature of the group's reaction brings Man to consider other perceptions of himself as well. It is only in light of this more refined awareness of self, provided by group interaction, that Man is able to gain a more complete awareness of his substance; and it is this more enriched concept of himself that enables Man to release his full positive potential to society.
>
> (Cohn 1967: 1)

Inherent in the preceding statement is the theory of an adequate self-concept and the significance of the group to individuals and their self-awareness. Utilizing the advantages provided by the group, group counseling provides an accepting climate in which members can test new and more effective ways of behaving. The process facilitates each member in discovering a new self and in revealing it to others.

The implications of this discussion for the educational system, as well as others, can be seen when one recognizes that individuals behave in terms of the self-concepts they possess. Even an individual's level of aspiration is a function of the kinds of self-concepts he or she holds.

As early as 1945, Lecky pointed out that children who are not considered bright by their parents, and who have, therefore, come to see themselves as stupid or incapable of learning, hold to this concept when they go to school. A given phenomenal self perpetuates itself by permitting only such perceptions as are consistent with its already existing structure. Rogers (1967) said in effect that the fundamental urge underlying all behavior was the need to preserve and enhance the phenomenal self. A tendency exists for individuals to regard themselves in certain, fairly consistent ways and to behave in such ways as will maintain their view of themselves.

Group counseling provides the individual with an opportunity to explore behavior patterns that may be the result of a limiting self-concept. Although many may provide lip service, few counseling programs have the development of positive self-concepts as one of their *major* functions. Because every individual experiences personal problems, group counseling can be utilized as a developmental approach for all students, not just problem cases.

Discovering Others

For those individuals who feel threatened by a one-to-one counseling relationship, the group provides a degree of anonymity, and the individual within the group can feel less conspicuous and "on the spot." When group members feel anxious and fearful, they may withdraw verbally from the interaction but still be very much involved in the group through the experience of other members. Thus, their withdrawal is not total.

Whether verbally active or inactive, group members discover that their problems are not unique to themselves and begin to feel less different, unwanted, and alone. They begin to relax and to be less defensive as they perceive themselves to be less isolated. The most terrifying part of working through developmental problems is the feeling of isolation and loneliness that comes from the delusion that no one else has ever experienced the same difficulties. This feeling is especially true of adolescents. However, when individuals discover through the process of group interaction that other members also have problems, a feeling of empathy and belonging begins to develop even if the problems shared are different (Kline 2003).

Realizing that personal problems are common is a process that helps group members to admit their own problems to full awareness and to deal with them in the context of a caring relationship. Thus, members' problems are no longer unique to them, and they discover that others share their journey.

Redefining Self

Individuals function most of their lives within groups. Against this background of interaction with others, one's self-concept is formed and oftentimes distorted. A distorted perception of self and self in relation to others often occurs in the dynamics of the family group relationship. Seemingly, then, the most effective place for dealing with adjustment difficulties is within a group relationship that incorporates the basic structure that originally created the difficulty.

Through the process of the group-counseling relationship, the group member discovers the meaning of giving and receiving emotional support and understanding in a different and more positive sort of way. Perception of self then can be redefined in a context similar to that which initially resulted in the distortion. The ongoing groups can recapitulate the family of origin and possibly provide the venue for a "corrective emotional experience."

Pistole (1997) outlined working through such distortions from an attachment theory perspective. Bowlby (1988) postulated that individuals' primary attachment behavior is mediated through a "working model" that is constructed between parent and child. The goal of group counseling, then, becomes to help clarify each member's attachment behavior and the distortions involved. The primary benefit of group counseling is the feedback from multiple sources and the opportunity to modify one's working model and form different, more healthy or secure attachments (Pistole).

Developing Interpersonal Awareness

Most problems are basically social and interpersonal in nature. Within the group-counseling relationship, members can identify with others and develop understanding into their own difficulties by observing the behavior of others. The group provides immediate opportunity for discovering new and more satisfying ways of relating to people. When individuals begin to feel safe, understood, and accepted, they will attempt social contact at greater feeling-oriented levels and in effect will try out new behaviors. Group members then are confronted with interpersonal relationships that provide feedback. Through this experience, individuals recognize and experience the possibility of change.

Immediate opportunity is thus afforded group members to test the effectiveness of their ability to relate to people and to improve their skills in interpersonal relationships. For some individuals, having peer group members present has a facilitating effect on their social behavior. To see and hear another person extending him or herself openly in an attempt to better understand self may encourage the cautious member to attempt similar behavior. When one person talks openly and honestly about feelings and attitudes denied in other social situations, the effect upon others may be contagious. In a group-counseling relationship, feelings and attitudes about self and others are examined in an immediate situation as the group brings into focus the individual's adequacy or inadequacy for social and interpersonal skills.

Reality Testing Laboratory

The group itself provides an immediate, firsthand opportunity for the group members to change their perceptions and to practice more mature social living. Since emotional difficulties and maladaptive behaviors that are not physiologically based often result from disturbances in interpersonal relationships, the group offers the most appropriate situation for their correction by providing an opportunity for reality testing.

Each member in a group counseling relationship is provided with multiple stimuli to work through problems or difficulties in a situation that more closely approximates the real-life situation. Yalom (2005) referred to the group as a matrix for reality. The group represents immediate social reality and enables members to test their behavior. In effect the group serves as a practice field in which members may become aware of their own feelings, how they feel and act toward others, and how others perceive and act toward them.

Group structure within a group-counseling relationship becomes an extremely flexible reality-testing base. In the larger society, individuals encounter rather rigid and fixed structural demands which are inhibiting factors in their striving for self-discovery and change. The flexibility experienced in the counseling group, which can be viewed as an immediate mini-society, is a freeing agent to individuals, providing an opportunity to experiment in their own way with reality as perceived by them. This exploring behavior is fostered by the absence of anxiety resulting from fear of punishment.

Experiencing Significant Relationships

In our society children learn at an early age that to withhold, repress, and deny awareness of feelings and emotions are considered appropriate behaviors. Consequently children do not know how to deal with their own feelings, to express themselves in a feeling or caring sort of way, or to respond to others out of the depth of their emotions. Within the safety of the group the individual, in the process of becoming less defensive, begins to experience fully, at an emotional level, another person, initially the counselor, who exhibits a kind of helping behavior unlike that which the individual has encountered previously.

The significant relationships that develop within the group are the basic contributors to behavioral change. Group members come to function not just as counselees but also as a combination of counselees at times in the sessions and at other times as helpers or therapists. Through the process of this experience, group members seem to learn to be better helpers or member-therapists. Although members may absorb some of the leader's attitudes and thus learn from the leader, helping behavior can emerge only after group members have made progress themselves in counseling. Therefore, giving help is basically within the person and not external to the individual.

A general agreement is that in a group-counseling relationship, group members learn to give as well as receive help. Unlike individual counseling, where the information flow and care are in one direction, in group, the information and direction of care comprise a multidirectional matrix, where each member participates in the giving and receiving of help. Experiencing the reality of being helpful to another person is especially growth-promoting to an individual who has felt worthless and rejected.

Dynamic Pressure for Growth

In the group-counseling relationship, a compulsion to improve is present. This drive toward sanity and health is so strong that groups "push" members toward normalcy. Group pressure to change or improve can be viewed as originating in the verbal interaction with other members that helps to reveal to members the inadequacies in their self-image and the distortions in their views of others. Within this pressured system, group members are often able to observe other members' behavior, give feedback, and thus encourage others to comment on their behavior. The feedback system provides impetus for growth. This pressure to move forward in a positive direction is a creative force that encourages members to move away from defensiveness and rationalization toward specific personal sharing that is for many members a new way of being.

Supportive Environment

As group members assist in the helping relationship, they realize the worth of human relations and feel less helpless and defensive. Experiencing the reality of being understood by others reduces barriers, and defense mechanisms become less acute. Group members then are encouraged to deal with their problems because they feel accepted and supported by the group. This process of being understood and accepted by others as a worthy person results in the group member beginning to view him- or herself in a more positive way, to perceive self as being worthwhile and acceptable. This change in self-image results in more positive kinds of behavior.

Experiences of trusting and being trusted can be extremely effective in meeting the needs of alienated individuals whose fears of our manipulative society have forced them to withdraw or to adopt maladaptive behavior patterns. The group provides an anchor to reality and a feedback system through which group members learn that different people will react to them in different ways.

Limitations of Group Counseling

Although group counseling has many inherent advantages and is often the preferred mode of counseling, the beginning group facilitator should be aware of the natural limitations to the effectiveness of counseling groups. Every person does not feel safe in a group, and consequently certain individuals may not be ready to invest emotionally in the group experience. To think that everyone will profit from group counseling would be a mistake. Some individuals just naturally feel more comfortable and safe in one-to-one relationships and will readily explore very personal issues they would be most reluctant to even mention in a group. Other individuals may be too angry or hostile to benefit from the therapeutic factors in a group.

Age also must be considered to be a limitation in that wide age ranges usually should be avoided when determining group composition, especially for groups involving children and teenagers. Children younger than age five usually do not possess the social and interactive skills necessary for most typical counseling groups to be effective. Even the most experienced play therapist often finds working with this age group in group play therapy to be a very trying experience.

Some individuals may use counseling groups as a place to hide. They go from emotional high to emotional high in various groups and seem not to be able to generate openness and emotional intensity outside the group in day-to-day relationships involving spouse, children, friends, or working relationships. They experience being cared for and appreciated in the group, and instead of transferring such experiences outside the group, they seek out other groups and begin the process again. For such individuals, the group is primarily a place to ventilate with no real focus on change or growth.

A particular type of counseling group may be appropriate for one person but not for another. Potential members who may not be ready for or suited to groups are those who show extremes in behavior that will sap the group's energy and interfere with forming close emotional relationships. Individuals who are verbal monopolizers, sociopaths, overly aggressive, extremely hostile or self-absorbed should probably be placed in individual counseling. Individuals who are out of touch with reality are not likely to benefit from counseling groups.

Types of Groups

In 2007, the Association for Specialists in Group Work (ASGW) delineated four distinct types of groups based on group goals, characteristics, and leader roles. These four types are task, psychoeducational, counseling, and psychotherapeutic. Deciding which type of group is appropriate is an important first step in creating a functional group. Each group, and its corresponding elements can be found in Table 1.1.

Basic Elements of Group Facilitation

The basic principles of a group discussion approach are essential in conducting counseling groups. The extent to which the group facilitator is sensitive to the needs of group members will be reflected in what the facilitator does to help members achieve a place of esteem for themselves in the group. Individuals value themselves more when they are responded to in ways that grant responsibility and convey respect for the person and a valuing of potential contributions. Whether the topic or focus of the group is content, feelings, or both, a group-discussion format allows individuals to experience the power of their own unique contribution in the peer relationship.

Individuals learn best when they become involved as participating and contributing members to the group. The question for the facilitator of the group, then, is "How can I help and encourage members to participate in the discussion?" Too often, members do not express their thoughts and questions simply because they are not encouraged to do so. If the topic selected by the facilitator or the group is to have personal meaning to the members, they must be encouraged to interact with the discussion or material and helped to make a practical application to their own personal world.

The key to this approach is the utilization of personally focused questions or reflections by the facilitator that helps members of the group relate to points brought out in the discussion to themselves. If what is being discussed and a responsive, responsible way of

Table 1.1 Group typology

Type of group	Group goal	Leader role	Size	Examples
Task group	Specific, measurable goal Improve efficiency in an established process	Facilitate agenda and goal setting Help move the group to the achievement of the specified goal Keep group focus May also provide organizational assessment and evaluation	12–15 members	Any committee Most meetings (i.e. faculty meetings)
Psycho-educational group	Remediate an identified skills deficit	Identify the skills deficit and set curriculum to address the deficit Impart new information and allow the group to process the integration of the new skills	12–18 (any larger and it may be difficult to process)	Parenting groups Skills for Living groups Interpersonal violence prevention groups Girl Power groups
Counseling group	Prevention, personal growth, inter- and intrapersonal awareness	Facilitate here-and-now interaction to illuminate inter- and intrapersonal patterns	8–12 members	Any process or person growth group that does not focus on a skills deficit
Psycho-therapeutic group	Remediate in-depth psychological problems and disorders	Explore and reconstruct problematic personality patterns Often works with multidisciplinary team for management of chronic conditions	8–10 members	Most groups in psychiatric hospitals and outpatient agencies May focus on one type of disorder (i.e. mood disorders)

life are to become relevant to members, they must be assisted in their struggle to explore their own personal world rather than given a hurry-up approach with the answers supplied by the leader. Questions or reflections that help group members to explore and to derive new meanings also help them to learn how to explore critically when they are outside the group. For the majority of members, the process of learning how to do something for themselves may be just as important as learning what the answers are supposed to be.

Contrary to popular opinion, most individuals are seeking a better understanding of themselves. When allowed to express their concerns, they reveal a desire to understand their own beliefs and attitudes. Understanding, however, is not something that can be given. Understanding results from the individual's own unique struggle to discover, to derive meaning.

How, though, can the facilitator know what the members of the group need to know or about what they are puzzled? The answer to these questions will emerge and the dynamics of a discussion approach will be facilitated by helping individuals to fulfill the following seven needs as group members.

1. Each Member Needs to Feel Important and Worthwhile

The facilitator can help by making certain everyone gets a chance to talk, to state ideas, and to be heard. Some members can be helped to participate by calling on them when they look as though they would like to talk but have not, or when other members keep interrupting or will not let the member "get in." The important action is for the facilitator to show interest in each member. Each member's contribution deserves equal consideration. The facilitator might respond to these situations by saying, "Norma, you seem to be thinking about something; could you share it with us?" Or, "Bob has something to say but he keeps getting cut off. Let's give everyone a chance."

2. Each Member Needs to Experience a Sense of Belonging and Acceptance

No place exists for "favorites" in group counseling. Each member wants to be wanted. The facilitator should avoid depending on certain members for answers or suggestions. Each member wants to feel needed. The facilitator can help by showing genuine interest in what each member has to say. Members know they belong when others show they are wanted in the group.

3. Each Member Needs to Feel Understood

The facilitator can help by restating or repeating what a member or several members have said when the group seems to be confused. Understanding another person implies that you give that person your full attention and listen so carefully that you can restate what that person has said to his or her satisfaction. Listen with the speaker, and try to understand how he or she "sees" the problem or situation. Even when the facilitator does not understand completely, to try to restate as much as possible so the speaker can fill in the gaps is helpful. Another approach would be to ask another member to explain what he or she thinks the speaker has said. Through observing the facilitator, other group members can learn how to listen, to understand, and to let the speaker know they understand. We only know someone understands us when they communicate their understanding to us. Therefore, a rule of thumb for the group might be that a member who speaks is always responded to by someone in the group.

4. Each Member Needs to Understand the Purpose of the Group or Topic of Discussion

The facilitator's role is to help group members to understand "what we are here for." The facilitator can help members to understand more fully by asking them to state what they think is the purpose of the group. The facilitator could ask, "What do you think the purpose of the discussion is for us?" Or, "How could learning more about this be helpful to you?" Wait for responses to such questions. At times, the facilitator may need to call on a member who has not spoken. However, for everyone to participate verbally each session is not necessary. As members hear other's ideas, new purposes that they had not thought of will begin to emerge.

5. Each Member Needs to Share in the Decision Making of the Group

What the group does should involve every member in some way. Sometimes the group may need the facilitator's help in resisting one or two members who try to push their ideas and force the group to agree with them. In such situations, the facilitator can help by saying,

"Marilyn, you and Beth are pushing hard to get the group to agree with you, but some members don't really seem eager to do so. How do the rest of you feel about this?"

6. Each Member Needs to Feel That the Group or Topic Will Be Helpful, That It Is Worth the Effort

The facilitator can help by asking members to tell the person on their right one specific way in which they think the group or topic could help that person or something they think would be helpful for that person to learn about self. The idea is to help each other to discover something worthwhile in the experience.

7. Each Member Should Be Able to See the Face of Other Members

An effective group discussion cannot be carried on if everyone is seated in rows. Arrange the chairs in a circle. Allowing people to face each other is psychologically conducive to interpersonal interaction and is, therefore, basic to the group-discussion approach. Such an arrangement stimulates participants to communicate with other members of the group and not just to the authority figure at the front of the room.

History of Group Counseling

Throughout this text, we take the position that group counseling is a unique intervention system that differs significantly from those procedures that can be described as *guidance* and those therapy processes commonly referred to as *psychotherapy*. Much of the difficulty in clearly delineating the functions of these processes stems from the fact that considerable overlap exists in training of group leaders, methodologies employed, and client population served.

Another problem is that during the process of professionalization within the fields of guidance, counseling, and psychotherapy, the terms—particularly among laypersons—have been used somewhat interchangeably. Added to this problem has been a plethora of popular literature appearing regularly in widely read national weeklies concerning all kinds of groups, hence one readily can see the possibilities for misinformation. Condensed "quicky" versions of various therapeutic intervention systems that focus mainly upon "therapies" that range from highly experimental to bizarre are presented to the lay public, often accompanied by visual reinforcers in the standard three-column synopsis.

More or less on a regular basis through the media, the public is treated to nude therapy groups, EST, sensitivity training (a generic term covering the widest range of activities from offensive nonsense to well-planned, systematic, self-awareness laboratories), and primal screams. The height of this cultural grab for instant intimacy caused many practitioners and clients to view group therapy with a suspicious eye.

Major professional organizations are continuing in their attempts to define, delineate, and professionalize the counseling/therapeutic functions. The American Counseling Association (ACA), the American Psychological Association (APA), and the Association for Specialists in Group Work (ASGW) have position papers and ethical guidelines that address the many problems of small-group work.

Association for Specialists in Group Work "Best Practice Guidelines"

On March 29, 1998, the Executive Board approved the ASGW "Best Practice Guidelines." These standards are intended to complement ACA standards in the area of group work by clarifying the nature of ethical responsibility of the counselor in the group setting and by stimulating a greater concern for competent group leaders. This document and the considerable strength represented by ASGW membership constitute a major step forward in the professionalization of group work in the USA. In 2008, ASGW published a revised version of these "Best Practices" (Thomas & Pender 2008; see Appendix C).

In an attempt to help clarify what we see as counseling in a small group, we offer the following definition from the ASGW professional training standards (ASGW 2000):

> **Group Work:** is a broad professional practice involving the application of knowledge and skill in group facilitation to assist an interdependent collection of people to reach their mutual goals which may be intrapersonal, interpersonal, or work-related. The goals of the group may include the accomplishment of tasks related to work, education, personal development, personal and interpersonal problem solving, or remediation of mental and emotional disorders.
>
> (p. 328)

Early Influences

Group counseling owes its historical roots to the influence of group dynamics and to the more established procedures used in group guidance and group psychotherapy. The virtual explosion of counseling-related groups since the mid 1960s has caused professionals within the field to struggle with defining and professionalizing the concept of counseling people in groups. Some argue that intensely personal problems are better dealt with in individual counseling.

Nevertheless, groups are a natural phenomenon in human history. Forerunners of organized groups include various religious movements, drama, and morality plays. Some historians cite Mesmer's work as a precursor of group treatment. Most, however, note the "class method" work of J. H. Pratt, a Boston physician, as the beginning of scientific group treatment (Flournoy 1934) in the USA. In 1905, Pratt used a directive-teaching methodology with his tubercular patients as he instructed them in hygiene. His original intention was to boost their morale through more effective cleanliness. The method more closely resembled what we think of as guidance today. It is doubtful whether Pratt fully understood the psychological impact of his group methods, particularly in the early stages. It soon became clear that his patients were deriving more benefit from the supportive atmosphere of the group than from the information imparted in the lectures.

Somewhat later, Alfred Adler and J. L. Moreno began using group methods in Europe. Adler would counsel children in front of a group, with the primary purpose of instructing other professionals in individual counseling. Again, the observation was made that, far from interfering, the group or audience, as they asked questions and interacted, had a positive impact on the counseling. This methodology continues to be used by present-day Adlerians with the dual purpose of teaching and counseling.

Before leaving Europe to practice in the USA, J. L. Moreno used group techniques with the street people of Vienna. He worked with children, displaced persons, and prostitutes as he found them in their environments. According to Gazda (1982: 10), Moreno was "very likely the most colorful, controversial and influential person in the field of group psychotherapy . . . Moreno introduced psychodrama into the USA in 1925; in 1931 he coined the term *group therapy* and in 1932, *group psychotherapy*."

Others who have had great influence on group therapy in the USA include S. R. Slavson, who in the 1930s introduced methods later to become known as *activity group therapy*. His methods were developed with socially maladjusted children. Rudolph Dreikurs applied

Adlerian principles in his work with family groups and children in Chicago. Carl Rogers and his client-centered or phenomenological approach helped popularize group work following World War II. A shortage of adequately trained personnel and a great need for reconstructive and supportive therapy accelerated the adaptation of client-centered principles to group work with veterans.

The exact origins of group counseling are somewhat obscure, owing to influences of group psychotherapy and group dynamics. Furthermore, many of the early writers used the terms *guidance, counseling,* and *psychotherapy* interchangeably. R. D. Allen (1931) appeared to have been the first person to use the term *group counseling* in print. Close inspection, however, indicates that the methods and procedures he described are what would be referred to as *group guidance* today.

Although practitioners attempted to clarify the terms *group guidance* and *group counseling,* considerable controversy raged during the late 1930s and 1940s. Group psychotherapy moved forward in 1942, when S. R. Slavson created the American Group Psychotherapy Association (AGPA). The APGA is the longest standing group professional organization and is dedicated to an interdisciplinary exploration of group psychotherapy practice and research. The organization publishes the *International Journal for Group Psychotherapy* and oversees a clinical registry of certified group psychotherapists.

With the proliferation of group counseling procedures during the 1960s and 1970s, the argument over terminology seems to be subsiding. The professionalization of school counselors and counselors in public agencies and private practice has added credibility and acceptability to group counseling procedures.

George and Dustin (1988) wrote about the influences of group dynamics and the National Training Laboratories (NTL) movement.

In the mid 1940s, a training group in Bethel, Maine, devised a method to analyze its own behavior. The leaders of this group had worked with Kurt Lewin, a psychologist at the Massachusetts Institute of Technology who had developed the idea that training in human relations skills was an important, but overlooked, type of education in modern society. Forming shortly after Lewin's death, the group focused on experience-based learning, that is, analyzing, discussing, and trying to improve their own behavior in the group situation. Observing the nature of their interactions with others and the group process, participants believed, gave them a better understanding of their own way of functioning in a group, making them more competent in dealing with interpersonal relations. The warm, caring relationships that developed among the participants led to very deep personal change in individuals.

As a result of these group experiences and the learning that resulted, those individuals organized the NTLs, which quickly became a model for training leaders in industry and education. The major impact of NTL was a new emphasis on the process by which a group operates, rather than on content. Group leaders placed far more importance on how something was said and the effects this had on other individuals than on the words themselves. Thus, participants in the group experience were not interested in learning content but were focusing on how to learn, especially within the area of interpersonal relationships (George & Dustin 1988: 2–3).

In 1971, Gazda, Duncan, and Sisson conducted a survey of the membership of an interest group in group procedures of the American Personnel and Guidance Association. One of their purposes was to clarify the distinctions among various group procedures. Gazda (1982: 23) summarized:

> Group guidance and certain human potential-type groups are described as primarily preventive in purpose; group counseling, T-groups, sensitivity groups,

[and] encounter groups . . . are described as partially preventive, growth engendering, and remedial in purpose; group psychotherapy is described as remedial in purpose. The clientele served, degree of disturbance of the clientele, setting of the treatment, goals of treatment, size of group, and length and duration of treatment are, accordingly, reflected in the emphasis or purpose of each of these three distinctly different groupings.

Finally, George M. Gazda, J. A. Duncan, and K. E. Geoffroy founded the ASGW, a division of the American Personnel and Guidance Association. In December 1973, Gazda was appointed its first president. ASGW has been instrumental in providing a professional organization devoted to the exploration and practice of group work in its many forms. In addition to the "Best Practices" document (see Appendix B), ASGW has also written comprehensive training standards (Appendix C) and diversity competencies for group workers (see Appendix D).

Significant Historical Dates and Events

1905: J. H. Pratt, Massachusetts General Hospital in Boston, offers first formal therapeutic group experience with tubercular patients.

1907: Jesse B. Davis, Principal of Grand Rapids (Michigan) High School, requires one English class per week devoted to "Vocational and Moral Guidance." Probably the first group approach used in school guidance.

1908: Vocational Bureau of Boston opens in January with Frank Parsons as director. After the death of Parsons, staff members begin to see vocationally undecided persons in groups.

1910: Sigmund Freud introduces his theories through lectures at Clark University.

1910: Clifford Beers publishes *A Mind That Found Itself.*

1914: J. L. Moreno, under the name of J. M. Levy, publishes a philosophical paper on group methods.

1918: Progressive Education Association established.

1918: Army alpha and beta tests used with the military.

1921: Moreno forms the "Theatre of Spontaneity," which was the forerunner of psychodrama.

1922: Alfred Adler uses collective counseling with prison and child-guidance populations. Forerunner of group counseling.

1924: F. Allport: social scientists involved in the investigation of small-group phenomena.

1924: K. Gordon compares individual and small group counseling.

1927: Hawthorne Study begins, directed by Elton Mayo.

1928: G. Watson performances.

1931: R. D. Allen publishes "A Group Guidance Curriculum in the Senior High School," *Education,* 52, 189–194. First use of the term *group counseling* in the literature. He was referring to group guidance procedures. Group counseling did not emerge until the 1940s.

1931: Moreno introduces the term *group therapy.*

1932: Moreno introduces the term *group psychotherapy.* Moreno devises an early form of group treatment known as *psychodrama.* This paves the way for the emergence of group therapy and group counseling.

1935: Trigant Burrow (psychoanalytic group analysis) focuses on biological principles of group behavior, a process he labeled *phyloanalysis.*

1936: Louis Wender: psychoanalytic group model.

1936: Muzafer Sherif: sociological fieldwork studies.

1930s: Alcoholics Anonymous (AA), the first major self-help group, begins.

1939: Paul Schilder (psychoanalytic orientation) focuses on interaction between individual group members.

1940: Kurt Lewin, influential founder and promoter of group dynamics, a field theory based on Gestalt principles of part–whole relationships.

1942: American Society of Group Psychotherapy and Psychodrama (ASGPP) established by Moreno.

1942: American Group Psychotherapy Association created by S. R. Slavson.

1942: Carl R. Rogers publishes *Counseling and Psychotherapy*.

1946: Lewin organizes an intergroup relations workshop in Connecticut that leads to the formation of the National Training Laboratories (NTL) in Bethel, Maine. There originates the Basic Skills Training (BST) Group, which later evolved into the training group (t-group) movement.

1947: Moreno founds the journal *Sociatry*, which changes its name in 1949 to *Group Psychotherapy*.

1948: Wilfred Bion, Tavistock Institute of Human Relations in Great Britain: group dynamic focus on cohesiveness and forces that foster growth or regression in groups.

1949: Slavson founds the *International Journal of Group Psychotherapy*.

1950: R. F. Bales begins looking at interaction process analysis and observes stereotypical roles emerging in groups.

1951: John Bell starts conducting group therapy for families.

1951: Rudolph Driekurs starts working with parent groups.

1951: American Personnel and Guidance Association (APGA) is founded.

1954: In *Brown* v. *Board of Education*, the US Supreme Court rejects the "separate but equal" doctrine previously established by *Plessy* v. *Ferguson* (1896).

1958: National Defense Education Act (NDEA) passed.

1958: Nathan Ackerman, Gregory Bateson, and Virgina Satir (1964) modify psychoanalytic group model for work with families.

1958: Helen I. Driver writes *Counseling and Learning Through Small Group Discussion*, the first textbook published in the field of group work.

1960: Carl R. Rogers, the most influential theorist, applies his person-centered techniques to groups and coins the term *basic encounter group* while working at the Center for the Study of Persons in La Jolla, California.

1961: Jack Gibb looks at competitive versus cooperative behavior in groups.

1964: Eric Berne applies transactional analysis (TA) concepts to group work and publishes *Principles of Group Treatment* (1966).

1967: Fritz Perls, leader in human potential movement, applies Gestalt theory in numerous workshops at the Esalen Institute on the coast of California.

1967: William C. Schutz, human potential leader, stresses nonverbal touching, hugging, and experiencing in groups.

1967: George Bach: conflict resolution through fair fighting; along with Fred Stoller, describes the power and need for marathon groups.

1968: George M. Gazda assumes the leadership role for Dwight Arnold in creating an interest group through APGA specifically for practitioners interested in group work.

1970: Jane Howard writes the book *Please Touch*, chronicling her personal journey as a journalist through several of the most popular "sensitivity groups" of the period. This books helps deflect some criticism of the encounter group movement but also emphasizes the importance of professional leadership and member selection.

1970: I. D. Yalom, based on his extensive clinical experience, posits ten "curative factors" available in therapy groups.

1970: *Carl Rogers on Encounter Groups* is published.

1971: I. L. Janus coins the term *group think* to demonstrate the power that groups can have on people to conform.

1971: Yalom and M. Lieberman study encounter groups and find that aggressive, confrontive, distant leaders produce the most casualties in groups.

1971: Robert R. Carkhuff develops highly researched model called Systematic Human Resources Development/Training (HRD/T).

1973: Association for Specialists in Group Work (ASGW) is officially formed as a division of the APGA, now the American Counseling Association (ACA). With Gazda as the charter president, the association is very active in promoting training standards and ethical guidelines for group leaders.

1980: "Ethical Guidelines for Group Leaders" adopted by ASGW.

1983: "Professional Standards for Training of Group Counselors" adopted by ASGW Executive Board on March 20.

1989: "Ethical Guidelines for Group Counselors," revised and expanded version, adopted by ASGW.
1998: "Best Practice Guidelines" developed by ASGW.
1998: "Principles for Diversity-Competent Group Workers" developed by ASGW.
2000: "Professional Standards for Training of Group Workers" revised by ASGW.

References

Allen, R. D. (1931). A group guidance curriculum in the senior high school. *Education*, 52, 189–194.

ASGW (2000). ASGW professional standards for the training of group workers. *The Journal for Specialists in Group Work*, 25, 237–244.

Baker, J., Parks-Savage, A., & Rehfuss, M. (2009). Teaching social skills in a virtual environment: An exploratory study. *The Journal for Specialists in Group Work*, 34, 209–226.

Bowlby, J. (1988). *A secure base*. New York: Basic Books.

Burlingame, G. M., Fuhriman, A., & Mosier, J. (2003). The differential effectiveness of group psychotherapy: A meta-analytic perspective. *Group Dynamics: Theory, Research and Practice*, 7, 3–12.

Cohn, B. (1967). *Guidelines for future research on group counseling in the public school setting*. Washington, DC: Guidance Association.

Erford, B. T. (2011). Outcome research in group work. In B. T. Erford (Ed.), *Group work: Process and applications* (pp. 312–321). New York: Pearson.

Flournoy, H. (1934). Chief steps in psychotherapy. *Psyche*, 14, 139–159.

Gazda, G. M. (Ed.). (1982). *Basic approaches to group psychotherapy and group counseling* (3rd ed.). Springfield, IL: Thomas.

Gazda, G. M., Ginter, E. J., & Horne, A. M. (2001). *Group counseling and group psychotherapy*. Boston, MA: Allyn & Bacon.

George, G. M., & Dustin, D. (1988). *Group counseling: Theory and practice*. Englewood Cliffs, NJ: Prentice Hall.

Kline, W. B. (2003). *Interactive group counseling and therapy*. Upper Saddle River, NJ: Merrill Prentice Hall.

Lecky, P. (1945). *Self-consistency: A theory of personality*. New York: Island.

Pfeiffer, J. W., & Jones, J. E. (1972). *Annual handbook for group facilitators*. La Jolla, CA: University Associates.

Pistole, M. C. (1997). Attachment theory: Contributions to group work. *Journal for Specialists in Group Work*, 22 (1), 7–21.

Shen, Y., & Armstrong, S. (2008). Impact of group sandtray therapy on the self-esteem of young adolescent girls. *The Journal for Specialists in Group Work*, 33, 118–137.

Steen, S. (2011). Academic and personal development through group work: An exploratory study. *The Journal for Specialists in Group Work*, 36, 129–143.

Thomas, R. V., & Pender, D. A. (2008). Best practice guidelines. *The Journal for Specialists in Group Work*, 33, 111–117.

Yalom, I. D. (2005). *The theory and practice of group psychotherapy* (5th ed.). New York: Basic Books.

2

DIVERSITY AND SOCIAL JUSTICE IN GROUP WORK

Never forget that justice is what love looks like in public.

Cornel West

Well, I could be wrong, but I believe diversity is an old, old wooden ship that was used during the Civil War era.

Ron Burgundy

The issue of diversity in group work has received mixed attention over the past several decades. Merta (1995) reported that Kurt Lewin's work to decrease racial tensions seemed to be the first concerted effort to apply group work to issues of diversity but also noted that this strand of inquiry and application largely disappeared after Lewin's death. In the early 1990s, group work once again focused on the issues of diversity as the mental-health field become more interested in the growing pluralist nature of our society (DeLucia-Waack 1996; Patterson 1996). In 1999, the Association for Specialists in Group Work approved *The Principles for Diversity Competent Group Workers* (ASGW 1999).

A Model to Facilitate Diversity and Social Justice Awareness and Action

Understanding how concepts of social justice and diversity can be melded into the process of group work can be a confusing process. Some authors posit that the struggles rest on issues of discomfort with the subject (Adams et al. 2007) or the fact that the topic itself is somewhat complicated and at times nebulous (Ratts et al. 2010). The purpose of this chapter is to illuminate importance of diversity and social justice in group work, while at the same time, to provide a framework for making the issues practical for the reader.

Ratts et al. (2010) created the "Dimensions of Social Justice Model" as a means for describing a developmental framework for conceptualizing the degree to which social-justice elements are integrated into the group experience. The dimensions range from less developed, where social justice is ignored, to more fully developed, where social-justice issues are acknowledged openly. This model provides an excellent backdrop for the conversation about social justice and group, and fits with later discussions about traditional group stage development (Chapter 8) and co-leadership relationship development (Chapter 6). The focus on group issues as a non-linear developmental process is a congruent theme throughout the book and provides a consistency to the learning of rather complex phenomena. Each of the five dimensions/stages in the model will be outlined below.

Naivety

Groups functioning in naivety are characterized by a lack of awareness of how issues of diversity impact the intra and interpersonal interactions within the group. In these groups, the group leader will assume that all interactions are universal and equal, ascribing little to none of the group communication, conflict, or feedback to social justice constructs. As Ratts et al. (2010: 162) state, "The belief shared by group leaders within this dimension is that good group work is good group work regardless of multicultural variables such as race, ethnicity, gender, sexual orientation, economic class, or religion." Group facilitators operating from this stage often are not trying to harm the group but instead just do not see the value of these factors in the group process. Despite this lack of insight, the consequences for the group include members not feeling understood or valued, feelings of oppression as the dominant discourse becomes the accepted group narrative and overall group stagnation as a result. As MacNair-Semands stated, "As such dynamics arise in our groups, therapists are given the chance to assist in the creation of healing experiences rather than allowing potential hurtful interactions to occur or repeat themselves" (2007: 62).

Example

A group counselor is hired to facilitate a short-term group at a local agency that is having trouble with morale and work-related relationships. During the pre-group interviews, one African American worker (Jane) and one Latino worker (Manuel) express their concern that the other workers and the supervisor, who are White, routinely leave them out of conversations, social gatherings, and important work opportunities. The group facilitator appreciates the information and decides that this pattern represents an issue of problematic communication and connection. Out of this conceptualization, the group leader never addresses the possible impact of race in this matter but instead works with the group to improve their level of interpersonal interaction and belonging (i.e. making sure everyone gets a turn to process and share in the group). As a result, Jane and Manuel never voice their concern about how they are treated and instead "play along" with the communication exercises. Although they may even feel temporarily closer to their co-workers, the underlying issue remains. They may even feel further confused or hurt because their issue was ignored.

Multicultural Integration

In this dimension, the group leader moves out of an ethnocentric lens and more fully recognizes the richness of the cultural elements of each member. Group leaders will view, and help each member see the unique flavors each member contributes to the group experience. Dialogues about each person's cultural identity are interwoven into the natural flow of the group and, in some cases, become the focus on group and individual goals.

As each member's identity is honored and explored, it is also important for group leaders to consider their own place in the matrix. As the de-facto "person in power," it is helpful to process how the group is perceiving this status and may be a good opportunity to share the power within the group. Several authors have explored different ways of power sharing from collaborating with group members on topic setting (Coker, Meyer, Smith and Price 2010) to direct processing about the use of power within the group (Burnes and Ross 2010; Debiak 2007).

This appreciation and inclusion of culture may seem like a stark contrast to the previous group, but this is the normal experience of illumination. In the first stage the light is off, while in this stage the light is on. With an awareness of the existence of the vitality of culture, the elements can be used to improve the potency of the group.

Example

Instead of trying to address the feelings of racial isolation as general communication issues, the group facilitator engages the group in a discussion about each person's cultural identity and how that impacts connections within the agency and, more specifically, in the group. The group leader understands that although the cultural pieces are at the heart of the present issue, the conversation may be a difficult one. Respecting the potential discomfort, the group leader will first create an atmosphere of safety. The group leader may employ activities that will help group members connect at gradually deepening levels. As the group's cohesion increases, the group leader increasingly folds in the issues of cultural identity as a way to help the members gain a deeper understanding of each other. Each person has an opportunity to share and feel valued for their unique background and perspective. Within this atmosphere of acceptance, it will also give Jane and Manuel an opportunity to voice their feelings and work directly with the cultural components.

Liberatory Critical Consciousness

In the last dimension, awareness and integration of diversity was the norm. However, there are times when developing insight into culture is not enough to fully address the issue. In these groups, movement into the third dimension is valuable as group leaders facilitate an awareness of how one's cultural identity has deeper and broader implications, both personally and as a member of the world community. As each member gains a more expansive understanding of self and the conditions that help form their beliefs, they are also exposed to other's learning as well. This micro- and macro-level insight provides opportunities to change but also places each person in the context of something bigger. As a result, an element of the potential growth comes from a move away from self-blame and instead toward understanding which aspects are outside of one's control.

Example

In the agency group, the expression and validation of each member's cultural identity had been experienced, but the group wanted more. As a result, the group leader used the developing dialogue to incorporate the impact of racism on our broader community and society. The group, using their external and internal group experiences, explored the role and dynamics of racism as a social issue. The result of the ongoing discussion produced a deeper awareness of the implications of racism on each member. Members from both non-dominant and dominant cultural groups were able to see how the racism that was negatively impacting the agency was a reflection of a greater societal norm. Jane and Manuel felt less likely to internalize the shame of being ostracized while White members felt less defensive because the message did not convey, "Racism is your fault." Instead, all parties could understand the consequences of the prevailing racial discourse and were primed to encourage change at several possible levels.

Empowerment

Knowledge of oppressive institutions and the will to change them does not necessarily translate into action. In the dimension of empowerment, group leaders build on the momentum of the previous stages and help create an atmosphere that promotes self-advocacy. Ratts et al. noted that as group members find their voice they "develop the confidence and skills needed to become self-sufficient members of society" (2010: 165). Because group is a social microcosm of the greater community, learning and experimenting self-advocacy skills in the group setting becomes the ideal place to begin this important process. The literature contains many excellent examples of integrating social-justice issues into a wide variety of group-work applications, and all highlight this stage as a vital part of the process, both for the individual and the greater community (Bhat 2010; Dickey & Loewy 2010).

Example

In our agency example, at this stage the members would be aware of not only how the issues of racism and oppression were operating within themselves, the group, the agency, and the larger community, they would also be eager for the opportunity to use that knowledge to cultivate a culture of change. This process would begin with each person stretching themselves beyond their typical internal dialogue by practicing a new voice within the group relationship matrix. This new experience of empowerment could be realized through a combination of group discussions via feedback or through role plays of scenarios that could provide the members with opportunities to identify old and new patterns of relating and advocating. Consider the following interaction:

GROUP LEADER: I would like you to role play a situation where Jake [the supervisor] is discussing a new project opportunity. Go ahead Jake, you start us off.

JAKE: OK, I would like to tell everyone about a new grant that we just received to provide support for a group of middle-school students.

JANE: This is a great example! This is something that I would normally be very interested in, but already I hear myself saying, "He doesn't want you to do it. So just be quiet." I was also aware that Jake really never looked at me while he was talking, so that reinforced my thought.

JAKE: Hmmm . . . I wasn't aware I didn't look at you. I can see how that could seem that I am discounting you. The weird thing is that I agree with you Jane. I know you like this population and would be great for this job. I guess I am not communicating it.

GROUP FACILITATOR: You have both identified internal messages that are interfering with your connection to each other and probably those around you. How can you change them and in turn, advocate for a larger change?

JANE: It is good to hear that he thought of me. I guess I would like to say, "Jake, I am really interested in that position." I would also like to know why he never looks at me, [*laughs*] but I guess I already told him that.

JAKE: [*laughs*] Yes you did. Although it was embarrassing to hear, I am glad you did it. I think I should approach people more and let them know how I am feeling so they do not have to guess.

STUART: I noticed that Jake wasn't making eye contact with Jane, and I didn't say anything. I am aware that I benefit from Jane's silence and her and Manuel's isolation by the larger group. I can remember several times when I received the project because they were invisible. I think I can change my voice to be more encouraging to them both. I can see that when I am silent about this issue, I just make it worse.

Social-Justice Advocacy

In the final dimension, the group moves beyond the confines of the group session and expands into the larger community to advocate for larger change. As the group members experience personal change and have an opportunity to practice those new ways of being within the group, the group may feel that the change then needs to grow and impact others in the community or society as a whole. The group members see working for a larger cause as an appropriate next step for their own growth. It is important to keep in mind a few caveats for this dimension:

- This dimension may not be appropriate for every group you facilitate.
- As a group facilitator, make sure your group is comfortable with outside-of-group advocacy. In the spirit of social justice, you do not want to force your ideas or values on the group. This would be oppression in action.
- Be aware that you will be stretching the "norms" of counseling practice. As such, you may feel internally anxious and may experience conflict with other professionals who are concerned about your approach.

Example

The agency group has experienced quite a bit of growth over time. Each member has gained insight into their own cultural identity and how it impacts them personally and professionally. As a group, they have learned new skills that empower each person to use cultural knowledge and social-justice tools to address issues within the agency. They have also explored how this issue is prevalent in the greater society and how their new skills have the potential to enact larger-scale change. In this dimension, the group decides they want to move beyond the group room and into that larger community. They connect with a local "End Racism" movement, becoming active in the organization's community efforts, sponsoring some events, and co-authoring three important grants. Through all of these activities, the group is reminded of the need for continuous reflection and gets to practice social justice in action.

Social Justice Elements of Group Leadership

As you strive to become a competent group leader, it is important to remember that social justice is a natural part of the group-dynamic fabric. To ensure that you are aware and remain attentive to these issues, Bemak and Chung (2004: 37–39) made several suggestions for improving your multicultural group skills. Some are summarized below.

1. Group Work Must Be Considered as Unique Counseling Modality

As was mentioned in Chapter 1, group is different from other forms of counseling. Learning group builds on the skills that you will use with individuals, couples, and families, but also requires a special set of skills. Due to the uniqueness of group, it is important to understand that diversity issues will manifest in a variety of new ways in group. Group leaders should not merely use the contexts learned from individual-based counseling but should evolve their understanding to how these issues are being experienced in the group, here and now, matrix.

2. Understand and Employ Diversity-based Skill Sets that are Important to Creating an Atmosphere Conducive to Social Justice

Here, one must have working knowledge of the multicultural competencies and standards (ASGW 1999) and develop the skill of infusing them into group work. Embedded in these standards are specific areas of competency one must address:

- the awareness of how White privilege impacts self and the group;
- the awareness of how oppression and any "ism" can impact self and the group;
- a working knowledge of a wide range of populations, not limited to racial, ethnic, gender, sexual, spiritual, political, and geographical identities, as well as an awareness that most, if not all, people are composed of a combination of these facets;
- an awareness of the inherent barriers that exist in our society to many individuals and groups and how these barriers may exist in the microcosm of the group.

3. Gain a Comprehensive Understanding of Your Own Culture and How It Impacts Your View of Others and, In Turn, How It Impacts Your View of Your Group Members

It is vital to commit yourself to a lifetime of introspection on the issues of how you identify yourself and where these beliefs originated. As you gain a more complete sense of self you can begin to address how these personal beliefs intersect with the greater community (macro level) and with the smaller group matrix (micro level). This greater sense of personal awareness will strengthen your willingness to consider the ways diversity and issues of social justice impact your group process and, in turn, increase your comfort level in bringing these issues into the awareness of your group members within the process.

Understand how issues discussed in 1–3 directly impact your group: If you understand that group is unique, commit yourself to knowing the knowledge and skills necessary to employ a diversity-competent approach and do the self-work to expand that awareness beyond an academic knowing, then you are prepared to fully use the power of group to explore diversity and social-justice issues. These "courageous conversations" (Singleton & Linton 2006) include a willingness to engage in discussions where differences of opinion and perception will emerge. Leaders must be open to conflict and comfortable with modeling risk-taking and dialoguing about issues of oppression and injustice. Leaders must also consider how the group is viewing the role of the leader and how those perceptions influence the dialogue.

Summary

As the mental-health field mirrors society and continues to see the human condition as an increasingly complex interplay of cultural elements, group work must continue to add to the dialogue. The "dimensions model" was outlined as a way for you to see the development of social justice in the life of the group. Aspects of leadership were also provided as ways for you to consider specific areas to focus on as you develop your leadership skills.

For beginning group workers, it can be overwhelming to learn the new skills set of group while also trying to conceptualize the vast variety of identities that exist and impact the interactions in the room. To be honest, this confusion is felt by even the most seasoned professional! We put the issues of diversity at the beginning of the book so you could be aware of the existence of these forces as you learn more universal dynamics of group. These elements do not exist outside of any group but instead are additional currents in the greater flow of the overall group. Rather than be overwhelmed by their presence we hope that you see them as vital to the process and can be addressed as a way of bringing richness to the experience.

References

Adams, M., Bell, L. A., & Griffin, P. (Eds.) (2007). *Teaching for diversity and social justice* (2nd ed.). London and New York: Routledge.

Association for Specialists in Group Work (1999). Principles for diversity competent group workers. *Journal for Specialists in Group Work*, 24, 7–14.

Bemak, F., & Chung, R. C. (2004). Teaching multicultural group counseling: Perspectives for a new era. *Journal for Specialists in Group Work*, 29, 31–41.

Bhat, C. S. (2010). Assisting unemployed adults find suitable work: A group intervention embedded in community and grounded in social action. *Journal for Specialists in Group Work*, 35, 246–254.

Burnes, T. R., & Ross, K. L. (2010). Applying social justice to oppression and marginalization in group process: Interventions and strategies for group counselors. *Journal for Specialists in Group Work*, 35, 169–176.

Coker, A. D., Meyer, D., Smith, R., & Price, A. (2010). Using social justice group work with young mothers who experience homelessness. *Journal for Specialists in Group Work*, 35, 220–229.

Debiak, D. (2007). Attending to diversity in group psychotherapy: An ethical imperative. *International Journal of Group Psychotherapy*, 57, 1–12.

DeLucia-Waack, J. L. (1996). Multiculturalism is inherent in all group work. *Journal for Specialists in Group Work*, 21, 218–223.

Dickey, L. M., & Loewy, M. I. (2010). Group work with transgender clients. *Journal for Specialists in Group Work*, 35, 236–245.

MacNair-Semands, R. R. (2007). Attending to the spirit of social justice as an ethical approach in group therapy. *International Journal of Group Psychotherapy*, 57, 61–66.

Merta, R. J. (1995). Group work: Multicultural perspectives. In J. G. Pinterotto, J. M. Casas, L. A. Suzuki, & C. M. Alexander (Eds.), *Handbook of multicultural counseling* (pp. 567–585). Thousand Oaks, CA: Sage.

Patterson, C. H. (1996). Multicultural counseling: From diversity to universality. *Journal of Counseling and Development*, 74, 227–235.

Ratts, M. J., Anthony, L., & Santos, K. N. (2010). The dimensions of social justice model: Transforming traditional group work into a socially just framework. *Journal for Specialists in Group Work*, 35, 160–168.

Singleton, G. E., & Linton, C. (2006). *Courageous conversations about race: A field guide for achieving equity in schools.* Thousand Oaks, CA: Corwin.

3

GROUP WORK AND THEORY

You will find only what you bring in.

Yoda

Theory in Group Work

Theory is an important aspect of counseling as it helps the counselor conceptualize and make sense of the countless pieces of information learned from the client. Theory is not some abstract, external set of techniques that is applied to clients but instead reflects the counselor's own philosophy on how people develop, how and why people struggle, and how change occurs (Fall et al. 2010). Because it arises from each counselor's own values and is then shaped and honed by existing, more developed theories, the development of one's personal theory is a very personal and complicated process.

In individual counseling, theory can serve as a priceless roadmap to change. In group, it serves the same purpose, but is even more useful given the increase in complexity and sheer volume of information the group counselor is expected to process in any given transaction. Due to the fact that theory rests within the values and philosophy of the counselor, who you are in individual counseling is who you are in group. This is great news! It means your theory does not have to change as you switch modalities, you just have to expand your lens to accommodate the information gained from interpersonal interactions that occur within the group.

Most people in graduate group courses have already taken a general theory course where they were exposed to a wide range of theories. This foundational knowledge will serve them well as they integrate and explore theory application from a group perspective. In this chapter, we will provide some examples of theory at work in groups and in the spirit of viewing theory development as a personal journey, we will each discuss our own use of theory in group work.

Examples of Theoretical Applications in Group Work

Person-Centered

Established by Carl Rogers, person-centered group therapy can be characterized by the climate of the group as influenced by the leader. The counselor must be congruent and demonstrate the core conditions of empathy, genuineness, and unconditional positive regard toward the group members. If the leader can relate to the group within the three conditions, a climate of growth will be established that will enable the members to reach their own potentials.

The person-centered approach is unique in its nondirectiveness and emphasis on the climate in the group. Although Rogers (1967) recognized both leader and member variables that affect group work, focus is placed on the client. Rogers also emphasized that members provide the interaction, motivation, and direction of the group. To many practitioners, the person-centered group therapist is viewed as passive, but that would be incorrect. Despite the focus on the members' interaction, *the client-centered therapist must be actively listening and continuously connected with the group and self* to maintain the climate of growth and to stay congruent.

Rogers (1967) constructed a model of stages of group development specific to the person-centered approach. According to Rogers, these are developmental patterns that occur during the life of a normal group and appear in the following order:

1. milling around;
2. resistance to personal expression or exploration;
3. description of past feeling;
4. expression of negative feelings;
5. expression and exploration of personally meaningful material;
6. expression of immediate interpersonal feelings in the group;
7. development of a healing capacity in the group;
8. self-acceptance;
9. the cracking of façades;
10. the individual receives feedback;
11. confrontation;
12. helping relationships outside the group sessions;
13. the basic encounter;
14. expression of positive feelings and closeness; and
15. behavior change.

In general, the leader will focus on maintaining a therapeutic climate by first providing and managing the core conditions within the leader's self. The resulting climate will foster the atmosphere of growth and change. The interaction below demonstrates a group interaction within a client-centered framework.

THERAPIST: I'm noticing that you seem upset and agitated today.

MARY: I just want to scream, I am so frustrated! I don't get it!

STEVEN: I sensed you boiling in your seat for a while now. If you want to scream, that's OK.

MELISSA: Yeah, I mean, maybe if you let your anger out, you would learn more about it. I would feel closer to you too. I'm not sure if closer is what you want, though.

WAYNE: I think what Melissa is saying is that if you open up, you might find your role in the group.

MARY: It took a lot for me just to admit that I was frustrated. I was really scared you all would laugh at me or kick me out of the group. Expressing anger is new for me, but it is a part of me. Thanks for accepting that part of me.

THERAPIST: I sense that the whole group has experienced a little bit of the genuine Mary.

Gestalt

Developed by Fritz Perls (Perls et al. 1951), Gestalt therapy focuses on removing the blocks that prevent individuals from living effectively. Group sessions are directed by the therapist, and emphasis is placed on here-and-now interaction. Polster and Polster (1973) viewed the group leader as the creator, the catalyst for each member to begin to take responsibility for each personal choice. Gestalt therapists rely on content provided by the members to develop a theme within the group. The leader encourages each member to experience the moment as fully as possible and to get in touch with any unfinished business within the self. To aid the members in the experience, a variety of techniques and experiments are employed by the leader.

All of the experiments that are applied to individual clients can be adapted for group work. The benefits of group are that as the therapist works with one member to resolve unfinished business, other members may vicariously be helped by participating in the here and now, experiencing and therefore beginning to work on their own unfinished business. Experiments such as language exercise, dream work, making the rounds, and the hot seat are all designed to get members to relate to self and others in the present and to take responsibility for what is instead of what could or should be.

The following interaction illustrates the Gestalt emphasis on present behavior and experience, as well as the directive nature of the leader.

THERAPIST: Leo, I notice when Mary was talking about her accomplishments, you seemed uncomfortable. Even now as I speak to you, your hands are clenching.

LEO: I wasn't aware of that. I was just listening, I guess. [*Hands still clenching.*]

THERAPIST: Tell me, what are your hands trying to tell you right now? Let your hands talk to you.

LEO: They would say, "I am really uncomfortable. I can't say what I'm feeling, I'm all tight and squished up."

THERAPIST: OK. Feel your lack of comfort. Let your hands clench and experience what you are trying not to say.

LEO: [*Unclenches hands*], I can't believe she got the job. I hate women!! I feel cheated.

THERAPIST: Leo, stay with that feeling and go around the room and express to each member how you have felt uncomfortable in this group. Begin with "I'm uncomfortable because . . ."

Adlerian

Based on the work of Alfred Adler (1956), individual psychology was best expressed in terms of group work by Dreikurs (1950). The Adlerian approach focuses on each member as a holistic, social creative being, whose every action has a purpose. Working with the individual's lifestyle, which is expressed through interactions in the group, the leader can monitor each member's behavior in the group and be able to get a clear picture of the purposes of the behavior. From an Adlerian perspective, the group acts as a social laboratory, and because all change occurs in a social context, the group is a perfect place to encourage behavior change.

Leaders can be free and spontaneous in their level of interaction within the group, with the overall goal of cultivating social interest in the group structure and individual members. Following the four stages of (a) establishing a relationship, (b) analysis, (c), insight, and (d) reorientation, the leader encourages members to use the social context of the group to explore the meaning of their behaviors and to attempt to modify selfish behaviors by utilizing more cooperation and therefore expanding social interest.

The following segment expresses the leader's attempt to focus the group on the purpose behind the current group behavior by attending to one member and utilizing an early recollection.

THERAPIST: Kim, I notice that each time Jade gets emotional, you make a joke. Could it be that you are uncomfortable with her level of emotion?

KIM: I don't know.

DAVID: I saw that, too. You like to stay in your head. Like feelings hurt you.

KIM: They don't hurt me, but I do get uncomfortable when anyone gets too deep.

THERAPIST: You believe you will lose control and get pulled under if the group gets "too deep."

KIM: Yeah, exactly.

THERAPIST: Kim, I wonder if you could remember the first time you felt overwhelmed by an intense emotion. Could you describe the time for the group?

KIM: I'm not sure if this is exactly what you mean, but when I was four [*pauses*] I was crying because I broke one of my favorite toys. My mom told me only babies cry. I felt stupid but at the same time scared that I would never stop.

THERAPIST: What happened next?

KIM: My mom would not talk to me until I stopped, so I stopped. I don't remember crying much after that time.

THERAPIST: Your belief of "I mustn't cry or I am not wanted" has seemed to have been generalized to others. I wonder if you are trying to save Jade from the pain you felt?

KIM: Yeah, maybe [*looking down*], but it's weird; I still like Jade even though she cried.

THERAPIST: Perhaps you have learned through her risk to express herself, and you can now choose what you want to do with that insight.

Rational Emotive Behavioral Therapy (REBT)

REBT as created by Albert Ellis focuses on the irrational beliefs of the members. In an REBT group, the leader confronts the members on their absolute and magical ways of thinking, which are heard in statements containing *must* and *should.* The leader is directive and focused, emphasizing acceptance of each member but not including warmth as a necessary component of the relationship. The leader disputes the irrationality of each member's beliefs and teaches each member how to dispute them on their own, enlisting the help of the group in the disputation process (Ellis 2001).

The protocol exemplifies the REBT use of disputation of irrational beliefs and the interaction among member during the process.

REHF: I feel like such an idiot when I get turned down for a date.

THERAPIST: You're telling yourself, "I'm an awful person!" Or, "I'm a total loser because I didn't get a date today!" Is that how it goes?

REHF: Yeah, it sounds dumb. I know I shouldn't be like that.

RITA: You "shouldn't" be like that? Who did you get that from?

REHF: Society, I guess.

GEORGE: Well, I'm a part of society, and I'm not saying that. I guess I'm a loser too for not getting a date last night! [*Laughs*],

TRUDY: Yeah, me too!

REHF: No. Not you all! I guess I just feel like I'm worthless if I don't have a date.

BEN: What's the worst thing that could happen if you don't get any more dates this month?

REHF: I would be worthless . . .

TRUDY: and . . .

REHF: And no one would want to be around me, you people included.

THERAPIST: Great, Rehf. We have something to test. Go around the group and tell each member that you don't have a date and ask them what they think and record their reactions.

REHF: OK.

General Considerations

In selecting a theory of group process, practitioners are encouraged to integrate the theory into one's own personality and beliefs. Alignment with a particular theory should be based primarily on a congruence between the counselor's beliefs and the tenets of the theory and less on what is convenient or popular to practice. As an illustration of what that intersection might look like, we have each taken some time to describe our own theory and how it applies to group work.

Garry's Group-Centered Theory

The group-centered approach is a function of the facilitator's attitude toward self and each group member. It is both an acceptance of self and each group member, and a deep and abiding belief in the capacity of each group member to be responsible for self in the process of exercising self-direction resulting in more positive behaviors. This attitude of commitment to the group member was expressed by Hobbs (1964: 158) as

> putting aside tendencies to evaluate what is good and right for other people. It requires a respect for their integrity as individuals, for their right to the strength-giving act of making and living by their own choices. And it requires, perhaps above all, a confidence in the tremendous capacities of individuals to make choices that are both maturely satisfying to them and ultimately satisfactory to society.

A significant objective, therefore, of the group facilitator is to help group members feel safe enough to change or not to change, for only when the person is free not to change will genuine change be possible.

A unique aspect of this group-centered approach is the belief that "man's behavior is exquisitely rational moving with subtle and ordered complexity toward the goals his organism is endeavoring to achieve" (Rogers 1957: 202). Therefore, what a person knows, some intellectual knowledge or some "important" information that the facilitator can provide is not what is important; how a person feels about self is what makes a significant difference in behavior. Each individual possesses a personal, perceptual view of self and the world that is for him or her reality and thus provides a basis for functioning in the daily experiences in which the person finds self.

Personality Theory

The group-centered theory of personality development is based on three central concepts:

1. the person;
2. the phenomenal field;
3. the self.

(Rogers 1951)

The person is all that an individual is: thoughts, behaviors, feelings, and physical being. The phenomenal field is everything the person experiences, whether or not at a conscious level. It is internal as well as external and forms the basis of internal reference for viewing life. Whatever the person perceives to be occurring is reality.

A basic proposition is that every person "exists in a continually changing world of experience of which he is the center" (Rogers 1951: 483). As the person reacts to this changing world of experience, he or she does so as an organized whole so that a change in any one part results in changes in other parts. Therefore, a continuous, dynamic intra-personal interaction occurs in which the person, as a total system, is striving toward actualizing the self. This active process is toward becoming a more positively functioning person, toward enhancement of self, independence, and maturity as a person. The person's behavior in this process is goal-directed in an effort to satisfy personal needs as experienced in one's phenomenal field that, for that person, constitutes reality. Personal needs, then, influence the person's perception of reality. Therefore, the person's perception of reality must be understood if the person and his or her behavior are to be understood. Thus, the facilitator avoids judging the person's behavior and works hard to try to understand the internal frame of reference of the person (Rogers 1951).

The third central concept of the group-centered theory of personality development is the self. Through interactions with significant others in the environment and from the total phenomenal field, the person, as an infant, gradually begins to differentiate a portion as the self. According to Patterson (1974), the individual can only become a person and develop a self in a society or group. The self grows and changes as a result of continuing interaction with the phenomenal field. Rogers (1951: 501) described the self structure as

> an organized configuration of perceptions of the self which are admissible to awareness. It is composed of such elements as the perceptions of one's characteristics and abilities; the percepts and concepts of the self in relation to others and to the environment; the value qualities which are perceived as associated with experiences and objects; and the goals and ideals which are perceived as having positive or negative valence. It is, then, the organized picture, existing in awareness either as figure or ground, of the self and the self-in-relationship, together with the positive or negative values which are associated with those qualities and relation-ships, as they are perceived as existing in the past, present, or future.

Awareness of self ushers in the development of the need for positive regard from others. This need for positive regard is reciprocal in that as a person satisfies another person's need for positive regard the person fulfills the same need. Satisfaction or frustration of the need for positive regard in association with self-experiences contributes to the development of a need for self-regard. This "sense of self-regard becomes a pervasive construct influencing the behavior of the whole organism and has a life of its own, independent of actual experiences of regard from others" (Meador & Rogers 1984: 154).

Group-Centered View of Personality and Behavior

Rogers (1951) articulated nineteen propositions regarding personality and behavior that provide a conceptual framework for understanding human behavior and motivation, and reflect the philosophical core of group-centered counseling. These propositions, summarized as follows, describe a group-centered view of the person and behavior of the individual and provide a basis for relating to members in the group.

Every person exists in a continually changing world of experience of which that person is the center. The person reacts as an organized whole to this field as it is experienced and perceived, which for the person is reality. As the person develops and interacts with the environment, a portion of the person's total private world (perceptual field) gradually becomes recognized as "me" (differentiated as the self), and concepts are formed about self, about the environment and about self in relation to the environment. The person has a basic tendency to strive to actualize, maintain and enhance the experiencing self. The resulting behavior is basically the goal-directed, emotionally influenced attempt of the person to satisfy his or her needs as experienced in the field as perceived. Therefore, the best vantage point for understanding the person's behavior is from the internal frame of reference of the person.

Most of a person's behavior is consistent with the person's concept of self, and behaviors inconsistent with the self-concept are not owned. Psychological freedom or adjustment exists when the self-concept is congruent with all the person's experiences. When this is not the case, tension or maladjustment is experienced by the person. Experiences that are inconsistent with the self-concept may be perceived as a threat, resulting in the person becoming behaviorally rigid in an effort to defend the existing self-concept. When there is a complete absence of any threat to the perception of self, the person is free to revise his or her self-concept to assimilate and include experiences previously inconsistent with the self-concept. The resulting well-integrated or positive self-concept enables the person to be more understanding of others and thus to have better interpersonal relationships (Rogers 1951: 483–524).

The Therapeutic Relationship

Before attempting to describe the therapeutic relationship, it is important to reiterate the group-centered philosophical position that there is an inherent tendency within each person to move in subtle directedness toward adjustment, mental health, developmental growth, independence, autonomy of personhood, and what can be generally described as self-actualization. It is the person's natural striving toward inner balance that takes him or her to where he or she needs to be.

Therefore, the focus of the group-centered counselor is on the inner self of the person, what the person is capable of becoming, not on the person's ways of being in the past. In this approach, the person, and not the problem, is the point of focus. Knowing about the causes or extent of the person's maladjustment is not a prerequisite for establishing a therapeutic relationship with the person. When we focus on the problem we lose sight of the person of the individual and in the process communicate to the individual that his or her problem is more important. Diagnosis of maladjustment is not necessary because this is not a prescriptive approach. What the counselor does is not based on a specific problem the individual may be experiencing (Landreth 1991). Having made this point, we can proceed to discuss a group-centered view of the therapeutic relationship.

If I am to be helpful to each group member, I must make contact with each person of the group at all levels of experiencing in our shared time together. I would like to gently touch each member's emotional world and also to hear as fully as I can his or her expressed thoughts and descriptions. I would like the total response of my person to convey to the group member the depth of my yearning to know and understand, to the extent to which I am fully capable, his or her experiential inner world of feelings and thoughts as known, experienced, felt, expressed, and lived out at the moment. I also want to hear that the other person has a longing to share what may be perceived by the person as a frightening part of his or her life, or as confusion, but may fear doing so because I or others may reject it. And so they venture forth in this relationship in ways that may seem to lack focus or direction as they experience this inner conflict of wanting to be heard and fearing evaluation and criticism. At such times, a tentative and perhaps almost imperceptible desire exists to share this vulnerable part of self in what may be an obscure or oblique manner that could easily go unnoticed because the message is so inconspicuous or veiled.

In many relationships, the person seems to be perhaps at that moment only vaguely aware at some deeper level of this underlying part of self or experience that he or she would like to share, perhaps not even at a conscious level in the immediacy of our experiencing relationship. At other times, I have sensed, at an immediate conscious level, a deep longing on the part of self heard and accepted. The person seems to be crying out, "Does anyone hear me? Does anyone care?" At these moments in our sharing together a developing relationship, I would like by my attitude, words, feelings, tone of voice, and facial and bodily expression—by the total person I am—to communicate my hearing, understanding, and acceptance of this deeper message in a way that will help the person to feel safe, accepted, and appreciated. In such moments, my response seems to very gently open a door the person has come to stand in front of in our journey together and by that gesture say to the person, "I'm really not sure, either, what is on the other side of the door. I understand that whatever is there may be frightening to you or something you had rather not face, but I am willing to walk through that door with you. I am not willing to lead you through the door, nor will I push you or follow you through the door. I will be fully present beside you, and we will discover together what is there. I trust you in this process to be able to face and cope with whatever we find there."

A young lady with whom I worked in a counseling relationship expressed her reaction to this kind of caring by writing, "One thing I have come to really appreciate about you is that you will allow me to be frightened, even though you and I both know there is no reason for me to be. You trust me, and I am coming to trust myself. Thanks for that." This kind of relationship is described by Rogers (1952: 70) as "the process by which the structure of the self is relaxed in the safety of the relationship with the therapist, and previously denied experiences are perceived and then integrated into an altered self."

The beginning of this movement toward a different self is facilitated when the warmth, interest, caring, understanding, genuineness, and empathy I experience are perceived and felt by the group member. Other members of the group are just as capable of experiencing these conditions, and when they are communicated they may have an even greater impact when perceived by the member of focus. In this climate of facilitative psychological attitudes (Rogers 1980), group members come to rely on their own vast resources for self-directed behavior and for altering their self-concepts and basic attitudes. Thus, the power to change resides within the group member and is not a result of direction, advice, or information I might have to offer. As expressed by Rogers (1961: 33), "If I can provide a certain type of relationship, the other person will discover within himself the capacity to use that relationship for growth and change, and personal development will occur." The relationship then can be described as therapeutic and a function of basic key attitudes of the group-centered facilitator, who is willing to know the group member(s) and to be known in the process of the developing relationship. According to Rogers (1967), the following conditions are necessary and sufficient for personality changes to occur:

- Two people are in psychological contact.
- The group member is in a state of incongruence, being vulnerable or anxious.
- The facilitator is congruent or integrated in the relationship.
- The facilitator experiences unconditional positive regard for the group member.
- The facilitator experiences an empathic understanding of the member's internal frame of reference and strives to communicate this experience to the member.
- The group member perceives, at least to a minimal degree, the facilitator's empathic understanding and unconditional positive regard.

In this approach, the person, and not the problem, is the point of focus. When we focus on the problem, we lose sight of the person. The relationship that develops in the group and the creative forces this relationship releases in the group member are the process of change and growth for the group member. It is not preparation for change. Rogers

(1959: 221) expressed this view as follows: "Psychotherapy is releasing an already existing capacity in a potentially competent individual." Although at times the past may be described by the group member in light of certain experiences, the present is considered to be more significant. In this process, the group member is responsible for him- or herself and is quite capable of exercising that responsibility through self-direction, resulting in more positive behavior.

Bob's Integrated Approach

Perhaps because of the complexity of human nature and the problems encountered in life, most group leaders of my acquaintance eventually evolve to an eclectic system of group facilitation. I chose the word "evolve" quite carefully because I believe that beginning counselors and group leaders need to select a single theory that fits their personality and style and to master it first. Through the process of mastery, the group leader can try interventions that are time tested and eventually select what makes the most sense and what works best for him or her. I am not convinced that an inexperienced group leader should choose eclecticism as an initial intervention mode. My personal bias is that the eclectic group leader needs to have good, solid reasons that are grounded in established theory in order to make consistent choices regarding what works best in groups.

My personal beliefs about how people learn and what motivates them to change have been most directly influenced by the following theorists and schools of thought. The influences of Carl Rogers (1951–1980s) and Robert Carkhuff, the neopsychoanalytic school, and particularly the work of Karen Horney, the Gestaltists, and more recently the conceptualization of Harville Hendrix (1988) will become apparent as I discuss my views on the development of human personality and the therapeutic process.

Personality Development

One of the most difficult arguments to settle is the age-old nature-versus-nurture issue. We continue to learn more about the ways in which genetics influence the human organism. Studies with twins and increasingly sophisticated research with chromosomes indicate that heredity may influence disposition and behavior much more than previously thought.

I believe that heredity and environment are intricately interwoven and most probably in a fashion that will remain somewhat mysterious. I continue to be impressed with the powerful role that learning plays in the development of human personality and in the choices people make as they journey through life.

Learning begins at least at birth. Some would suggest that a very primitive kind of learning may even begin during gestation. The human brain is capable of processing hundreds of sensory inputs per second. The most complex and intricate computer in existence pales in comparison to the enormous capacity of the human brain. Naturally, we do not consciously process each piece of data that impacts the brain. That would literally be overwhelming. Nevertheless, some brain researchers believe that every experience we have is stored somewhere in the brain.

I chose to begin my discussion of human personality with the brain because I believe that all of our developmental experiences shape who we are and who we become. I think that early experiences are the most significant because they are being charted and stored in emotion that is uncontaminated by the higher processes of thinking and evaluating that develop later as the cerebral cortex and its functions become more prominent. The older and more primitive limbic system of the brain is the repository of feelings and emotions. In this portion of the brain, our memories of early and unevaluated experiences are stored—both positive and negative.

This primitive part of the brain is relatively uncritical and is most interested in having needs met: safety and security, warmth and nurturance, excitement and sex. The cerebral cortex is a more highly evolved part of the brain that gives rise to our ability to think logically and critically, evaluate, decide, and organize our lives. It also, for better or for worse, helps us control the more impulsive nature of the limbic or primitive brain.

As we "learn" about what culture considers appropriate behavior, we also learn to moderate our primitive wishes and desires. Because most of us have difficulty remembering in exquisite detail some of our early experiences before age five or so, my belief is that many of our personality-shaping experiences have been sublimated or repressed so that they are no longer part of our conscious awareness. Nevertheless, they remain, at an unconscious level, powerful influences upon our current perception of ourselves and our world.

Our uniqueness as individuals has to do with the delicate interplay between that naturally affective part of self and the way in which we choose to manage our lives—our perception of ourselves in our world. How we perceive ourselves is the sum product of our internalized experiences, both those of which we are aware and, perhaps more importantly, those that have been filed away in our brains but are no longer available to us consciously.

Our most demanding early needs also are the most influential in setting the course of our eventual development and feelings about self. The basic needs for safety and security can be clinically observed throughout the life span. They are powerful motivators and at some level probably play a part in most of the major decisions we make in life—from choices of occupation or career to the selection of our mate.

To me, the recognition that infants enter the world crying and howling is no wonder. We have excised it from one of the warmest and most nurturing environments imaginable —the womb. In that desirable place, all needs were met instantly and continually. It was warm, safe, and secure, a condition that will never be duplicated again. We sometimes return to that comfortably protective fetal position while sleeping or when experiencing pain. This regressive behavior also can be observed in severely withdrawn mental patients and in some ways can be interpreted as adaptive behavior. I use the example to illustrate the importance that I believe feelings of security play in the development of healthy personalities.

If we are wise enough to choose our primary caretakers carefully and to have been reared by warm and nurturing parents, we will have a decided advantage in developing in a healthy and positive direction. However, because even the most sensitive of caretakers could not possibly ever meet all of our needs, life becomes a process of learning the skills necessary to deal with and adapt to frustration. The manner in which the human organism perceives the world through those early and needy experiences will heavily influence its perception of the world as a secure, warm, and nurturing environment that can be trusted, or as a world that is distant and cool, perhaps even a hostile one that needs to be guarded against.

These early experiences with frustration of our needs give rise to an anxiety that will govern whether we move toward other people in a dependent manner, move away in a distant and isolated or independent way, or move against others with a hostile or aggressive personality orientation.

Horney first talked about these basic personality styles, and they are similar to what Hendrix (1988) later labeled *fusors* and *isolators* in relationships. The theory is that dependent or fusor personalities will move toward others in an attempt to ward off the anxiety associated with early childhood wounds. Perhaps as a child the fusor did not receive enough nurturance from the significant caretaker and therefore grew up literally craving an unusual amount of affection, reassurance, and physical contact. Fusors typically fear abandonment, so they will seek and demand closeness, togetherness, and teamness.

Counterdependent or isolator personalities may have been overprotected or rejected as children and therefore adopt an independent, "I don't need anybody" personality. Isolators become extremely uncomfortable and anxious in relationships that they perceive to be too demanding of their time and energy. They frequently will state that they need personal space, freedom, and their own individuality in a relationship. What they fear most is being overwhelmed, suffocated, or engulfed by another person.

Basic personality styles, although acted out in an unconscious manner, have important implications for current relationships and the group. Adults have most likely developed many layers of defense in order to avoid things that they fear most—abandonment or engulfment. Ironically, when fusors and isolators grow up, they tend to seek each other out as romantic partners. This can be seen as an attempt to heal those early childhood wounds. Paradoxically, although an isolator may be initially attracted to the fusor, who seemingly possesses the natural warmth and acceptance that he or she was denied in childhood, as it later becomes apparent that the fusor also has strong needs for closeness and intimacy, the isolator will begin to experience an inner panic because the fusor has become so demanding and clinging!

The converse is also true: As the fusor moves forward with insistent affiliation needs, the isolator, in response, begins to distance. Thus begins an intriguing dance played out through the unconscious needs of the two confused participants. In effect, fusors become isolator-phobic, and isolators become fusor-phobic.

What we need in order to get better is a healing of those childhood wounds. In essence, we need that which we most fear! Those childhood wounds are the result of unfinished business with our primary caretakers. We go through life attempting to get closure on those situations that have been left in our background but that continue in a very real sense to influence current behavior. When we enter relationships that have the potential to become powerful and significant in our lives, they are measured against the background of our experiences. That is, we project our unconscious agenda onto the person or the group: "This person can make me whole" or "This group of people can help me grow."

Against this theoretical backdrop of individual personality, I do group work. I tend to conceptualize groups as reconstructed families where early wounds can be reexamined and in some cases played out. A person's basic personality style will be apparent in the group because issues of boundaries, trust, power, and intimacy will activate the same defenses and roles as will the "real" world.

The Therapeutic Relationship

My own personality best suits me for the "good father" role as a group facilitator. I believe that Rogers was essentially correct regarding the core interpersonal conditions, and although I feel they are necessary, my own personal role in the group tends to be broader than that and will vary with the levels of maturity and insight available in the group members. My inclination is to respond to group members with immediacy and gentle confrontation to both members' strengths and weaknesses. I attempt to remember that old wounds are best healed with nurturing and gentle care. People can get plenty of aggression, anger, and confrontation in the streets and even in their families. The group should be, I believe, above all a safe place. Through my manner of acceptance and respect, I try to help create an atmosphere that is secure and safe so that members can trust me, other members, and primarily themselves.

I believe that group members deserve the best of me, so I attempt to be well rested and fully available to them emotionally. I attend to their messages as carefully as I can.

Being fully available means, however, that I am going to do more than just listen and nurture. Carkhuff's (1969) research into the interpersonal conditions and the concept of wholeness is the model I use for personal availability in the group. Although I will not be intrusive with my personal values—at least not consciously—I give myself permission to be fully human in the group. That means that sometimes I will share my likes as well as dislikes, and my personal biases, prejudices, and opinions. In my work with group members I will be respectfully confrontational and immediate with my reactions.

Because in most cases, I am functioning at higher interpersonal levels and depth of insight than are my group members, I will assume somewhat more responsibility for helping to create a therapeutic climate in the group. I am mindful, however, that I am still only one person in a collection of individuals, and so my impact is limited. The climate or atmosphere in the group is an ongoing concern of mine, and so "how we are together" is always an issue that is available for inspection by the group.

Finally, I would like to say that all of my life experiences have in some way prepared me for group facilitation. That includes all of the laughter and tears, the highs and lows, wins and losses, elations and sorrows—all are part of me. In many ways, the most significant concentrated learning experience has been my own personal therapy. Actually experiencing the process that my group members go through has aided me most in being able to create for them a trusting and growing atmosphere.

Kevin's Adlerian Approach

People live and grow in groups, so it is only natural that people would best change in groups. Alfred Adler was one of the pioneers in the field of group work, not because he focused his psychology on group dynamics but because he recognized the social embeddedness of human beings. Most of his early work and teaching were done in a group format, much like a town hall meeting, where he would treat individuals in group settings. Although a complete exploration of Adler's theory is beyond the scope of this book, I will outline a brief discussion of Adler's philosophical approach to development and then illustrate how I integrate these ideas into the group work I conduct.

Personality Development

Adlerians believe development is a fluid process that focuses on the individual's striving from inferiority to superiority. At birth, we are all naked and helpless. This "inferior" state produces inferiority feelings that motivate us to strive to connect and belong (superiority). When we are infants, this striving is necessary for survival. Later on in life, it helps us form relationships with others. For these basic inferiority feelings, we each creatively discover ways that work best within our given environment to belong. We develop strategies for belonging, known as our style of life, that we continue to use for the rest of our lives. The style of life, one's blueprint for belonging, can also be called one's *personality*.

Our first society, our first group, is our family. People do not create their personality in an individualized vacuum. Instead, we create ourselves in a social setting. As we take the lessons we have learned out into the real world, we once again apply our strategies to other social groups. So from an Adlerian perspective, every person is best understood in a group/social context. It is important to note that one's environment does not determine one's style of life. Instead, how one perceives one's environment becomes the most important aspect of personality development. The creative power of the individual helps explain general examples such as how some people succeed in overcoming poverty and also specific examples of how siblings can be so different despite growing up in the same home.

Throughout one's life, each person strives to belong and succeed in what Adlerians call the tasks of life. These tasks represent spheres of existence that are universal aspects of everyone's life. The tasks are love, work, friendship, self, and spirituality. I believe you can learn quite a bit about anyone by exploring how that person attempts to meet each task.

Adler considered the social aspects of humanity so central to health and maladjustment that he coined the term "social interest" to describe the dynamic of belonging and contributing to one's society. Social interest is an innate potentiality in all people, and it can be seen in one's style of life. People whose life strategies include social interest will behave in ways marked by cooperation and mutuality. Those with limited social interest will behave in ways that better themselves at the detriment of others or in ways that withdraw from social commitments. Social interest is a concept unique to Adlerian theory, and understanding its emphasis on social connection makes it easy to see why Adlerian theory is such a nice fit for group work.

People enter counseling because one or more of the tasks of life are not being fulfilled in ways that are satisfactory to the person. Adlerians believe that people become discouraged when their strategies of succeeding in life are not working out for them in the present. Symptoms such as anxiety and depression often are created to act as excuses for not meeting the tasks of life. For example, " I am too anxious to work" or "If only I was less depressed, then I could form a real relationship." When faced with this discouragement, people often need help to face the tasks of life in new and creative ways. Understanding one's creative power to change can be the antidote to discouragement and pave the way to change. For a more detailed exploration of Adlerian theory and its philosophy, please refer to Fall et al. (2004), Sonstegard and Bitter (2004) or Dinkmeyer and Sperry (2000).

Therapeutic Relationship

My main focus in group leadership is to present to each group member as an interested collaborator in their change process, however they might define that process. It is through this spirit of collaboration that the group can begin to feel safe to risk sharing and connecting with each other. Collaboration in group may include discussing and deciding on group rules together, facilitating the group to set its own agenda, and minimizing advice giving. Imparting information may be appropriate, especially in psychoeducational groups, but I always emphasize and pay special attention to the process and the desires of the group at any given moment.

Fostering a collaborative environment helps group members warm up to the ideas of self-responsibility and teleology, two focus points of Adlerian counseling. *Self-responsibility* is the philosophical belief that each person is accountable for his or her own actions, thoughts, and feelings. *Teleology* is the principle that states that all of our actions, thoughts, and feelings are created for a purpose. The purpose highlights our life strategies, our chosen method for striving. Taken together, these two pieces are very powerful agents of change within a group. By exploring one's purpose of behavior and serving to hold members accountable for these behaviors, members can begin to change what they have control over: themselves. Group can be even more powerful in this effort because as a group leader I can harness the power of the group to collaborate in these explorations and help them hold each other accountable for their own "stuff." These efforts help groups stay on task, defend less, and grow more. In my work with adolescent males and domestic violence offenders, these elements have proven invaluable. In my groups, even though both populations are prone to blaming others for their issues, an observer would rarely hear members focusing on how parents or spouses are the real cause of their problems.

I also believe that to be effective I need to be a good model of social interest. Beyond creating a collaborative environment, I try to be present and genuine with my group members. If I am noticing or feeling something in the group, I am immediate and share that with the group. I do not believe that the group leader has to always be right. In fact, part of being human is making mistakes, so I actually enjoy it when a group member calls me on something that I missed. It provides an opportunity to model cooperative ways of handling mistakes.

Overall, I am drawn to Adlerian theory because it resonates with my own natural way of viewing human change. The deep understandings of human nature embedded in lifestyle analysis are useful to me and my insight into the group members. The emphasis on responsibility, to me, is a message of empowerment. It says, "Regardless of what you are going through, you have the power to change." I like that. The leadership style allows me to be active or to listen to the process. I can be confrontational and collaborative at the same time.

Developing Your Own Style

We included a brief discourse of our own approaches to group to illustrate that each person has his or her own way of making sense of the group experience. There is no one right way. Instead, what seems to make the difference is how well your group leader persona matches up with your real self. In lay speak, if you are faking it, it is going to show. As you read the remainder of the text, you will be bombarded with new information about the group process. We would encourage you, as you immerse yourself in group knowledge, not to forget the elements that make you an effective helper. These elements include your beliefs about how people develop, become maladjusted, and change. If you keep yourself at the forefront of this new exploration, we believe you will more easily begin to develop a sense of what you look like as a group leader.

References

Adler, A. (1956). *The individual psychology of Alfred Adler*. Edited by H. L. Ansbacher & R. Ansbacher. New York: Basic Books.

Carkhuff, R. R. (1969). *Helping and human relations: A primer for lay and professional helpers*, vol. I. New York: Holt, Rinehart & Winston.

Dinkmeyer, D. & Sperry, L. (2000). *Counseling and psychotherapy: An integrated individual psychology approach* (3rd ed.). Columbus, OH: Merrill/Prentice Hall.

Dreikurs, R. (1950). *Fundamentals of Adlerian psychology*. New York: Greenberg.

Ellis, A. (2001). *Overcoming destructive beliefs, feelings, and behaviors*. Atascadero, CA: Impact.

Fall, K. A., Holden, J. M., & Marquis, A. (2010). *Theoretical models of counseling and psychotherapy* (2nd ed.). London and New York: Routledge.

Hendrix, H. (1988). *Getting the love you want: A guide for couples*. New York: Holt, Rinehart & Winston.

Hobbs, N. (1964). Group-centered counseling. In C. Kemp (Ed.), *Perspectives on the group process* (pp. 156–161). Boston, MA: Houghton Mifflin.

Landreth, G. L. (1991). *Play therapy: The art of the relationship*. Muncie, IN: Accelerated Development.

Meador, B., & Rogers C. (1984). Person-centered therapy. In R. Corsini & D. Wedding (Eds.), *Current psychotherapies* (4th ed., pp. 142–195). Itasca, IL: F. E. Peacock.

Patterson, C. (1974). *Relationship counseling and psychotherapy*. New York: Harper & Row.

Perls, F., Hefferline, R., & Goodman, P. (1951). *Gestalt therapy: Excitement and growth in the human personality*. New York: Dell.

Polster, E., & Polster, M. (1973). *Gestalt therapy integrated: Contours of theory and practice*. New York: Brunner-Mazel.

Rogers, C. (1951). *Client-centered therapy: Its current practice, implications, and theory*. Boston, MA: Houghton Mifflin.

——— (1952). Client-centered psychotherapy. *Scientific American*, 187, 70.

——— (1957). A note on the nature of man. *Journal of Counseling Psychology*, 4, 202.

——— (1959). A theory of therapy, personality, and interpersonal relationships as developed in the client-centered framework. In S. Koch (Ed.), *Psychology: A study of a science* (pp. 184–256). New York: McGraw-Hill.

——— (1961). *On becoming a person*. Boston, MA: Houghton Mifflin.

——— (1967a). The conditions of change from a client-centered viewpoint. In B. Berenson & R. Carkhuff (Eds.), *Sources of gain in counseling and psychotherapy* (pp. 71–85). New York: Holt, Rinehart & Winston.

——— (1967b). The process of the basic encounter group. In J. F. Bugenthal (Ed.), *Challenges of humanistic psychology* (pp. 263–272). New York: McGraw-Hill.

——— (1980). *A way of being*. Boston, MA: Houghton Mifflin.

Sonstegard, M. A., & Bitter, J. R. (2004). *Adlerian group counseling: Step by step*. New York: Brunner-Routledge.

4

HOLISTIC LEADERSHIP TRAINING

Practice, practice makes perfect. Perfect is a fault and fault lines change.
Michael Stipe

Group Leadership Styles

Although the development of group theory and leadership intervention styles has been refined and differentiated greatly over the past thirty-five years, the early and classical leadership studies conducted by Lewin et al. (1939) and White and Lippitt (1968) provide a generic framework from which to evaluate group leadership. Essentially, they were looking at the dimension of group member participation in decision making. They identified three types of leadership for their studies: (1) authoritarian, (2) democratic, and (3) laissez-faire.

The Authoritarian Leader

This type of leadership style is autocratic and places a great deal of emphasis on leader power and authority. The leader often behaves in a highly directive manner and favors task completion over process issues. Although the group leader may initially consult with the group on mutual goals, the leader often determines and assesses the best way to achieve those goals. Authoritarian leader characteristics are most effective with psychoeducational groups and task groups.

The Democratic Leader

This type of leader, as the term reflects, is egalitarian in orientation. Group climate and cohesiveness are stressed, and participation by all group members in establishing goals and directions is encouraged. Valuing process over content, the democratic leader welcomes process input from the group and serves as more of a knowledgeable resource person. Counseling, psychotherapy, and psychoeducational groups work well with this type of leadership style.

The Laissez-Faire Leader

This type of leader takes a very passive role in the group. The group itself becomes responsible for its own direction and purpose. The leader serves as a technical consultant who will offer process interpretations and assistance if requested. These leadership characteristics are useful in support groups and in later stages of the group process when group members take on more responsibility for the work.

Lewin et al. (1939) and White and Lippitt (1968) found that interesting differences emerged, particularly as related to group member satisfaction, aggressiveness, and group-task efficiency. Authoritarian and democratic groups were noted as tending to stay with their tasks about equally, whereas laissez-faire-led groups were generally less conscientious. When the leaders absented themselves from the groups, authoritarian groups wandered from the task, democratic groups continued at about the same pace, and the laissez-faire groups tended to *increase* their work.

As might be expected, authoritarian groups fostered more dependency upon their leader, were more discontented and openly critical, and made more aggressive demands. Friendliness and cooperation were characteristic of the democratic groups, and, in general, group members expressed a preference for democratic leaders above the other two styles.

A close relationship exists between leadership style and group efficiency and satisfaction. Group members seem to want and expect an identifiable leader who fulfills certain developmental group needs. Fall (1997) explored the role of the leader in the facilitation of psychological safety and found that, across the life span of a group, the members attributed the facilitation of psychological safety to the leader, more often than to self or others. This seems to indicate that although a democratically oriented group with shared responsibility is most desired and effective, the leader should be identifiable as opposed to being an "equal" member of the group.

Each group leader must explore and define what is the most effective and congruent style for him or her. The process of determining a "proper fit" in terms of leadership style is one that requires experience and practice. We recommend that the leader in training experiments with several different approaches while under supervision. The most effective and satisfied leaders are those who find a relatively comfortable style that blends their own personality with a solid base of theory.

Kottler (1983) wrote about a group leader as a "fully functioning model." His group leader is a person who projects an image of a formidable individual who is fully in charge of his or her personal world. The leader exudes self-confidence, expertise, worldly experience, and serenity. Kottler defined "personal mastery" as the development of skills necessary for a happy existence. He further explained,

> Personally masterful therapists are busy persons, intensely concerned with their well-being and that of their fellow humans. They are action-oriented truth seekers who pursue the unknown and take productive risks in the search for a more satisfying life. Most important, they are in a continual state of improved change, ever working to become more personally masterful.
>
> (Kottler 1983: 92)

In addition, there are some corollary assumptions implicit in the personal mastery model.

1. The more personally skilled group leaders become, the more professionally effective they are.
2. The group leader is in a constant state of change, as are all group members. Each client concern and interaction conflict forces the leader to look inward, asking the question, "Have I worked this problem through for myself?" Although using group time to work through personal struggles is clearly unethical, the group leader cannot help but use the time between sessions to personalize relevant struggles to bring them toward successful closure.
3. The more effective group leaders become at solving personal problems, the better teachers they can be at facilitating such outcomes in clients. The group

leader should have learned ahead of time how to work through any concern with which a group member may have difficulty.

4. No mere human has ever reached perfection. Every group leader ought to be engaged in a rigorous self-training process aimed at teaching higher levels of personal mastery. Identifying behaviors in need of improvement is the first step in making constructive changes.

(Kottler 1983: 92–93)

Kottler concluded with a list of group leader characteristics to aid in self-evaluation. They include self-confidence, risk-taking, humor, flexibility, creativity, internal discipline, flow (being immersed in the present), freedom from negative emotions, honesty, energetic enthusiasm, and compassion.

Techniques and strategies in the group are frequently associated with specific theoretical approaches. Gestalt, existential, and narrative approaches all utilize techniques that are unique to that particular theory. Group functions, on the other hand, particularly in process-oriented groups, are more broadly based and comprise issues with which all group leaders need to be concerned. Group climate, cohesion, levels of trust, and interaction patterns fall into this category.

Finally, the accomplished group leader will engage in an ongoing assessment of his or her own relationships with individual group members and the group as an entity. The concept that leader relationships are a critical dimension in an effective group leads to the following discussion of *interpersonal skills*.

Rationale for Interpersonal Skills Training

Interpersonal skills are constellations of behaviors that define and may circumscribe the quality of person-to-person relationships. It is the concept of looking carefully at how people behave with one another qualitatively. Most often, interpersonal skills are defined as communication skills, and most systematic study has been devoted to verbal and nonverbal communication transactions. The study and quantification of interpersonal skills have been impacted most directly by psychotherapy and communication theory.

The concept of interpersonal skills development and subsequent training implies that these skills are acquired rather than latent. Because of this focus on learning, consequently, the impact of culture, environment, social expectations, and societal and personal values are of interest to therapists and communication theorists.

Historically, the groundwork for incorporating an interpersonal dimension into therapy was laid by the neo-Freudians who departed from Sigmund Freud's heavy reliance upon innate biological explanations for behavior. Alfred Adler, a social democrat, was the first to view humans as essentially social beings whose behavior is purposive and goal-directed. The later work of Karen Horney, with her emphasis upon the cultural impact in the formation of neurotic conceptions of self, and—most important—the interpersonal theory of Harry Stack Sullivan, provided pathways for future theoreticians to explore the more subjective worlds of their patients.

The work of F. C. Thorne and his eclectic approach to psychotherapy further broadened attempts to provide a more balanced and integrated method of looking at human behavior. With the publication of Carl Rogers' *Client-Centered Therapy* (1951) and its almost total focus upon the subjective, phenomenological world of the client, the relationship between the therapist and client became primary, and the process of relationship development came under more intense scrutiny. A major historical contribution was Rogers' attempt to identify the necessary and sufficient conditions of therapeutic personality change.

In addition to his concern with a client as a "whole person," Rogers gave impetus to the concept that there is a central core of "facilitative" conditions crucial in developing a constructive relationship between therapist and client. He identified these conditions as therapist-offered empathy, warmth, and genuineness.

Charles B. Truax and Robert R. Carkhuff (1967: xiv) focused intensive research efforts toward identifying new knowledge of the ingredients of effective counseling and psychotherapy that result in client benefit. The primary methodological breakthrough from their impressive volume of research was the development of a reliable series of scales for the measurement of the identified interpersonal conditions of accurate empathy, non-possessive warmth, and the therapist's self-congruence.

Concurrently, communication theorists were synthesizing the complex information available from a number of interdisciplinary fields into a set of principles that can be applied to interpersonal communication. Samovar and Rintye (1970) emphasized that human speech exhibits common elements and that human attention is highly selective. They posited that humans actively seek consistency between their self-image, behavior, and perceived information, and that they maintain perceptual consistency by distorting information or avoiding data they cannot change.

Samovar and Rintye (1970) contended that active listening on the part of the receiver of information produces better retention. Social roles and statuses influence communication in organizations, and no symbol or word has a *fixed referent*—that is, the "meaning" of the word is attached to the sender or receiver rather than to the word itself. They also addressed the issue of how nonverbal language contributes to human communication. They considered these principles basic to the study of interpersonal communication.

Building upon the work of Rogers and Truax, Robert R. Carkhuff (1983a) refined the interpersonal rating scales and expanded the list of interpersonal communication dimensions. Carkhuff and his associates developed an interpersonal helping model primarily for use in therapeutic settings but theoretically applicable to all human interactions. Their model, which is essentially training and learning oriented, focuses initially on the skill of discrimination or the ability of the person to fully understand the message sent in both content and process. The ability to receive a message accurately depends upon the receiver's level of attention. They have demonstrated techniques to improve a person's attending skills.

How a person responds to a message is critical to the continuance of constructive communication and lays the foundation for initiative action. Six interpersonal conditions impact the effectiveness of communication: three facilitative and three action conditions.

Facilitative Conditions

When these conditions are offered in communication at observably high levels, they tend to facilitate one's effort to explore and understand oneself.

- *Empathy.* This is the ability to merge temporarily with another person and see the world through that person's eyes. It is the ability to understand the experiences and feelings of the other person.
- *Respect.* This is the ability to communicate caring for and belief in the potential of another person.
- *Concreteness.* This is the ability to assist another person to be specific about the feelings and experiences that person is talking about.

Action Conditions

When these conditions are offered in communication at observably high levels, they tend to lead one to initiate and take action upon one's own ideas.

- *Genuineness.* This is the ability to be one's real self in a relationship with another person.
- *Confrontation.* This is the ability to tell the other just the way it is and to point out discrepancies between words and actions and perceived realities.
- *Immediacy.* This is the ability to understand the feelings and experiences that are going on between oneself and another person.

Basis Assumptions in Helping

Interpersonal skills development can really be seen in the total design as an essential first step in the maximizing of each person's potential capacity toward what Carkhuff (1983b) termed *human resource development.*

The obligation of each person in helping situations is to accept the *right* to intervene at the critical points in the life of another person and, at the same time, take full *responsibility* for the level of help that he or she is willing to offer. When we have decided that we want and intend to be more than a mere "sounding board" off which others can bounce feelings and meanings, we also must accept the awesome responsibility for mobilizing all of the helping skills we have available to us in order to ensure a successful completion.

This statement means that we will make a commitment to becoming as effective in helping as is in our power to become. It means that we will do the things necessary— incorporate the essential physical, intellectual, and emotional skills—that will allow us to offer potent and functional help and to serve as efficient models and teachers through our actions as well as our words.

Let us examine two basic assumptions underlying the helping process.

Helper–Helpee: The Universal Relationship

Essentially, all transactions between two or more human beings can be broken down into helper–helpee roles. One person in the transaction will tend to be the helper (or the "more knowing" person), and the other will be the helpee (or the "less knowing" person). The critical factor in the helper–helpee relationship is the sum of interpersonal effectiveness brought to bear in the situation, as measured by a person's total impact—physical, intellectual, and emotional. An additional dimension is that the roles are not necessarily fixed or static and that they may change or reverse according to the kind of help that is sought and the relative "knowingness" of the persons involved.

The helper in a transaction will be the more knowing, whether in any one or a combination of two or more of the three areas:

1. *physical*—in that, through general physiological conditioning, the helper is able to demonstrate high levels of energy and endurance;
2. *intellectual*—in that, having the appropriate and relevant information, the helper can creatively apply it to the situation;
3. *emotional*—in that the helper is fully aware of his or her own personal feelings and interpersonal impact and can act compassionately and decisively as the situation and circumstances require.

Relationships Are "For Better or for Worse"

The second major assumption in human transactions is that they can be "for better or for worse"—constructive or destructive. The primary question is, "Where do we fit in as helpers?" When a person seeks our help, does he or she leave the transaction in better condition or worse? Ultimately, in our efforts to assist, have we helped the other person grow, or have we retarded growth? The relationship that we provide for the other person will be, as a result of the level of the interpersonal skills we offer, either additive or subtractive in the helpee's life.

In summary, the helper–helpee is a universal relationship that can assume many configurations, that is, parent–child, doctor–patient, leader–follower, friend–friend, and so forth. In addition, the level of the relationship or "help" offered will influence individual growth—either "for better," in a healthy, constructive fashion, or "for worse," in an unhealthy, deteriorative, destructive direction.

Philosophical Foundations for Interpersonal Skills Development

This model envisions a person as a developing, striving, growing organism who ultimately is a product of the levels of "help" received from the environment. That is, a person will respond to and grow in either a "for better" or "for worse" direction according to the effectiveness of the models to whom he or she assigns *significance* in life. Most usually, this model is the parents or primary caretakers. Later on, as a child's world expands, it will include significant teachers, coaches, counselors, aunts and uncles, peers, and others. Given inherent biological determiners, the child–adolescent–adult will, in effect, model behavior and learn appropriate or inappropriate skills from the people in his or her personal world.

Such a theory of personality focuses upon conscious growth and integration as the central motivating forces. Putting this idea more concretely,

- The most potent example of a person's total effectiveness is one's level of functioning in the world—not wishes, desires, or self–reports, but observable behavior.
- The person is mainly a product of the skills and behaviors that are learned from the world.
- The person's ego (or that part of personality structure that sorts out and integrates internal needs with the reality of the world) is seen as moving toward fulfillment of potential and growth.

The central thesis of this model is that the life of the "whole person" is made up of actions that fully integrate the emotional, intellectual, and physical resources in such a way that these actions lead to greater and greater self-definition or integration. In a sense, then, the fully functioning "whole person" is the person who can say and understand the implications of "I know who I am, and I know what I can do."

The Whole Person

The interpersonal skills model is committed to the fully functioning, integrated, whole person as illustrated in Figure 4.1. In terms of "helping," the fully integrated, whole person will be able to better generate and sustain high levels of help because of superior capacities, as demonstrated by the three areas:

THE "WHOLE" PERSON

INTELLECTUAL
Information
Creativity

PHYSICAL	EMOTIONAL
Body Image	Intrapersonal Understanding
Energy	Interpersonal Skills
Endurance	

Figure 4.1 Fully functioning, integrated, whole person

1. physical: high energy levels and the ability to tolerate and endure hardships;
2. intellectual: synthesizing relevant data and creatively applying them to the circumstance;
3. emotional—being able to offer appropriate dimensions of interpersonal responsiveness and initiative.

Perhaps the best way to capsulize the whole person or effective helper is with the following paragraph:

> The effective helper is a person who is living effectively himself and who discloses himself in a genuine and constructive fashion in response to others. He communicates an accurate empathic understanding and respect for all of the feelings of other persons and guides discussions with those persons into specific feelings and experiences. He communicates confidence in what he is doing and is spontaneous, intense, open and flexible in his relationship with others and committed to the welfare of the other person.
>
> (Carkhuff 1983b)

The Growing Person

Latent forces seem to be available in an advanced technological society that are constantly at work to encourage and promote mediocrity. In a highly specialized and institutionalized society, reward systems seem designed to regulate human behavior in such a way as to stifle imagination and creativity. The fully functioning person recognizes these latent forces and becomes involved in a continual program of learning, relearning, and acquiring new and more effective skills. The group leader understands that to stand still or to "play a pat hand" is not really standing still at all—but moving backward. No such thing as a holding pattern exists.

Growing persons accept the proposition that staying "fully in the moment" is an ability that requires continual upgrading of skills. Being full and complete means accepting the challenge of depending fully on oneself when situations develop, as opposed to manipulating or controlling people and events. This behavior means dealing with people honestly and in an up-front manner, rather than by cunning and guile.

The key to confidence in the situation is the development of a wide range of abilities or, put another way, increasing our repertoire of responses. The person with the widest range of response to any situation stands the greatest probability of success. As we increase our repertoire of responses, we multiply the number of options available to us.

Concerning functionality, the truly integrated person knows that in critical situations we want the most skillful person in the driver's seat. That is, we must learn to concede to functionality where it exists and encourage its growth where the potential is present.

By way of illustration, let us say you are confronted with choosing between two players (A and B) to be the quarterback for your team. All other things being relatively equal, you find that A is a mechanically sound and adequate quarterback. In addition to being mechanically sound, however, player B seems able to infuse the team with a greater desire to perform well. He is an exciting leader. Choosing player B to quarterback the team will increase the probability of winning because he has *additional skills* to ensure a successful delivery. The most functional person in the situation should play quarterback.

An Overview of Interpersonal Skills Development

We begin our exploration of interpersonal skills with a schematic presentation of the overall model as presented in Table 4.1. As suggested in Figure 4.1, when we begin to examine carefully the kinds of things that happen between two people in an interpersonal relationship, we need to focus upon *discrimination* (the ability to listen and understand) and *communication* (the ability to respond accurately to what we have heard). In addition, the model includes six dimensions that occur to some extent (or at some level) in all human transactions. These dimensions are *empathy, respect, concreteness, genuineness, confrontation*, and *immediacy*.

Carkhuff and Berenson (1977) have researched each of the dimensions and found that persons (therapists, counselors, teachers, parents, students, and lay helpers) who offer high levels of the interpersonal conditions tend to create an atmosphere or climate for growth. Conversely, persons who offer low levels of these same conditions tend to retard or inhibit an individual's growth. This process has been demonstrated in the physical, intellectual, and emotional areas, but here we will primarily be concerned with the quality of verbal responses that the group leader is offering members.

Let's look at what we mean when we say *high* or *low* levels. In determining whether a response is high or low, we use a five-point scale where each of the responses can be scaled

Table 4.1 Schematic model for interpersonal skills

Discrimination and communication of the facilitative/responsive and action-oriented/initiative dimensions

1. Empathy (understanding someone)
2. Respect/warmth (caring for someone)
3. Concreteness (being specific)
4. Genuineness (being honest and open)
5. Confrontation (pointing out discrepancies or "telling it like it is")
6. Immediacy (being in the here and now)
7. Preferred mode of treatment or effective course of action (self-understanding)

Table 4.2 Scale to evaluate overall helping effectiveness

Helpfulness	*Scale*	*Level of communication*
Additive responses	5.0	All conditions are communicated fully, simultaneously, and continually.
Area of additive empathy	4.0	Some conditions are communicated at a minimally facilitative level, and some fully.
Interchangeable	3.0	All conditions are communicated at a minimally facilitative level.
Subtractive responses	2.0	Some conditions are communicated, and some are not.
	1.0	None of the conditions are communicated to any noticeable degree.

by trained raters for content and feeling. The scale to evaluate overall helping effectiveness is provided in Table 4.2.

Responses that fall below level 3.0 on the scale are judged to be subtractive, deteriorative, or destructive to the person who is seeking help. Responses that are at the 3.0 level are called *interchangeable responses* in that they (the stimulus statement from the helpee and the response from the helper) can be laid side by side and could have been said by either the helper or the helpee. The helper at level 3.0 attempts to simply restate or reflect back to the helpee as accurately as possible his or her *expressed* feeling and meaning. The higher levels (3.0 and above) are termed *additive empathic responses*—when the helper goes beyond what the helpee has expressed in an attempt to add to the exploration and self-understanding.

The area of additive empathic responses between levels 3 and 4 on the scale is where the majority of good helping occurs. This is the area where the skillful helper will spend most time and energy facilitating the deeper self-exploration of the helpee. It involves going beyond what the helpee has presented. To be additively empathic, the helper assists the individual in taking personal responsibility for his or her part in the problem. In effect, this means that the helpee cannot put the meaning off onto someone or something else. It involves ownership or internalization of his or her position in the problem.

No value occurs in problem-solving until the focus person internalizes and "owns" responsibility for self. This frequently involves letting go of some of the more primary ego-defense mechanisms such as denial, blame, projection, and rationalization.

Subtractive responses on the five-point scale are "for worse," and according to Carkhuff and Berenson (1977), the overall average for various samples of the population is below 3.0, or the minimally facilitative level (that is, lay helpers scored 1.49, the general public scored 1.58, graduate students in psychology scored 2.35, classroom teachers scored 2.10, high-school counselors scored 1.89, and experienced therapists scored 2.13) (Carkhuff & Berenson 1977: 31), we can see that we are paying a heavy price in our interpersonal relationships.

Interpersonal Skills for the Group Leader

Most of us find ourselves in "helping" situations several times each day. Some of us literally make a living from helping. Others are less directly involved with providing professional help, but most people are engaged in some form of service to other people. The range of possible therapeutic situations in which we find ourselves is almost infinite, that is, counselor–client, teacher–student, nurse–patient, parent–child, police officer–citizen, airline flight attendant–upset traveler, ad infinitum.

We believe that the critical determiner as far as the help we offer to others is ourselves. When we are called upon for help, the impact we have on the person or the effectiveness of the helping transaction will be related directly to the level of interpersonal skills we offer to the other person.

More concretely, we might ask ourselves the question "If I didn't have the uniform, or the professional role, or the set of procedures, or the guidelines, what would I be able to offer to another person?" The answer is always the same: me.

Our major focus is on an exploration of the personal qualities that each of us has available to us and the level or degree to which we offer these personal qualities to others in helping situations.

We could summarize by saying that each of us finds ourselves in multiple situations where we are called upon to help. Furthermore, let us assume that each of us wants to maximize our potential as potent and effective helpers. From this base, we can proceed to further explorations.

Discrimination

What can we, as group leaders, do to increase our levels of response and make a significant difference in the lives of our group members? The first skill we need to examine is *discrimination.* Developing high discrimination (or attending) skills means that we will tend fully to the message that is being sent and all of its parts. Not only do we listen to the content, or *what* is being said, but also to the feeling, or *how* it is being said. To do this, we need to listen to another person not only with our ears but also with our eyes. We need to hear not only the words (verbal) but also the feeling (nonverbal).

The first step in improving the quality of our responses is to make a good discrimination of what and how something is being said to us. The key is to attend carefully to all of the cues—content, feeling, verbal, and nonverbal.

Some people in our world tend to be naturally high discriminators. This person would be the kind of individual who is inclined to be quiet and observant of the behavior of others. This individual is what we might call a *responsive personality type*—one who carefully watches others and then acts according to his or her perceived expectations. As a predominant mode of behavior, this could be dangerous if carried to its neurotic extreme because it can result in behavior that is initiated only in response to others—loss of personal definition, and ultimately incorporation of a self-concept from the "outside in," so to speak. By practicing our attending skills, we can train ourselves to be better, clearer, finer discriminators by listening to and fully being with the other person.

Communication

Discrimination, although it is the foundation for higher-level interpersonal relationships, is of relatively little therapeutic value in helping if it stands alone. Discrimination, although it is a necessary and even crucial step in helping, is not enough. After the careful discrimination has been made comes the next, and most important, step—that is, *communication.* This is the step where we respond to our helpee in terms of what our best discrimination tells us he or she is saying—or asking for. In a sense, we can make a judgment on how good our discriminations have been by evaluating the level of response that we communicate back to the helpee—or the other person in the transaction. At this point, the five-point scale is meaningful. Now we can look at the stimulus (S, or the statement presented by the helpee) and also look at the response (R, or the statement given back to the helpee by the helper) and determine its effectiveness on the scale—its additiveness or subtractiveness.

Overall, helping involves discrimination and communication. Both of these skills can be trained, practiced, and improved. As you might expect, discrimination is somewhat easier to train because it is a relatively passive behavior. Discrimination involves *sensing* and *knowing*—fully attending to another person to determine as accurately as possible what is being said. Communicating back to the helpee is a more active behavior and, as such, demands a certain amount of risk on the part of the helper. We can never be truly effective helpers until we accept the risks of deep, active involvement with our helpees.

Summarizing, discrimination involves total *alertness*, and communication involves *acting*.

Group members will first want to know that their leader indeed can help them—that the helper is more functional, "more knowing" and able to deliver the appropriate help. We relate back to what was said earlier about functionality. The initial discrimination that the helpee will make is physical. He or she will want to know if the helper respects self enough to present a competent, ordered, and attractive physical picture.

Let's assume that the group member has decided to stay and run a few more tests. The next question asked or felt, however vaguely, is "Will I be understood—can he or she understand me?" Helpees frequently feel confused and upset—not able to sort out their thinking and feeling. This very fact often makes them anxious and fearful. At this point, the group member is not interested in judgments, advice, or "being told what to do." He or she is interested in being cared for and understood as completely as possible. Being understood by another human being, at this particular point, helps to answer the question "Am I still OK?" The group member wants the helper to respond in a nonjudgmental, unconditional way. He or she wants to feel understood (empathy) and cared for (respect).

When offered to the helpee at interchangeable levels, these two conditions, empathy and respect, are called the *building block dimensions* in that they communicate and promote deeper and deeper levels of mutual trust. As empathy and respect are communicated, the helpee will learn to trust at deeper levels and feel free to explore self and problems more intensely.

The group member also will progress toward deeper self-exploration and self-understanding as the leader focuses sharply upon what is being said—and not said—and guides the helpee into personally relevant material in specific terms.

At the point where trust has been established and self-exploration has been facilitated, a kind of self-understanding frequently occurs. This is often a cognitive or intellectual understanding of self or the problem. In the interpersonal skills model, this level of understanding is achieved when the group member can respond to self just as the leader would. In other words, the helper and helpee have become verbally interchangeable. Some therapists refer to this point as *insight*.

The interpersonal skills model goes beyond most insight therapies to an action or initiative stage. What is being said, in effect, is that "there is no understanding without action." Put another way, we could say that it is possible to "understand" ourselves or our problems, but the real proof of our understanding is how we put our insights into action through appropriate and constructive behavior.

Also, at this point the leader, after having demonstrated understanding and caring and after developing a bond of trust, can become increasingly conditional or initiating with the helpee. At this point, the helper is established as a strong reinforcer for the helpee and can become increasingly genuine, confrontive, and immediate—more interchangeable or reciprocal as the helper–helpee team begins to work together to develop plans, programs, and effective strategies to reintegrate the helpee with his or her thinking, feeling, behavior, and world.

Helping from the Point of View of the Helper

From our previous discussion, we can see that the process of helping is essentially seen in two major phases—discrimination and communication. These two phases also relate directly to the interpersonal conditions that are emphasized in each phase.

Facilitative or Responsive Dimension

The facilitative or responsive dimension includes the conditions of empathy, respect, concreteness, and, to a somewhat lesser extent, genuineness. These "core" conditions, when offered at high levels, tend to meet the group member's initial need for nurturance or unconditionality and aid in the process of trust building and self-exploration.

The responsive dimensions, as the term implies, tend to take persons where they are and communicate to them that we understand their frame of reference or "where they are coming from." Let us look at each of the responsive conditions briefly.

Empathy

The communication of empathy involves the helper communicating back to the helpee that he or she knows and understands both the *feeling* and *meaning* of the helpee's expression and experience.

By focusing intently upon the content that the helpee is presenting and the manner in which the content is communicated, we can begin to respond to both parts of the message. At level 3, or the interchangeable level, we will want to communicate back to the helpee that we understand the expressed feelings and meaning. In a sense, we are asking the helper to *reflect* back to the helpee, as accurately as possible, what the helpee is meaning and feeling. At higher (or additive) levels, the helper will go beyond the helpee's expression and add noticeably in communicating understanding in a way that the helpee is not able to do for him or herself.

Here are some further guidelines for judging empathic accuracy. At the responsive level 3, or the interchangeable level, the helper reflects

- the helpee's verbally expressed feeling;
- the helpee's obvious feeling experience; and
- an understanding of the environmental stimulus or content.

Additive levels of empathy draw upon the helper's ability to integrate this information and experience and guide the helpee in

- identification of the helpee's behavior pattern;
- the helpee's feelings about self as a result of interaction with the environment;
- the helpee's expectations of self;
- the helpee's basic beliefs about self; and
- incorporating the new feelings or reactions to new meanings.

Helpee stimulus: "It's gotten so that I get nervous whenever we get an invitation to a party. I start to worry and fret a whole week in advance."

Interchangeable response: "Just the anticipation of going to a party makes you feel anxious and tense."

Additive response: "The anticipation of a party really makes you uptight and sort of scared. Like you won't be able to handle it all, and that leaves you feeling confused and frustrated."

Respect

The communication of respect involves the helper communicating back to the helpee a concern and regard for the helpee—his or her feelings, potentials, and experiences. The helper communicates respect at level 3 by indicating a positive regard and caring for the helpee's feelings, experiences, and potential to grow. The helper communicates an appreciation of the helpee's ability to express self and deal constructively with life experiences. At higher levels, the helper's responses enable the helpee to feel free to be him- or herself and to experience being valued as an individual.

Respect communicates that the helper cares and values the helpee's ability to work through problems in a constructive way. At the highest levels of respect, the helper will initiate communication that causes the helpee to realize his or her full potential for growth.

Helpee stimulus: "It makes me so darn mad. I know I'm a better basketball player than most of the guys on the team, and every Friday night I buy a ticket to get in to watch them play."
Interchangeable response: "You get pretty angry when you feel that you could be playing and contributing instead of sitting in the bleachers."
Additive response: "You're pretty angry at yourself for sitting around and letting a good opportunity pass you. You've got a lot more than you're using right now, and you want to find a way to test that ability."

Concreteness

In communicating concreteness, the helper guides and directs discussion into personally relevant material in specific terms and concrete terms. At the minimally effective level, or level 3, the helper, at times, enables the helpee to discuss personally relevant material in specific terms. The helper may not always develop the area of inquiry fully. The communication of concreteness requires that the helper make a fine discrimination in terms of the helpee's cognitive and affective readiness to discuss personally relevant material in increasingly specific and concrete terms.

These are the major responsive or facilitative dimensions and are usually communicated first in helping relationships. They assist the helpee in self-exploration and understanding and in laying the groundwork for the helper to become increasingly initiative and conditional in the relationship as the helper–helpee team begins the upward-outward process of reintegration with the real world.

Helpee stimulus: "I suppose I'm not so different—I guess most people get pretty uptight and nervous when there's a lot of work to do."
Interchangeable response: "You're really hoping that your own uptightness won't get out of hand—that most people feel about the same as you do."
Additive response: "On the one hand, you still hope that your anxiety will just go away and at the same time it's pretty frightening to think that it might get out of control—overwhelm you."

Initiative or Action-Oriented Dimension

The initiative or action-oriented dimension includes the conditions of genuineness, confrontation, and immediacy. After the helpee has experienced the feeling of being understood and cared for and has demonstrated an increased self-awareness by becoming more and more interchangeable with the helper, he or she is ready to translate self-understanding into a concrete plan of action.

At this point, the implications for the helper are to become more "conditional" and, in a sense, more of a reciprocal person in the helping relationship. Let us look at the specific conditions that can be offered at higher levels during this later stage in helping.

Genuineness

The communication of genuineness consists of the helper expressing his or her honest feelings to the helpee in a constructive manner. Perhaps a good way to illustrate what we mean by *genuineness* is to think about the opposite of being genuine—that is, being unreal or phony. Being honest and open with real feelings in helping requires a good discrimination of the helpee's ability to handle your openness. An individual can be highly genuine and real with feelings and meanings and yet the total impact of an interchange can be destructive to the helpee. The key to helpful genuineness is being appropriate and constructive with feelings. At the lowest levels of genuineness, the helper often responds defensively or in a "professional" manner or role. The helper offering low levels of genuineness may sound rehearsed or preplanned.

At level 3, or the minimally facilitative level, the helper provides no "negative" cues or, for that matter, "positive" cues to indicate a truly honest response. In other words, the helper indicates attentive listening, but responses do not reflect that he or she is either *insincere* or, on the other hand, *deeply involved.*

At higher levels of genuineness, the helper indicates honest responses (either positive or negative) in a nondestructive way. The helper is being honest, spontaneous, and constructive.

Helpee stimulus: "It's almost surprising to me. I know it's what I've been working toward, but I can really care for someone, and someone cares for me."

Interchangeable response: "You weren't really sure it could happen to you. That you could care for me and allow me to care for you."

Additive response: "It's really an amazing and awesome feeling to know that I care for you deeply and for you to care for me. It really makes me feel good to know that you understand and accept my caring."

Confrontation

Confrontation involves the helper focusing upon helpee discrepancies. Types of confrontation include the following:

- real versus ideal self;
- insight versus action; and
- helper versus helpee experience.

Modes of confrontation include the following:

- experiential;
- didactic;
- confrontation to strength;
- confrontation to weakness; and
- encouragement to act.

Unfortunately, the cultural violence of the 1960s and early 1970s helped create an emotional response to the word *confrontation*. Too frequently, it is equated with anger and conflict. As can be seen by the definition here, confrontation involves focusing upon *discrepancies* in ideas and behavior and is not necessarily accompanied by any particular affect. As we inspect the definition, we see that there are three major types of confrontation and five major modes or methods.

At the minimally facilitative level, the verbal and behavioral expressions of the helper, although open to helpee discrepancies, do not relate directly or specifically to these discrepancies. For instance, the helper may simply raise questions without pointing to the diverging directions of the possible answers.

At higher levels, the helper attends directly and specifically to helpee discrepant behavior and confronts the helpee directly and explicitly in a sensitive and perceptive manner whenever discrepancies occur.

Helpee stimulus: "I've been on diets a hundred times. Tried about everything. I can lose weight, but then I gain it back. I don't seem to have the willpower to stick to anything."

Interchangeable response: "You've proven you can take the weight off—it's keeping it off that bothers you. This pattern raises some questions about your ability to stick with a program."

Additive response: "This 'on-again, off-again' pattern raises some real questions about yourself. It's a question of whether you can work only for short periods of time—or whether you can persist and endure. Whether you can make a commitment to real and lasting change."

Immediacy

The communication of immediacy involves the helper focusing upon the "here-and-now" ongoing relationship between the helper and helpee. At the lowest levels of immediacy, the helper's responses disregard helpee expressions that have the potential for relating to the helper. The helper may disregard, remain silent, or just not relate the content to self.

At the interchangeable level, the helper remains open and alert to interpretations of immediacy but does not relate what the helpee is saying to the immediate moment. The helper may make literal responses or reflections that are open-minded but that refer to no one specifically.

At additive levels, the helper relates the helpee's responses to self either in a tentative manner or, at the highest levels, in a direct and explicit way.

Helpee stimulus: "I don't know, I've seen two other counselors and it didn't seem like it helped much. Maybe I'll just have to learn to live with this. Nobody seems to have the answers."

Interchangeable response: "It's pretty discouraging to you. You've tried before, you're trying again, but you're just not sure that anyone can help you."

Additive response: "You're pretty discouraged at this point, partly with yourself and partly with me. You were hoping that I would be different than the others, but right now you're just not sure."

Summary of Helper's Strategy

In summarizing the helper's strategy through the implementation of the dimensions in an interpersonal relationship, we see a group leader who is keenly aware of self and his or her personal impact on the helpee. The helper is able to make fine discriminations of the helpee's needs and is able to respond to those needs at an appropriate level.

The helper sees self both as a person who can be nurturing and facilitative and as a person who can initiate new material and add directionality to move the helpee to higher and higher levels of growth and self-fulfillment. The overall plan is to facilitate self-exploration and understanding, and to strategize with the helpee in devising effective programs or courses of action to remedy destructive behavior patterns and encourage the incorporation of new and effective modes of living. A helper accepts the responsibility for becoming a potent force to the helpee and is willing to "go the extra mile" in order to maintain potency and increase his or her own personal growth.

Through a personal philosophy of being real and offering him- or herself in a relationship at the highest levels, the helper discloses self as a person.

Effective Leadership Training

The Association for Specialists in Group Work (ASGW 2000; see Appendix B) and the Council for Accreditation of Counseling and Related Educational Programs (CACREP; 2009) provide specific guidelines for effective leadership training. Both agree that students should engage in a comprehensive learning system that includes both didactic instruction and hands-on learning that gives students an opportunity to experience the role of a member and a facilitator. University programs have various creative ways of fulfilling the spirit of these elements of training, and this section highlights some of these approaches.

Many programs manage the experience of being a group member by having the students participate in a "personal growth" group. Approximately one half of the allotted class time is devoted to group counseling, labeled a *laboratory group.* Normal class size is sixteen students, so that, when divided, there are two laboratory groups of eight members each. Groups meet for one and a half hours weekly during the regular academic semester and twice weekly during summer sessions. The laboratory groups are led by senior doctoral students or hired licensed practitioners. Having outside facilitators effectively avoids the dual relationship concerns that may occur when the group is led by the instructor.

The laboratory group component of the course is designed to be a nonevaluative component of the course. Students are encouraged but not required to participate as fully as they can in helper and helpee roles, and to test and explore their skills in a direct fashion. Grades are not assigned for laboratory-group participation.

Prescreening for group membership suitability is limited to acceptance into the master's degree program. Group counseling is a required course, and all candidates participate. Although most students are eager for the experience and graduates consistently rate the experience highly, it is probable that the laboratory groups would be even better were the course elective.

Group members are asked to keep detailed personal journals that focus upon their own in-depth self-exploration in addition to the process of the group itself. Riordan and White (1996) pointed out that logs can help integrate group experiences and were found helpful by a majority of group members studied. Particularly for some members, this assignment increases their personal awareness and facilitates the critical examination of the group process.

Other methods of the group-member experience exist, but this seems to be the most common practice. The next section describes four different approaches to the leadership-training component.

Observation Model

The observation model allows students to observe master group leaders facilitate a group. As the students watch, they take notes and can be directed by the instructor to notice specific process and leadership dynamics. Conyne et al. (1997) noted that the level of detail and analysis can be a real advantage to this approach, because students get to see good examples of the dynamics they have learned about in class. When the group has ended, the students and often the group leader can process the day's issues. The observation model can be used with live groups, where the students watch behind one-way glass in a process observer position outside the group (fishbowl) or with videotaped sessions.

The observation model allows students to learn directly about group without being confronted with the anxiety and responsibility of leading a group. This distance frees the student to focus on what is going on with the group without having to be worried if they are "doing the right thing." The instructor can also immediately focus on different group elements depending on the need of the student. For example, if one student seems to be struggling with the issue of process versus content, the instructor can point out examples of this during the group or direct the student to specifically look for examples. At the same time, another student may need more attention to attending skills, and the instructor could make individualized recommendations to him or her using the same group. The observation method, in this way, provides a very flexible learning laboratory.

Programs that employ the observation model must consider several disadvantages. The most obvious challenge is trying to substitute observational learning for the potency of participant learning. Without experiencing the real-time power of the group, something seems to be lost in the translation. Even though the observer may only be separated from the group by a small pane of glass, most people would agree that the feel of the flow is much different inside the room. Observational models may have implementation problems if the group leaders and group members are not readily available. Students may have to be very flexible in order to observe the group off-site. If a group is found, the facilities must be equipped with observation rooms. Unfortunately, many are not, which means the models must adapt by using the fishbowl or taped approach.

Field-Based Model

Landreth and Berg (1979) noted that in order to deal more effectively with the anxiety most novice group leaders feel regarding the initiation of an actual group, a more direct experiential approach can be helpful in addition to skill training. Dameron and Engels (1990) and their colleagues listed a direct, hands-on group leadership experience as a master's-level counselor competency.

This field-based leadership experience is typically rated as one of the most potent learning activities available to the students. Though there is usually the anticipated anxiety of a first group-leadership experience, follow-up feedback has been exceptionally positive. Although data have not been analyzed in a systematic way, written feedback is gathered anonymously at the conclusion of each course. Over the past twenty years, students have consistently rated the "out-of-class" group co-leadership experience as one of the top two learning experiences available to them through this course.

Students are asked to get to know their classmates early in the semester with the ultimate goal of selecting a person with whom they can work as a co-leader. Students who live in relatively the same geographical areas tend to choose each other initially simply out of convenience. To a large extent that seems to work, but the course instructor reserves veto power over co-leader matches where personality types might conflict or in some way be unsuitable. Self-selection works rather nicely, and the privilege of instructor veto power is seldom exercised.

When co-leader teams have been agreed upon, students are asked to go directly to the community to generate a group to work with for a minimum of six sessions. This requires the students to plan and organize their thinking and presentation to the people who are potential members. In some cases, they must also "sell themselves" to the administrator of the school or agency where they hope to lead the group.

In a large metropolitan area, there are many potential placement sites for graduate students to do groups. Typically, schools (public and private), churches, social agencies, college dormitories, nursing homes, and detention facilities provide intact populations from which to select group members. The instructor keeps a list of placement sites where personnel have been cooperative and helpful in generating groups.

Although direct, on-site supervision is not provided by the university, student co-leaders are required to make audiotapes of each session. The students have the availability of the doctoral-level laboratory group leaders and the course instructor for help should they encounter difficulty in their groups. The audiotapes are used by the co-leaders to go back over their sessions and do self-evaluations of their leadership interventions.

The preceding group experience fulfills all of Stockton's (1992) criteria for a competent leadership program in the following ways:

- Training students to identify selected interpersonal and intrapersonal events that define group process at each stage of development is met through the didactic and experiential components.
- Providing students with an array of interventions and helping them understand the rationale for the interventions in terms of influencing group process and development are met through lecture/demonstration, feedback in supervision, and co-leadership modeling.
- Providing feedback and encouragement to students to help them risk intervening is facilitated through supervision and the processing of the lab and out-of-class group experiences.

The entire experience is time- and energy-demanding. Students find themselves motivated to read and attend carefully to class activities related to organizing and initiating groups. The payoffs, however, are considerable. Student feedback has indicated that if they attend faithfully to administrative and organizational details, the vast majority of group co-leadership experiences are positive and growth producing. Also, once the initial anxiety of beginning a group has been overcome in a relatively safe environment, the chances are increased greatly that these counselors will continue to lead groups in their eventual professional settings.

At the conclusion of the co-leadership experience, each student is asked to submit a short, independently derived summary of the group experience. This summary includes group member appraisal, a session-by-session analysis of content and process, the conclusions they have drawn regarding organizational details, and the insights they have developed into themselves as group leaders.

Through a combination of in-class skill practice and then applying the skills to a real live group, leaders have an opportunity to practice a number of group-specific intervention skills, including the following:

- providing to potential consumers a clear and understandable definition of group counseling and a general description of methods, procedures, and expectations;

- screening for readiness of prospective group members;
- developing an effective working relationship with a co-leader;
- operationalizing procedures for closing individual sessions and terminating a fixed-duration counseling group.

Regarding group process, the novice leader will have the opportunity to:

- facilitate therapeutic conditions within the group;
- deal with various member roles and possibly disruptive members;
- intervene at crucial moments in the process of the group;
- intervene with group members' self-defeating behaviors;
- interpret nonverbal behaviors within the group; and
- practice appropriate linking, pacing, and interpreting skills during the group process.

Although the advantages of this approach seem clear, there are a few caveats. First, because the students are working with real clients, the need for malpractice insurance is an issue. Students should be well trained in ethics, specifically with regard to confidentiality and informed consent. Professionally crafted professional disclosure statements outlining the purpose of the group and the student status of the group leaders should be given to every potential member of the group. Finding groups could also pose a problem in some communities, and the ethical standards related to competency might also need to be addressed. Most of the concerns can be mediated by good communication between the instructor and the community resources and by ongoing supervision and consultation among students and the instructor.

Simulated Group Counseling Model

The simulated group counseling model (SGC) is designed to combine the elements of group member experience and leadership training into one experience. In SGC, the students form one group and rotate playing the roles of member, leader, and observer (Bruce-Sanford 1998; Romano 1998). Each student participates in the roles for two sessions. While playing a member, students are encouraged to develop issues different from their own personal issues. Although there seems to be the possibility of confusion due to all of the switching and transitions, Romano (1998) reported that the flow and developmental sequences are very similar to those of actual groups.

SGC seems to be much easier to implement than the other models. The class is available as a group, so the logistical issues are minimal. The format of the model meets the standards in that it supplies students with experiences of the member and the leader. The instructor can serve as a constant process observer to help facilitate leadership learning and group process insight.

In addition to the possible issue of role confusion, the biggest concern is with problematic dual relationships that may develop as students move through the member role. Although students are instructed to use personas that differ from their own, leakage may occur. Instructors who use this model must consider the following questions: "How will I know when students are playing a role or playing self? Do students know how to detect and manage role slippage? What mechanisms are in place if slippage occurs?" (Fall & Levitov 2002: 127). Ethical instructors keep in mind these questions and remember that the purpose of the experience is on training and not personal counseling.

Group Actor Model

The group actor model is also a hybrid, combining elements of the three previously discussed models. Students form co-leader pairs and are responsible for co-leading one group session. While the co-leader pair is facilitating the group, the other students observe the group (observational model). In this model, the students learn from direct and observational learning. Each session may be videotaped for later review in or out of class.

The success of the approach is largely determined by the quality of the actors. Potential actors can be recruited from university drama departments or even psychology departments. The instructor meets with each potential actor, discusses elements of informed consent, and helps the actor create a persona appropriate for the group. Levitov et al. (1999: 254) created the following criteria for actor selection:

- at least one year of on-campus acting experience;
- prior success with psychologically complicated roles;
- experience with improvisation;
- enthusiasm and interest in the work.

Once the group of actors is chosen, the group meets. Although each co-leader pair changes each week, the group members and the co-leaders are to act as if it is an ongoing group. To help with this challenge, the instructor consults with the actors before and after each session to help them get into character and recall elements of the previous session. These consultations also allow the instructor to emphasize various group dynamics, if needed. For example, if the instructor would like to focus on group conflict, he or she might ask the group actors to consider intermember frustrations or hostility. Once every student has the opportunity to co-lead, the actors meet with the students and process to experience through direct feedback.

The actor model provides the advantage of giving the students direct group-leadership experience with the decreased risk associated with novice counselors treating real clients. It provides a realistic yet safe group experience that also avoids the possible role slippage that could occur when students role-play clients (Fall & Levitov 2002).

The primary disadvantage of this model is the necessity of finding good actors. This model is more time-intensive for the instructor, who must recruit, orient, and direct the actors through the experience. Advocates of this approach maintain that the extra time is well worth the amount of learning that can be attained through this approach.

Summary

ASGW Professional Training Standards

The Executive Board of the ASGW approved a revised document that had been in study and preparation for several years. A broad survey of trainers of group counselors throughout the USA was conducted in order to ascertain prevailing education practices. Then began a process of synthesizing the data received from all sections of the country into a practical and usable set of professional standards that can be used for guidance in establishing and maintaining a program for training professional group leaders. Individuals who had significant impact upon the original document include Jeffrey Kottler, George Gazda, Robert Cash, Robert Berg, Don Martin, Garry Landreth, and Marguerite Carroll (see Appendix C).

CACREP Professional Standards

Counselor training programs in the future will most likely be guided by the training standards developed by CACREP. Incorporated in 1981, the council is the primary accrediting body of the American Counseling Association (ACA). The independent council was created by ACA and its various divisions to provide guidelines for excellence in graduate-level counselor training programs. Although the scope of the council's standards is broad and reaches into virtually every aspect of a counselor training program, they do, in section II relating to program objectives and curriculum, address in a general sense the components of a curriculum for group leader training.

GROUP WORK—studies that provide both theoretical and experiential understandings of group purpose, development, dynamics, theories, methods, skills, and other group approaches in a multicultural society, including all of the following:

a. principles of group dynamics, including group process components, developmental stage theories, group members' roles and behaviors, and therapeutic factors of group work;

b. group leadership or facilitation styles and approaches, including characteristics of various types of group leaders and leadership styles;

c. theories of group counseling, including commonalities, distinguishing characteristics, and pertinent research and literature;

d. group counseling methods, including group counselor orientations and behaviors, appropriate selection criteria and methods, and methods of evaluation of effectiveness; and

e. direct experiences in which students participate as group members in a small group activity, approved by the program, for a minimum of ten clock hours over the course of one academic term. (CACREP 2009, p. 13)

The evolutionary status of accreditations standards for professional group leaders is evidenced by the relative thoroughness of the documents issued by professional accrediting agencies.

Group Counseling Competencies

In 1990, Dameron, Engels, and their colleagues at the University of North Texas compiled a comprehensive guidebook designed to present competencies, behavioral performance guidelines, and assessment scales in all the major counseling specialties. This widely used handbook was the forerunner of the initial counselor accreditation efforts and was published and sponsored by the Association for Counselor Education and Supervision (ACES).

Appendix E provides the specific guidelines related to group leadership as given in the handbook edited by Dameron and Engels (1990).

In their classic 1939 study of three generic leadership styles, Lewin, Lippitt, and White noted differences in group member satisfaction, aggressiveness, group-task efficiency, and dependency in response to *authoritarian, democratic,* and *laissez-faire* leadership.

The developmental work of Adler and Sullivan, in departing from classical Freudian psychoanalysis to a more interpersonal orientation, and the more recent work of Thorne, Rogers, Truax, and Carkhuff are noted in the historical background to interpersonal group work.

Carkhuff's work (1983a) with an interpersonal model that expands upon Roger's "necessary and sufficient" conditions to include an action dimension includes the philosophical foundations and a scale for measuring levels of interpersonal dimensions offered by the helper.

Training group counselors should include supervised practica, skill acquisition, and an experiential component typically conducted in the field. The experiential component in the training of group counselors can add measurably to laboratory-directed skills. With a minimum of organization, instructors can create a program design where students can have both a membership and co-leadership experience within a traditional group counseling course. These experiences, although demanding time and energy of the students, have consistently been evaluated as beneficial and constructive.

The further professionalization of group leaders was assisted in 1998 with the revision and adoption by the Association of Specialists in Group Work of the document entitled "Professional Standards for Training of Group Counselors." The document provides a definition, leader knowledge, skill competencies, and the minimum number of supervised clock hours required for entry-level (master's degree) group leaders.

References

Association for Specialists in Group Work (2008). ASGW best practice guidelines. *The Journal for Specialists in Group Work*, 33, 111–117.

Bruce-Sanford, G. (1998). A simulation model for training in group process. *International Journal of Group Psychotherapy*, 48, 393–400.

Carkhuff, R. R. (1983a). *Helping and human relations: A primer for lay and professional helpers*, 2 vols. Amherst, MA: Human Resource Development Press.

—— (1983b). *The development of human resources*. Amherst, MA: Human Resource Development Press.

Carkhuff, R. R., & Berenson, B. G. (1977). *Beyond counseling and therapy* (2nd ed.). New York: Holt, Rinehart & Winston.

Conyne, R. K., Wilson, F. R., & Ward, D. E. (1997). *Comprehensive group work: What it means and how to teach it*. Alexandria, VA: American Counseling Association.

Council for Accreditation of Counseling and Related Educational Programs (2009). *CACREP accreditation standards and procedures manual*. Alexandria, VA: Author.

Dameron, J. D., & Engels, D. W. (1990). *The professional counselor: Competencies, performance guidelines, and assessment* (2nd ed.). Alexandria, VA: American Counseling Association.

Fall, K. A. (1997). The characteristics of psychological safety in group counseling. Doctoral dissertation, University of North Texas, 1997.

Fall, K. A., & Levitov, J. E. (2002). Using actors in experiential group counseling leadership training. *Journal for Specialists in Group Work*, 27, 122–135.

Kottler, J. A. (1983). *Pragmatic group leadership*. Monterey, CA: Brooks/Cole.

Landreth, G. L., & Berg, R. C. (1979). Overcoming initial group leader anxiety: Skills plus experience. *Personnel and Guidance Journal*, 58, 65–67, 87.

Levitov, J. E., Fall, K. A., & Jennings, M. E. (1999). Counselor clinical training with client actors. *Counselor Education and Supervision*, 38, 249–259.

Lewin, K., Lippitt, R., & White, R. (1939). Patterns of aggressive behavior in experimentally created "social climates." *Journal of Social Psychology*, 10, 271–299.

Riordan, R. J., & White, J. (1996). Logs as therapeutic adjuncts in group. *Journal for Specialists in Group Work*, 21 (2), 94–100.

Rogers, C. R. (1951). *Client centered therapy*. Boston, MA: Houghton Mifflin.

—— (1957). The necessary and sufficient conditions of therapeutic personality change. *Journal of Consulting Psychology*, 22, 95–103, 61.

Romano, J. L. (1998). Simulated group counseling: An experiential training model for group work. *Journal for Specialists in Group Work*, 23, 119–132.

—— (1999). Simulated group counseling for group work training: A four year research study of group development. *Journal for Specialists in Group Work*, 25, 366–375.

Samovar, L. A., & Rintye, E. D. (1970). Interpersonal communication: Some working principles. In R. S. Cathcart & L. A. Samovar (Eds.), *Small group communication: A reader* (p. 62). Dubuque, IA: Brown.

Stockton, R. (1992). *Developmental aspects of group counseling: Process, leadership and supervision* (videotape, 3 parts). Alexandria, VA: American Counseling Association.

Truax, C. B., & Carkhuff, R. R. (1967). *Toward effective counseling and psychotherapy: training and practice.* Chicago, IL: Aldine.

White, R. K., & Lippitt, R. (1968). Leader behavior and member reaction in three "social climates." In D. Cartwright & A. Zander (Eds.), *Group dynamics: Research and theory* (3rd ed., p. 57). New York: Harper & Row.

Yalom, I. D., & Liebermann, M. (1971). A study of encounter group casualties. *Archives of General Psychiatry*, 25, 16–30.

5

THE GROUP LEADER'S INTERNAL EXPERIENCE

Before I do anything I ask myself, "Would an idiot do that?" And if the answer is yes, I do not do that thing.

Dwight Schrute

The experience of facilitating a group is an integrative process of melding theory, counselor self-understanding, and practical experience. Such an integration can result in reduction of anxiety as counselors begin to trust the person they are in the process of coping with a group. The internal anxiety will be examined in this chapter, while the structural resistance to facilitating groups will be discussed in Chapter 8.

Ethical Standards for Group Leaders

The group counselor is expected to have a complete knowledge and understanding of the ethical standards established by professional organizations related to counseling and group work. In most cases, that would mean the ethical standards of the ACA and, specifically for group leaders, the ASGW. Ethical guidelines and standards of professional practice are usually agreed-upon regulatory postulates based upon a unifying set of moral principles that the majority of practitioners can support. These typically include the concepts of nonmaleficence (do not harm), beneficence (work actively for the good of the client), autonomy (promote the independence and self-sufficiency of the client), justice (be fair to all parties involved), and fidelity (make sure that promises are kept). Ethical codes represent the consensus values of a profession. Because values are core issues, knowing the values of the profession of group work and comparing them to your own internal process is a vital first step in becoming an effective group facilitator.

The ASGW and the AGPA have both established specific ethical guidelines which are intended to govern the professional behavior of the group counselor, and adherence to those standards is expected as a condition of membership in the association.

We believe that the most effective way of helping beginning group counselors engage in the process of learning ethical decision-making involves four key elements:

1. **Personal individual counseling.** This experience can initiate a process of internal focus and examination that will assist in the self-understanding that all counselors need in order to work effectively with others. Although we may not always be totally comfortable with where we are in the challenge of handling life's hurdles, the attitude of self-examination is worthwhile in keeping group leaders from becoming rigid and inflexible.

2. **Specific course instruction and training**. As we continue to accumulate a widening body of evidence regarding helpful procedures in group work, it becomes increasingly important to ensure that leaders are familiar with a range of intervention techniques that are unique to working with people in groups.

3. **Participation as a member in group counseling**. Participating as a member in a group experience can afford the leader in training with the opportunity to directly observe and experience the group as it develops through stages. Although this is not the primary reason for being in a group, the member has an opportunity to watch another person facilitate the group. Also, the member can utilize the experience to continue the personal process of self-study.

4. **Supervised experience in facilitating a group**. This final training piece gives the new group leader an opportunity to test his or her developing intervention and group management skills with a live group suitable to the new leader's developmental skill level.

Each of these training components can assist the leader in moving toward a position of increased clarity in the ethical decision-making process.

Personal Standards

In addition to suggesting that group leaders adhere to a generally accepted code of ethics, Gazda (1982: 88–89) suggested guidelines for group leader qualities that could form the basics for personal ethical standards. They are as follows:

- The group leader should have a clear set of group rules that guide him or her in the leadership of his or her group.
- The group leader should be self-confident and emotionally stable.
- The group leader should possess high perceptual and communication skills.
- The group leader should have a well-conceptualized model for explaining behavioral change.
- The group leader should have evidence that he or she has received training commensurate with his or her group practice.
- The group leader should have evidence that his or her leadership is effective, that is, post-treatment and follow-up data of group members illustrate that they have benefited from membership in the leader's group.
- The group leader should possess the necessary certification, licensure, or similar evidence of qualifications generally accepted by his or her discipline.
- The group leader who does not possess professional credentials must function under the supervision of a professionally qualified person.
- The group leader should attend refresher courses, workshops, and so on to upgrade his or her skills and obtain evaluation of others regarding his or her skills and/or level of functioning.

The development of an effective objective position on ethics is largely dependent on the counselor's self-understanding. Prospective group counselors should examine carefully their own needs that are being met by facilitating a group. A counselor who is unaware of his or her own emotional needs is very likely to inappropriately use the group to meet those needs and will thus be less emotionally available to group members. We consider this a basic ethical issue in that the primary purpose of the group is to meet the needs of group members. Such counselor variables are crucial, and personal limitations must be recognized.

Ethical guidelines and professional standards of practice are designed to provide a consensus position on the minimally acceptable standards for practitioners. No set of guidelines, regardless of how complete and detailed, will cover every conceivable dilemma presented to the practicing group leader. When the codes are silent or fail to address an issue, the group leader must depend upon his or her personal moral code to guide professional decisions.

The following is a brief list of ethically oriented questions often posed by beginning group leaders. In some cases, the codes provide specific guidance and in others they are vague and require further context for ethical decision-making. What does the ethical group leader do when people in the group begin dating each other? Or when

- a member engages in joking but thinly veiled threats against another member?
- a member comes to the group intoxicated or high?
- a group member talks about intent to commit suicide?
- a member asks the leader out socially?
- a group member breaks confidentiality?
- the group facilitator becomes overwhelmed with personal problems?
- the group "gangs up" on one member?
- a member stops coming to group without any notice?
- an upset or angry member leaves during the course of a group meeting?
- a group member discloses that he or she is HIV positive and has not informed his or her partner?

The ASGW Ethical Guidelines

The ASGW Ethical Guidelines provide guidance in the general areas of:

- counselor competence;
- recruitment and informed consent;
- screening and orientation of group members;
- preparation of group members;
- voluntary participation;
- psychological risks;
- confidentiality;
- experimentation, research, and tape recording;
- protecting member rights;
- leader values and expectations;
- insuring member opportunities in the group;
- treating members equally;
- personal relationships;
- promoting member independence and development of personal goals;
- use of alcohol and drugs; and
- providing help after sessions and follow-up.

For a copy of the guidelines, see Appendix G.

Two Common Ethical Dilemmas

Confidentiality

Most counseling ethical codes and guidelines consider confidentiality to be the most binding of ethical principles. The confidence that group members place in the primary rule of confidentiality sets the stage for the development of trust among members and cohesion in the group. Trust and cohesion are the building blocks for productive work in the group.

Group members need to know the importance of adhering to a norm of confidentiality in the group. This needs to be clearly stated at the beginning of the group, when new members are admitted, and at various times during the life of the group. The issue of confidentiality needs to be reaffirmed as the group progresses to deeper levels of commitment and disclosure. We have found it useful to explain and define confidentiality and to provide members with examples of ways in which confidentiality can be broken in inadvertent and seemingly innocent ways. After there is a clear understanding of the rule, we ask that each member take a personal responsibility for his or her own confidentiality. Remind the group that confidentiality is difficult to police and enforce, so they must respect the privacy of their fellow members.

The counselor/group leader should make members aware that he or she can be personally responsible only for his or her own confidentiality and can never guarantee confidentiality from each of the members. Leaders need to make each member personally aware of the consequences of intentionally violating the rule of confidentiality.

Although members may want to share their personal journey in the group, we also caution about that. Although ethically appropriate for a member to talk about his or her personal insights into self and his or her own growth experiences, we have found it useful to coach group members to talk about what they have learned in the group rather than how they learned it. Linde et al. (2011) noted the need to explore the issue of confidentiality with the group and that members will agree with the importance of keeping group material confidential. This helps protect the integrity of other group members and the group process.

Dual Relationships

According to the ASGW ethical guidelines (1989), group leaders are to "avoid dual relationships with group members that might impair their objectivity and professional judgment, as well as those which are likely to compromise a group member's ability to participate fully in the group." Within the guidelines, counselors are given specific examples of possible detrimental dual relationships:

- combining the teacher and counselor or supervisor and counselor roles;
- bartering counseling for goods or services;
- socializing outside of counseling sessions,
- becoming sexually involved with a client or former client;

In all dual relationships, the counselor must weigh the potential risk to the client. The key factor in determining the effect of a dual relationship lies with use of the power differential that exists within the counseling relationship. Counselors must guard against using the power of the relationship in an exploitative manner to fulfill their own needs. When in doubt, Haas and Malouf (2005) described some early warning signs that a counselor may be misusing the power of the relationship:

- inordinate levels of self-disclosure by the counselor;
- eager anticipation of the group's session;
- desire by the counselor to extend the span of the group or of a particular member's stay in the group, despite a completion of goals;
- desire or behaviors by the counselor to please, impress, or punish the group or any particular member.

Counselor educators face the dual-relationship issue when attempting to train beginning group leaders. Participating in an experiential counseling group is an effective and often-used strategy in the training of group counselors. However, an ethical dilemma arises when a student is required to participate in a group and share personal issues in a group where the leader is also a professor who will assign the final grade for the course. According to the ASGW (1989), if a student is required to participate as a group member, the amount or quality of the participation cannot be graded. Steps that can ensure ethical group training include using advanced students, under faculty supervision, as group leaders or using externally led and supervised groups.

Due to the difficulties and confusion associated with the blurring of different roles, counselors are also encouraged to avoid providing counseling services to relatives or close acquaintances or bartering counseling for goods and services. Unequal expectations and the pressure of special attention create tension on the effectiveness of the leader and the group. The possible effects of disappointment, resentment, and the loss of the relationship can be avoided by both parties if the counselor makes a referral to another group. An explanation of the ethical standards and the possible harmful effects of the dual relationship can also be helpful to a relative who is seeking guidance. An explanation and providing services *pro bono* or on a sliding scale can be advantageous to those clients who are seeking barter.

Sexual contact between counselor and client is unethical and, in many states, illegal. Remley and Herlihy (2009) outlined the devastating effects that sexual relations with a mental-health professional could have on a client ranging from mistrust to suicide. Consequences also exist for the counselor. Counselors who engage in sexual contact with their clients could face lawsuits, felony conviction, fines, and license revocation.

The unequal power distribution inherent in the counselor–client relationship demands that the counselor be aware of sexual issues as they surface during the group, both from the clients and from within the counselor. When faced with sexual feelings for a member of the group, ethical counselors will seek supervision and personal counseling. Pope et al. (1993) encouraged therapists to work through personal feelings of guilt and shame surrounding the attraction by dealing with the issue directly. If the issues cannot be resolved, the leader can arrange for another counselor to facilitate the group. When a group leader is the target of sexual feelings from a client, the feelings should be handled within the context of the group in an open, honest, and warm manner. The focus can be on how to achieve intimacy with appropriate persons outside of the group setting.

To prevent misunderstandings of expectations between client and counselor, leaders can make a statement concerning keeping the relationship between counselor and member on the professional level. Leaders can inform clients that a professional relationship exists in the confines of the group session and does not extend to social gatherings or functions. Leaders can safeguard themselves.

The ethical issue of dual relationships is also important within the intermember relationships. Members are discouraged from participating in a group with a professional or personal acquaintance unless the group is for that purpose. Clients who enter the group with preformed relationships are more likely to hold on to those relationships and form subgroups, which can lead to group friction or a decrease in openness among the members. In addition to discouraging clients from beginning group with known associates, leaders should also attempt to prevent clients from initiating intimate contact among the members outside of group. Due to the intimate nature of personal growth and exploration within many groups, clients are likely to explore the dynamics of close relationships. The leader can point out from the beginning that the group's function is to explore but not to create or provide intimate relationships within the group.

Overall, dual relationships are difficult to avoid, but the effects could be severe to both the counselor and the client. The gray area of the ethical code creates a dilemma for the counselor who must deal with the issue of dual relationships on a frequent basis. In general, avoid all dual relationships, making liberal use of the referral option. If one cannot be avoided, evaluate the possible effect the relationship may have on the client, consult regularly, and always seek supervision.

Getting in the Laboratory: The Importance of Practice

If it is indeed true, as most writers in the field of counseling propose, that the person of the counselor is a significant variable in the counseling process (Cavanagh & Levitov 2002; Fall et al. 2010; Kottler & Brew 2003), then the prospective group counselor must be provided supervised experiences that allow the person of the counselor to be utilized as a therapeutic agent in the role of group facilitator. How else can the prospective group counselor experience fully the person he or she is as a group leader without being a group leader? Although we agree that a sequential, skill-acquisition approach as discussed by Ivey et al. (2007) is a necessary and valuable first step, we question the effectiveness of programs that provide only didactic and laboratory-group membership experiences for the prospective group counselor.

High on the list of the unspoken fears of counselors is a lack of trust in the group and self-doubt regarding an ability to "handle" the group. Such reactions promote apprehension and reluctance to start a group and conceivably could also be detrimental to the success of the group if the counselor allows such feelings and reactions to persist without being verbalized, explored, and integrated. The logical place to deal with such feelings is in a setting similar to that which precipitates the feelings—a position of leadership in a group. To do otherwise is to be inconsistent with a basic rationale for group counseling.

As early as 1961, supervised experience in group counseling was considered to be a minimal necessity for counselor preparation. Since that time, accreditation standards (CACREP), ASGW Best Practice Guidelines and other authors have reinforced the importance of supervised group experience within training programs (Rubel & Okech 2006; Wilson et al. 2004). In keeping with long-standing recommendations in the field, counselors in our group-counselor training program are required to organize and facilitate an ongoing counseling group in a setting similar to that in which they anticipate working. In addition to the supervised leadership experience, counselors are asked to keep a diary of their reactions to the experience and to write a self-exploration paper. Our experience has been that the following diary excerpts resulting from initial group leadership experiences are typical of changes in attitudes, concepts, and perceptions of beginning group counselors.

Once the individual enters the group-counseling setting, learning about self can truly begin in the same manner that inter- and intrapersonal learning occurs for group members. In the interaction, observation, and reflection of the group experience, group counselors can gain a perspective of "self as facilitator" that adds to and often transcends that which was learned in the classroom. The following section explores some different types of learning about self that can transpire through participating in the group experience.

Learning About Self

The first excerpt is an example of the group leader's need to assume responsibility for the group members.

> I learned several things about myself and the way I lead a group. I felt all along that I was trying too hard to *lead*, or structure. This was especially true at the beginning of our first two or three sessions, because they were sitting there without talking much. This is something I need to work on because sometimes I didn't let the group go where it wanted to go. Another thing I tended to do was to respond too quickly myself, not giving the rest of the group an opportunity to act as helpers.

This feeling of pressure or anxiety is related to the counselor's need to "make something happen." Low-level structuring or ice-breaker activities are usually enough to help the group get going. After that, the counselor's best investment of energy is to actively facilitate interaction by encouraging, reflecting, listening, clarifying, and linking.

The next group leader summed up perhaps the most healthy resolution to the problem of responsibility and control because this person found a direct relationship between self-trust and the ability to trust the group to provide its own direction.

> I have come a long way with my group, in learning to accept deep feelings in myself and others. More important, I feel that for the first time I trust and accept myself. I have come to feel very comfortable in the group without feeling the need for establishing myself as the authority. I have learned to trust the group. There were a few times when I found myself questioning more than I should.

The next excerpt is provided by a group leader who is learning to trust self without the roles and symbols of status.

> I have learned that I must be myself in a group rather than concentrating on the role of group leader. When I started relaxing in my group, the members began to relax. I found myself to be much more facilitative when I quit worrying about what I was supposed to be doing as a group leader. When I relaxed my role, other members began to be more facilitative.

Learning About Group Process

The group leader in the next excerpt addressed the issue of group-member responsibility and how it was resolved. The importance of patience in group work is fully evident.

> Overall my group was a good experience for me and, I think, for the group members. The thing that stands out most in my mind was my frustration because of what I thought was a lack of progress after the first group session. I had certain expectations that were not being met, and I blamed myself for the lack of success. I offered a minimum of structure for my high-school seniors and after the first two sessions of very superficial kinds of talk, I was seriously considering initiating some kind of direct and forceful approach. I was going to try to push them into something that I considered serious and worth exploring. However, I did not use any more structure in the third session and much to my relief we made real

progress. We got to some personal feelings and the group began to jell. I am glad I didn't push them as I was about to do. I have learned to have a little more faith in the group process.

The next excerpt is shared by a counselor who was in touch with the potential power of a group and the energy required to stay in tune with all of the things going on in a group. In the opening sentence are suggested at least some of the things that a group can be.

> Working with a group is scary, fun, and challenging. I was surprisingly comfortable. It was tremendously frustrating a lot of the time because so much material was presented—far more than could be dealt with in the time allotted. It was a draining experience. I learned that I prefer some structure in early meetings, and in later sessions I feel more free to allow the group to branch out in any direction. The potential within the group for disclosure sometimes frightened me afterwards, but I was never totally at a loss as to how to respond as I had feared would be the case.

The next group leader tended to see the group leader's function more as that of a member—albeit a member with good facilitative skills. This counselor was able to take a personal dynamic (shyness) and through sensitive projection make it work to the advantage of some group members. In addition, this counselor recognized the significance of group interactions.

> Felt relaxed, easy in the group—fit in smoothly as a member—able to help establish climate of acceptance, comfort, safety—able to help those who were a little shy to begin to share themselves freely—felt good about that. I, too, am a little shy and quiet in new situations, and I really appreciate it when someone helps me to get into the swing of it. I'm learning more about tuning in on interactions not just individuals.

As these group leaders discovered, anxiety that results in trying too hard to make things happen, assuming too much responsibility for the group, and lacking faith and trust in the group inhibits the group process. Although frustrating to the beginning group counselor, these important lessons are possible only through experiencing and being personally open to learn about self in relationship to the group. Effective group facilitation is much more than knowing theories and techniques of group counseling. Counselors' recognition and acceptance of their personal needs are crucial to the group process. The more fully group counselors can be themselves in the group, the more effective they will be in attempting to help members to be themselves, and this can be discovered best by "getting your feet wet" in that first group counseling experience.

Taoism and Group Process

When discussing the internal experience of the group leader, students often remark on the inherent complexity of group. There just seems to be so much going on at once; how do we keep up with it all? There is an old saying in group work, "Trust the process." It seems simple enough, but what does that *really* mean? Group seems so complicated and hectic that it is often hard to trust the process.

For many years, I (KAF) have used the basic tenets of Taoist philosophy as a way to help add depth and clarity to the idea of trusting the process. It is antithetical to the premise of Taoism to think that this section in the book could "teach" you how to "correctly" apply the basics of Taoism to group. Taoism and its application are phenomenological explorations. In class, my students read *The Tao of Pooh* by Hoff (1982) and process the reading as an instructor's manual for group leadership. In the spirit of the exploration of process, a few passages are included below, and you are encouraged to personally explore how each reflects your understanding of the process of group.

> A clear sunny day can suddenly shift to thunder and lightning, a raging storm can suddenly give way to a bright moonlight night. The weather may be inconstant, but the sky remains the same. The substance of the human mind should also be like this.
>
> (Daoren)

> At birth a person is soft and yielding, and at death stiff and hard. Therefore, the hard and inflexible are friends to death. The soft and yielding are friends to life. An unbending tree breaks. The hard must humble itself or otherwise be humbled. The soft will ultimately ascend.
>
> (Lao Tzu)

> Whilst developing creativity, also cultivate receptivity. Retain the mind of the child, which flows like running water. When considering any thing, do not lose its opposite.
>
> (Lao Tzu)

> Once you face and understand your limitations, you can work with them, instead of having them work against you and get in your way, which is what they do when you ignore them, whether you realize it or not . . . your limitations can be your strengths.
>
> (Hoff)

> The existence of the leader who is wise is barely known to those he leads. He acts without unnecessary speech, so that the people say, "It happened of our own accord."
>
> (Lao Tzu)

> At the Gorge of Lu, a great waterfall plunges for thousands of feet, its spray visible for miles. In the churning waters below, no living creature can be seen. One day K'ung Fu-tse [Confucius] was standing a distance from the pool's edge, when he saw an old man being tossed about in the turbulent water. He called to his disciples, and together they ran to rescue the victim. But by the time they reached the water, the old man had climbed out onto the bank and was walking along, singing to himself. K'ung Fu-tse hurried up to him. "You would have to be a ghost to survive that," he said, "but you seem to be a man instead. What secret power do you have?" "Nothing special," the old man replied. "I began to learn while very young, and grew up practicing it. Now I am certain of success. I go down with the water and come up with the water. I follow it and forget myself. I survive because I don't struggle against the water's superior power. That's all."
>
> (Hoff 1982: 68–69)

Encountering Carl Rogers: His Views on Facilitating Groups

The goal of person-centered counseling, developed by Carl Rogers, is for each person to become more congruent. As this chapter is about exploring the internal self of the emerging group leader, we thought it would be nice to hear Rogers' own perspective on group. Rogers' views are presented as expressed in a telephone dialogue seminar with graduate students in the Department of Counselor Education at the University of North Texas.

QUESTION: Dr. Rogers, there are twenty counseling graduate students, sitting in a circle here this morning, and we are all eager to interact with you about your approach to facilitating groups. Because each person is involved in facilitating a group, a current topic is the facilitator's own feelings. How do you keep in touch with your own feelings, Dr. Rogers, when you are facilitating a group? Also, how do you handle your feelings in the group?

CARL ROGERS: I suppose I have the same kind of difficulty that everyone does in really keeping in complete touch with what is going on at the gut level in me. I think I have improved over the years, partly because that is something you can't accomplish in yourself overnight. Often with me, if I am not in touch with my feelings, I realize it afterward. I notice this particularly when I get angry, which always has been something of a problem for me. Sometimes after a group session, I begin to realize that I was very angry with a member, but I did not realize it at the time. Fortunately, in an encounter group, I usually have a chance to meet the person again and express that feeling. I am quite pleased whenever I can be aware of my anger right at the moment it occurs. Then, as to what I do about it, I have kind of a "rule of thumb" that helps me. In any significant relationship, whatever persisting feelings I have, I had better express to the person toward whom they are directed.

In some strictly casual relationships, such as those with clerks in a store, it doesn't make much difference whether I express my feelings or not. In deep relationships, such as those often experienced in an encounter group, however, or in a persisting relationship with a staff member, a colleague, or a member of the family, I have found that I had better express persisting feelings, whether negative or positive, because they will leak out around the edges anyway. The other person will be aware that I am feeling something I am not expressing and won't be sure what because they are getting a rather confused message from me. So if it is anger, dislike, or whatever the persisting feeling might be, I think I had better express it.

One other thing that is important to me is that so often we pile up our feelings, and then they come out as judgments of the other person. If I let my anger pile up, then it might come out in calling the other person names or by making some judgment about the person, and that, I think, is not helpful. If I express it as my feelings, that gives the person a chance to respond, and we can enter into fruitful dialogue.

Confrontation

QUESTION: Do you consider what you have just described to be a form of confrontation? If not, do you consider confrontation to be appropriate once the initial basis of trust and respect is established within a counseling relationship?

CARL ROGERS: Let me explain my situation. I have learned a great deal about myself and about how to counsel with people because I have become more heavily involved with groups, but I am not doing any individual counseling now because my schedule just doesn't permit it. Part of what I will say is speculation. I am quite certain even before

I stopped carrying individual counseling cases, I was doing more and more of what I would call confrontation. That is, confrontation of the other person with my feelings. I don't know what your definition of confrontation is, but mine is to confront the other person with my feelings in relation to their behavior or some specific thing they did.

For example, I recall a client with whom I began to realize I felt bored every time he came in. I had a hard time staying awake during the hour, and that was not like me at all. Because it was a persisting feeling, I realized I would have to share it with him. I had to confront him with my feeling, and that really caused a conflict in his role as a client. It was my problem, but I was bringing it up to him. So with a good deal of difficulty and some embarrassment, I said to him, "I don't understand it myself, but when you start talking on and on about your problems in what seems to me a flat tone of voice, I find myself getting very bored." This was quite a jolt to him, and he looked very unhappy. Then he began to talk about the way he talked, and gradually he came to understand one of the reasons for the way he presented himself verbally. He said, "You know, I think the reason I talk in such an uninteresting way is because I don't think I have ever expected anyone to really hear me." He then told me some of his background to explain this reaction. Now that was a very valuable confrontation. We got along much better after that because I could remind him that I heard the same flatness in his voice I used to hear. Saying something like that would bring up some old issues again, he would become much more alive, and as a result I was not bored.

Co-Counselor Group Facilitation

QUESTION: How do you feel about using a co-counselor in a group, and do you feel it's best if this person has differing views? What type of person do you feel most comfortable with in a group as a co-facilitator or co-counselor?

CARL ROGERS: A number of years ago, I preferred not to have a co-leader in my group. I would rather form my own relationship with the group and handle it that way. Then I tried working with a co-leader; it was a very valuable experience for me and the group. For me, some difference in approach between the two co-leaders is very helpful. I wouldn't want to see a carbon copy of me being my co-leader. I would like to work with a person of somewhat different approach. Then, on the other hand, I suspect there are leaders I could not work with because their approaches would be so diametrically opposed we would not be comfortable working with each other. What I say to anyone who is co-leading with me is "Let's each of us work in the way that seems natural to us. If I don't like what you are doing, I will say so, and if I do something you don't like, you do the same." I think it does an enormous amount of good for a group to find the co-leaders are human and can differ openly and work out their differences right in front of the group. That helps the group members to do the same sort of thing.

When I think about the kind of person I like to work with, I think about Bob Tannenbaum at UCLA. I have worked with him two or three times, and I like very much to work with him because he is better at stirring up people's feelings than I am. I think I work very well with a group that is already having some feelings they would like to express. With an apathetic group that really has nothing to say, or express, Bob is very good at sort of provoking relationships. If I knew exactly what he did to stir things up, I would tell you. He is just a sparkling person. People react to him and begin to express feelings if he is in a group. That helps a group to move further and more deeply. He happens to be the kind of co-leader I like to work with, but for someone else it probably would be a different type of person.

I do think there are a number of advantages to working with a co-leader. For example, I think of one incident where I got very angry with one member of the group. Although I am sure there was some irrationality in my anger, the co-leader was very helpful in understanding my point of view and also the point of view of the group member. He handled us both as participants during that interchange, and I think that is one of the advantages of having a co-leader. We both received help in resolving the problem.

Nonverbal Group Exercises

QUESTION: In various kinds of groups, nonverbal communication exercises are used a lot. Do you have any reactions to that?

CARL ROGERS: Yes, I do. I have a lot of respect for the wide use of nonverbal communication, body contact, and that sort of thing, but I am not particularly good at nonverbal exercises myself. The environment I was brought up in was too inhibited, and although I don't like to do anything that is not spontaneous, this part of me has experienced slow growth. In recent years, I have become a lot more spontaneous. I will go across a group and put my arm around someone who is in pain, but I don't do much to stimulate nonverbal communication. I just think it is a mistake for any group leader to try a procedure with which he is not comfortable. The group will pick the discomfort up in a minute and will know the leader is going beyond what is comfortable. I really regret I am not as skilled in that realm as I would like to be.

QUESTION: Dr. Rogers, do you place any limits on nonverbal techniques when you evaluate some of the more experimental things being done?

CARL ROGERS: My personal judgment is it is quite possible to be very cultish about body movements. The worst example is the nude marathon, where the assumption is if you take off your clothes, you are also removing your inhibitions. I think that is a lot of bunk. Publicity seekers have entered that field and gotten reams of publicity about it for all of us. I don't like anything that makes a cult out of groups. On the other hand, I have seen someone like Joyce Weir take a group and begin with them very gently doing different kinds of body movements. In her groups, anyone has a chance to opt out. In other words, you can choose not to participate if you wish.

I don't like the idea of limits where everyone must do the same thing. If members of a group began to do something I didn't like, I would feel very free to express my reaction. Then what the members do about it becomes a group consideration and is not just up to me. I have never had to face that situation, so I don't like to say exactly what I would do because I have never had a group run away with the idea of body movements.

Extended Group Sessions and Marathons

QUESTION: Since we have such a limited amount of time to invest in counseling, how do you see this time best used if we are going to work with groups? For instance, would one twelve-hour session or four three-hour sessions be more profitable? What is the most appropriate way to use our time if we can use it as we want?

CARL ROGERS: My answer to that keeps changing a little as time goes on. Personally, what I like and what I think is most effective is an intensive experience of approximately twelve hours, which I distinguish from a marathon, followed by briefer follow-up contacts of perhaps two or three hours. We have in the whole group movement tended to put too little emphasis on the follow-up. I think sessions of shorter duration are very important and necessary in working with students, but I like the intensive longer sessions. First, I prefer a whole weekend, with evenings off for rest, if I can get it, then later follow-up contacts.

QUESTION: Dr. Rogers, what is your reaction to marathon groups? Do you have any recommendations as to how a counselor might prepare to become a marathon leader or facilitator, and what is your reaction to marathon groups for couples?

CARL ROGERS: If you are interested in marathon groups, the best thing would be to become a participant in some marathon and see what your reaction is. I don't particularly care for marathons, but that is not a criticism. I think partly it is because I need some sleep and don't relish going twenty-four hours straight. I have tried marathons once or twice, and it has not seemed to me to be preferable. An intensive twelve hours with a group is grueling enough and seems to me to be as effective as a marathon.

You asked what I think about marathons for couples. I don't favor marathons for couples. In a couples' group, one of the good things that happens is in the hours between sessions or in the late evening or early morning hours, each couple begins to digest and assimilate what they have gained from the group. I would really prefer, especially in couples' groups, to meet with the group on an intensive, but not marathon, basis. On the other hand, if a group could only get away one day, then it might be better to have a marathon than to simply have a ten- or twelve-hour session during the day. I have never really tried that. But I feel that if a group could only get away for one day and were eager to get as much out of the experience as possible, then they would enter the marathon with a very good attitude and that would make a great deal of difference in whether it would work.

Owning and Expressing Feelings

QUESTION: Dr. Rogers, you said your reaction to the marathon is based on your becoming tired. Do you also feel this is a crucial issue for the participants you have been with?

CARL ROGERS: One of the arguments that is often stated for the marathon is that people get so weary their defenses drop, and they express attitudes they otherwise would not have revealed. That may be an advantage, but it is also one of the disadvantages. I like for individuals to be responsible for what they express in a group. If the member can say to himself or herself afterward, "Well, I did not really mean that. I was so fatigued it just came out of nowhere," then I don't believe the experience is going to be helpful. Being responsible for the feelings expressed is one of the things that makes any type of counseling or group encounter helpful. For example, when I carried an active client load in counseling, I can think of one or two clients who would come in somewhat drunk, and while drunk they might express attitudes and discuss things they wouldn't reveal in a sober state. But then, in the next interview, they would back away and say, "That wasn't really me. I had a little too much," and so forth. So I don't think the expression of feelings can be helpful unless the person is willing to stand behind the expression of feelings.

QUESTION: I really did appreciate your answer to that question, Dr. Rogers. How free do you feel to react to what group members do in the group? For instance, if you perceive that one member in the group is manipulating the group, would you bring this out or would you wait for one of the group members to react?

CARL ROGERS: I would certainly wait for a time to see if a member of the group did object. If I felt the group was too fearful or was not strong enough to handle the member, then I am sure my feelings would begin to build up and I would express my feelings. I would not be trying to protect the group so much. It would just be that if I knew a person was manipulating the group, and no one was objecting, then I couldn't help but object. I would be guided by my own feelings. I think, ordinarily, I would like to give the group a chance to handle such a situation rather than give them the feeling I would handle it for them.

A Different Rogers in Groups?

QUESTION: I would like to change the subject a bit. I have watched you work several times in groups and what I am seeing is a different Carl Rogers than the picture we have in an individual counseling session. Can you tell us how you are different in a group, why you are different in a group, and what kind of behavior you are trying to elicit that you don't in an individual session?

CARL ROGERS: First, let me pick up on the last part of your question. I don't think in either individual counseling sessions or an encounter group I try to elicit something. You speak as though it were a conscious objective on my part, and to me that makes a difference. If I was doing something with a member, thinking, "This will cause her to react a certain way and to move in a particular direction," I would not like myself for that.

I do believe spontaneous reactions to be an influence on people; that is certainly true. I like myself best in a group when I am not using any planned procedure. One thing I don't like about myself in the file, "Journey into Self," was that I was clearly anxious at the beginning of the group and I was not aware enough to just say so. Instead, I gave a much longer introduction to the group than I would normally do. I just talked and talked, and I would have like[d] it much better if I had been more aware of my anxiety and said, "Oh boy, I am really somewhat scared, but I think we will all get along." That, therefore, expresses my doubtful feelings better than the long speech I gave.

As to the differences in my behavior, yes, I do behave differently in a group than I did in individual counseling. I think if I went back to individual counseling, I would behave somewhat differently now than I did then. The main difference as I see it is that I would be more expressive of my own feelings. I would let things enter the relationship more than I used to. Let's see, why is that? I think it is that I have grown somewhat more free through my participation in groups. Then, too, there are some feelings that I have in a group that I must confess I have never been aware of in an individual counseling situation. I don't ever recall being really angry at an individual client; I am not bragging about that, I am just saying as far as I can recall, that is the truth. Yet in the more complex situations of a group, I can become quite angry at an individual's behavior. Usually the individual's behavior toward others is what stirs up anger in me, so perhaps that is why it didn't occur in the individual counseling situation. There is no doubt that work with groups and my own personal growth ha[ve] made me realize my feelings have a perfectly good place in the relationship as well as my being very sensitive to the feelings and attitudes of the other persons. Let me put it this way: I think any expression of real feeling certainly has influence on another person.

The Counselor's Expression of Values in the Group

QUESTION: Often in your writings, you have stated or implied a counselor should not make personal evaluations or judgments in a counseling situation. When you are working with someone and you feel what that person is doing is wrong, how do you handle that?

CARL ROGERS: Well, whether it is because of my personality or my experience in counseling, I am not judgmental in interpersonal relationships as many people are. The way I would say it is there are few things that bug me or shock me, while for some other people I know, there are many things that bug them and shock them or arouse strong feelings. If that is the person's attitude, then it is possibly better that it be out in the open than trying artificially to keep it covered up.

You used one word I don't think I have ever used, or at least I hope not. "The counselor should be nonjudgmental." I don't tell counselors what they should do. I describe the relationships that seem to me to have been the most productive of personal growth. To put it in more graduated terms, I would say yes, the less judgmental a counselor is, the more likely he is to produce a climate in which growth will occur. But if in fact he is feeling judgmental and evaluative, then I would be inclined to say bring it out in the open, as something in you. Say something like "I think I should let you know to me that seems wrong," which is different from saying, "That is wrong." The latter really is basically a judgment on the other person, but to let that person know your values would be better than trying to keep it to yourself. If you think it is wrong, the other person is going to pick up that attitude, I am sure.

The Future of Group Work

QUESTION: Dr. Rogers, we have seen a tremendous movement in personal growth through groups. Would you comment about what you see in the future for groups and what you would like to see?

CARL ROGERS: The thing I would like to see happen in the whole group movement is to see it multiply in its various forms, I have been primarily involved in encounter groups aimed toward personal growth, but there are task-oriented groups, organizational development groups, and other varieties of groups or new forms that might emerge. One thing I would hope would occur in the lower levels of education is that an encounter group would become unnecessary because the whole climate of the classroom would be of a sort that both intellectual thoughts and highly emotional feelings both could be expressed; then the whole person could be attending class, not just his head. Those are two things I would like to see develop out of groups. I think the group movement has a lot of implications for our culture because it is a counterforce against all the impersonal qualities of our technological civilization.

Summary

This chapter focuses on the internal experience of the inexperienced group leader and suggests direct, supervised experience to overcome initial anxiety. Carl Rogers presented some of his views on facilitating groups, including the use of his own feelings, confrontation, co-leadership, nonverbal exercises, extended sessions and marathons, and owning and expressing feelings. Also, Rogers told about how he differs in group from in individual therapy, discussed the expression of values in the group, and concluded by speculating about the future of group work. He was hopeful that interpersonal groups can provide a counterforce to the latent impersonal qualities of a technological civilization.

References

Association for Specialists in Group Work (1989). *Ethical guidelines for group counselors*. Alexandria, VA: Author.

Cavanagh, M. E., & Levitov, J. E. (2002). *The counseling experience* (2nd ed.). Prospect Heights, IL: Waveland.

Fall, K. A., Holden, J. M., & Marquis, A. (2010). *Theoretical models of counseling and psychotherapy* (2nd ed.). London and New York: Routledge.

Gazda, G. M. (1982). *Basic approaches to group psychotherapy and group counseling* (3rd ed.). Springfield, IL: Thomas.

Haas, L. J., & Malouf, J. L. (2005). *Keeping up the good work: A practitioner's guide to mental health ethics* (4th ed.). Sarasota, FL: Professional Resource Press.

Hoff, B. (1982). *The tao of Pooh*. New York: Dutton.

Ivey, A. E., Pedersen, P. B., & Ivey, M. B. (2007). *Group microskills: Culture centered group process and strategies*. Belmont, CA: Wadsworth.

Kottler, J. A., & Brew, L. (2003). *One life at a time*. New York: Brunner-Routledge.

Linde, L. E., Erford, B. T., Hays, D. G., & Wilson, F. R. (2011). Ethical and legal foundations of group work. In B. T. Erford (Ed.). *Group work: Process and applications* (pp. 21–38). New York: Pearson.

Pope, K. S., Sonne, J. L., & Holroyd, J. (1993). *Sexual feelings in psychotherapy*. Lawrenceville, NJ: Princeton.

Remley, T. P., & Herlihy, B. (2009) *Ethical, legal and professional issues in counseling* (3rd ed.). New York: Prentice.

Rubel, D., & Okech, J. A. (2006). The supervision group work model: Adapting the discrimination model for supervision of group workers. *The Journal for Specialists in Group Work*, 31, 113–134.

Wilson, F. R., Rapin, L. S., & Haley-Banez, L. (2004). How teaching group work can be guided by foundational documents: Best practice guidelines, diversity principles, training standards. *The Journal for Specialists in Group Work*, 29, 19–30.

6

CO-LEADERSHIP

Rationale and Implementation

> Sometimes the only way you can feel good about yourself is by making someone
> else look bad, and I'm tired of making other people feel good about themselves.
> Homer Simpson

According to Bernard et al. (1987: 96), co-therapy can be defined as "two or more mental health professionals working collaboratively in the treatment of the same entity." The co-therapy model has long been employed to improve both training and the therapeutic experience. Although psychotherapy pioneers such as Alfred Adler and Sigmund Freud used multiple therapists to enhance treatment, writing on the subject of co-therapy by these practitioners is sparse (Dreikurs et al. 1984). Hadden (1947) first commented on co-therapy more in terms of training group therapists than discussing the impact on clients. Later, Lundin and Aronov (1952) are credited with the first reference to the effect and possible benefits of the use of more than one leader in a single group and thus opened the door for the future examination of the use of co-leaders in counseling groups.

Over the past seventy years since its inception, co-therapy has been widely practiced as a treatment option for group counselors, and a number of authors have discussed the benefits and limitations of this approach (Bernard 1995; Gafni & Hoffman 1991; Roller & Nelson 1991). In the only survey of co-therapy practices, Roller and Nelson (1991) reported that 85 percent of their sample used co-therapy in their practice of group counseling. Fall and Menendez (2002) reviewed the literature on co-leadership and reported that although co-leadership is widely practiced, the positive and negative outcomes of this modality have been largely ignored by research. However, the research that has been done demonstrates the efficacy of the co-leader approach (Kivlighan et al. 2011). Expanding beyond the definition of co-therapy that was originally applied to individual and family counseling, Roller and Nelson (1991: 3) defined it in this way, "A form of psychotherapy in which the relationship between co-therapists becomes a crucial factor in the change process." Here, the agent of change and the reason for choosing the co-leader option is focused on the nature of the relationship between the leaders. This chapter provides an overview of the anecdotal evidence of advantages and disadvantages of co-leadership. We also outline specific ways to foster a healthy co-leadership relationship.

Advantages of Co-Leadership

Two Heads Are Better Than One

In any group session, there are many things to attend to at any one time. Group leaders understand that group (as a whole), subgroup, individual, and leader dynamics are occurring simultaneously. In addition, each of these elements has process and content aspects to each interaction. That is quite a bit to attend to on an ongoing basis! Breeskin (2010: 5) noted, "An individual therapist, no matter how skilled, cannot conceivably keep up with the richness of group experience." Co-leadership benefits the leaders by providing an extra set of eyes and ears to absorb all of the group interactions. In theory, there is a greater chance that the team will attend to all the important pieces of the interaction and provide a greater level of insight. Often, one leader will facilitate the current dialogue while the other serves as a process observer. Obviously, the benefit to the group members lies in the available therapeutic potency of the leaders' attentiveness; deeper material can be processed if material is not being "missed" by an overwhelmed leader.

Continuity of Treatment

Emergencies occur in the lives of all people, and group leaders are not immune to this wrinkle of life. Family responsibilities, illness, and clinical crises are some common reasons why group leaders might cancel group. Canceling group can be a logistical nightmare for group leaders because they must contact all the members of the group. Co-leading allows the group to continue if one leader must miss group.

Modeling a Healthy Relationship

Many people who enter group are struggling with interpersonal relationships in their present lives. Going back to past relationships, many of those same people grew up in homes where the spousal relationship was chaotic or uncommunicative. Co-leadership provides an excellent opportunity for group members to experience a healthy relationship as exhibited by the co-leader pair.

To model a healthy relationship, a co-leader must demonstrate respect toward the other co-leader. Respect manifests in good listening skills, trusting your partner, and managing conflict in a healthy manner. The last element, managing conflict, seems to impact the group in an intense manner. Much like many parents in the world, some co-leaders believe that "we should not fight in front of the children (i.e. group members)." Although we do not encourage you to fight and argue in front of the group, group members (and children) can learn valuable lessons about how to reach an agreement or agree to disagree by observing co-leaders work out an issue.

I (KAF) was co-leading a domestic-violence-prevention group for men, when my co-leader said something with which I disagreed. Like many interpersonal issues, it was not that I thought she was wrong and I was right; it was more that I saw the issue a different way. I waited until she had finished her point, and I said, "Sally, I see that issue a little differently. Would you mind if I share my idea with you and the group?" She respectfully agreed, and I shared my viewpoint. At the end of our brief discussion, neither one of us had changed our perspective, but we each could honor and appreciate the other's point of view. The group members seemed shocked. One person stated he thought I was going to start "freaking out" any minute because she would not "see things my way." We processed this incident, and most of the group members reflected that respectful disagreement was not something they were accustomed to experiencing. We were able to take that small interaction and refer to it on several occasions during future groups and made process comments every time we or group members disagreed in respectful ways.

Disadvantages of Co-Leadership

The disadvantages of co-leadership focus mainly on the consequences of dysfunction within the co-leader relationship. The first two disadvantages note the most common problems, and the third highlights a more practical concern.

The Group Likes Me More

Power struggles between the co-leaders damage both the co-leadership effectiveness and the group process for the members. Fall and Wejnert (2005) noted that evidence of a power struggle includes making responses that undermine the other co-leader's input, ignoring members who seem connected to the other co-leader, and paying extra attention to those members who do not seem to "like" the other co-leader, thus creating leader-based subgroups. The dialogue illustrates the conflict:

MEMBER A: I agree with what you [Co-leader 1] said about the way I come across as arrogant to others. I'm glad you called me on it and just didn't sit back and let me ruin the group.

CO-LEADER 1: It took a lot of courage to own that aspect of yourself. Your ability to handle my feedback also shows tremendous growth.

CO-LEADER 2: Well, I'm a little worried that you did not listen to the feedback from the other members of the group. It would have been nice if you could have come to that conclusion on your own, without Co-leader 1.

Another characteristic of power struggles is a dysfunctional communication pattern known as *tandeming* (Gallogly & Levine 1979). Tandeming occurs when the co-leadership pair sees verbal interaction as a way to gain legitimacy and power within the group. As a result, whenever one facilitator speaks, the other follows up. For example:

GROUP MEMBER: I guess I am a little scared to share these aspects of myself. I am usually a very private person.

CO-LEADER A: That is completely normal. Sharing is a risk.

CO-LEADER B: Yes, and it is normal to be anxious about any risk.

GROUP MEMBER: I want it to change. I'm not saying I won't share, but I need to ease into it.

CO-LEADER B: The nature of the process is that, as you share, you will get more used to it.

CO-LEADER A: Yes, each time you share will bring you closer to that comfort you seek.

In tandeming, the co-leaders are not necessarily contradicting one another; instead, they have identified verbal interaction as a valuable means to connect to the group, and in the infancy of the relationship, each is trying to connect as much as possible. The similarity of the co-leader messages could be conceptualized as the co-leaders' use of identification to connect and validate the other co-leader. The problem that arises from this dynamic is that the feedback is doubled and may lose its potency, or the group may wait to hear both group leaders before responding. In addition to the effects of tandeming on group member interaction, if the co-leader messages are contradictory rather than validating, then the pattern becomes evidence of a competitive power struggle that distracts from the group process (Fall & Wejnert 2005).

Incompatibility Issues

As should be apparent by now, co-leadership derives its therapeutic power from the relationship between the co-leaders. When the co-leaders are incompatible, the relationship will not grow and the therapeutic value of co-leading diminishes. Two common types of co-leader incompatibility include personality differences and theoretical clashes.

We are sure you have worked with people who you found very annoying. In your day-to-day existence, most people exist on a continuum ranging from very likable to very dislikable, in your opinion. When two co-leaders find themselves leading a group where one or both find the other co-leader very dislikable, both the group and the co-leader relationship suffer. In simplest terms, authoritarian leadership styles clash with laissez-faire approaches. Leaders who enjoy structure will conflict with those who enjoy more open-ended process. Leaders who use humor rub more serious leaders the wrong way. Personality polar opposites do not tend to work well in co-leadership situations unless each person is willing to spend a large amount of time processing the differences and finding ways to respect those differences for the betterment of the group.

Theory differences are an offshoot of the personality conflict, primarily because theory represents one's inner philosophy about the change process and, therefore, should be consistent with one's personality. However, because many practitioners do not take the time to think deeply about theory, it is possible that some basic differences about what constitutes change and how to get there may arise in co-leading teams.

It is important to note that some theoretical approaches do not work well with others. The reason lies in how they define change and the process by which one achieves the growth. For example, a person-centered group leader believes that change comes from creating a group environment characterized by unconditional positive regard, genuineness, and empathy. Group process reflects this belief, and the leader will engage in activities that honor that goal through active listing, reflecting, and process observation. On the other hand, a cognitive behavioral group leader sees maladjustment as distorted thought patterns that can be modified through learning cognitive restructuring techniques. Arising from this belief, cognitive behavioral group leaders spend group time teaching the basics of cognitive therapy and practicing the techniques using group-member examples. Imagine the counseling train wreck that would occur trying to honor both those approaches in counseling. The result would be confusing for the group members and frustrating for the group leaders.

The Money Issue

When deciding to co-lead a group in private practice, one must consider the income the group will generate. Although it is true that the group will serve more clients in an hour's time, it is also true that

- Group members will pay less for the group than for individual counseling.
- Group sessions often run for one and a half hours.
- Group leaders must factor in planning and debriefing time.
- If your private-practice office is not large enough to accommodate a group (many are not), you may have to travel to another office to meet with the group, so you must include travel time.

A quick calculation can show you how money can be an important practical issue in the decision to co-lead. Let us say that you are leading a middle-school to high-school transition group for adolescent boys and girls. You decide to lead the group yourself and do a comparison of possible individual versus group income. The group will have eight members who will pay $30 per one and a half hour group. Your income will be $240 a week. If you saw individual clients during that time, you could see two clients at your normal fee of $90 for an income of $180 per week. Group looks like a great deal!

Now let us factor in co-leadership. A simple calculation would divide the group income by two. In this example, you would earn $120. As you can see, just with the addition of a co-leader, your income is not as good as if you saw individual clients. Each time you factor in a possible complication such as travel and planning time, you are losing money. Just thirty minutes added to the beginning and end of group for planning (this is very conservative) will cut into your profit. If you unwisely neglect the planning time, you will increase the chance of the first two disadvantages occurring within the co-leader relationship.

To offset this disadvantage, some practitioners will increase the fee or the number of members in their group. Another strategy is to hold the group during a time that you have trouble scheduling individual clients. However, some practitioners will co-lead a group regardless of the slight dip in income because the group is rewarding or acts as a change of pace from individual counseling.

How to Pick a Co-Leader

To reap the benefits of co-leadership while minimizing the disadvantages, one must focus on the co-leader relationship. As McMahon and Links (1984: 385) stated, "Therapists who are of the opinion that the co-therapy relationship has minimal therapeutic value, fail to understand the potential for this type of therapy." It may surprise you to know that the co-leader relationship is a developmental process much like that of the group. In fact, the group literature is replete with excellent descriptions of developmental models that track co-leadership growth (Brent & Marine 1982; Dugo & Beck 1991; Fall & Wejnert 2005; McMahon & Links 1984; Winter 1976). These models can be used in the same manner in which group developmental models are utilized: to assess co-leader progress, troubleshoot any problem areas, and reinforce positive movement.

In addition to consulting developmental models for ideas about how to manage co-leadership, Nelson-Jones (1992: 58) offered these practical suggestions for choosing a co-leader:

- Always interview your prospective co-leader. Many co-leader teams are created out of convenience. Although that is not a very effective way to choose a compatible co-leader, it is the reality of the field. Even if you are placed with a co-leader, set up a pre-group leader session to discuss the other items on this list.
- Work with people who have theoretical positions similar to your own. You each need to understand the underlying philosophies that guide and define your definitions of the change process.
- Work with leaders with whom you can have a cooperative and honest relationship. You initially will not know this until you openly disclose your way of doing things and your hopes and dreams for the group, then hear your co-leader's reflections. Assess yourself during the interview: How much did you hold back?
- Share all aspects of planning and running the group. Disclosing and cooperating cut down on surprises within the group. Agree to use the planning time to discuss any planned activities and conceptualize member progress.

- Commit time to working with each other before and after each group session. Bridbord and DeLucia-Waack's (2011) research concluded that this was a vital aspect of co-leader satisfaction. Most good co-leader teams I (KAF) know spend at least one hour processing and working on the group. Some spend more. We would encourage you to consider attending supervision of your co-leadership, especially if you are new to co-leading or are co-leading with a new person. Making supervision a part of the co-leadership process early increases the chance that you will sidestep any relationship problems and provides the team with an outlet should problems occur.

The Developmental Stages of the Relationship

As mentioned in the previous section, it is widely accepted that the co-leadership relationship progresses through predictable stages of development. As you will learn in Chapter 7, groups form and evolve through similar stages of development as well. Paying attention to the stages can provide an excellent method for assessing relationship progress and highlight obstacles that need to be addressed in order to facilitate flow and growth. In the remainder of the chapter, the stages of group are applied to the stages of a co-leadership relationship. We will use the same stage concepts to ease learning, but be aware that the group and the co-leadership relationship do not necessarily evolve in the same time frame. It may useful to "jump ahead" to Chapter 7 and read the discussion of group stages to get a complete feel of the stages.

Precommitment Stage

Initial Testing of Limits

In this phase, the co-leader team experience the anxiety of beginning a new group. Even if the team has worked together before, this new group is a unique experience. It is normal for each person to feel anxious and uncertain as the journey begins. As Fall and Wejnert (2005: 315) pointed out, the main developmental task for co-leaders at this stage is answering the question, "How are our strengths and limitations going to fit together within this group?" As co-leaders attempt to get a feel for self and other within the group, the struggle for identity may manifest in problematic communication patterns, such as tandeming, discussed earlier.

To strengthen the co-leadership relationship and ensure smooth transition into the next phase, co-leaders are encouraged to do the following:

1. Expect anxiety and be aware that this is a normal part of the beginning stage of development. It does not mean you are an inferior professional. In fact, it only means you are a normal human being reacting to a new and exciting opportunity.
2. Engage in pre-group and post-group discussions with your co-leader. As discussed earlier, this provides an excellent opportunity to work on the relationship and process what is going on in the group.
3. If the relationship is new, considering supervision or a third party to process the discussion might be helpful. Having an objective person who is also knowledgeable about the importance of the co-leadership relationship can be a powerful catalyst for the developing relationship.

Tentative Self-Disclosure and Exploration

As the co-leaders get to know one another and begin to develop a sense of identity within the group, deeper levels of working begin to emerge. Through session work and outside group processing, each co-leader should be experiencing a greater knowledge of self and of the other co-leader, both professionally and personally. As depth increases, the need to "play nice" is replaced by the desire to "be real." In relationships, this is a positive sign, as both parties are no longer afraid of the relationship blowing apart but are instead willing to risk to take it to a deeper level. To test the relationship's durability, conflict must be experienced and resolved. If conflict is avoided, the relationship will stagnate. Even worse, the group will experience the leader's lack of comfort and will be unable to handle conflict as a group, thus paralyzing the group. If the co-leaders are willing to experience conflict but handle it poorly (fight and demean each other in group), the group will feel an enormous amount of anxiety regarding conflict and either avoid it or replicate the attacking behavior of the leaders. Neither is good for the group.

In this phase, it should be easy to see the potential impact and influence the co-leader relationship has on the group. Co-leaders that ignore the developing relationship do so at the group's peril. To increase the probability of progress into the next stage, co-leaders are encouraged to do the following:

- Understand that appropriate resolution of conflict is a normal and necessary part of relationship development. Explore your own gut reaction to the word "conflict." Explore past relationships to get sense of how you handle conflict and consider how those patterns might manifest in the co-leader relationship and in group.
- Continue to meet with your co-leader before and after group. It is in these meetings that you can openly discuss your own insights into conflict and collaborate on how it will be processed in group. Make sure you are attending to how conflict is emerging and being dealt with in both the co-leader relationship and in the group.

Commitment Stage

Congruent with the elements of these stages in group work, the commitment stage for co-leader development will feel like the "Golden Age" of the relationship. The specific phases outlined in this stage, depth exploration and understanding, commitment to change, and growth and working toward increased effectiveness, will be experienced as overlapping phases that differ only in the amount of cohesion and trust experienced by the co-leading team. As the relationship emerges from conflict resolution at the end of the precommitment stage, the team gets better at processing conflict, inside and outside of group, are comfortable with the unique identities of each co-leader, and power struggles are minimal. In this stage, each co-leader will feel as if the other co-leader is very interested in the personal growth and success of the other, which may come through support, encouragement, or confrontation.

One phase in this stage, preparing to leave group, deserves special attention. In most cases, this phase will run in parallel to the group development, and it is important to remember to prepare the co-leadership for termination just as you are preparing the group. This discussion of how the co-leadership is going to say good-bye can be processed in the pre- or post-group meeting. Much like in groups, it is typical for this topic to create some anxiety within the relationship and it is vital that the co-leaders not collude in ignoring the issue to avoid the anxiety.

Termination

Termination is the last stage in the relationship, characterized by bringing closure to the experience. With termination processing, the key word is "balance." If co-leaders ignore termination, then the effect on the relationship and on group can be devastating, as group members may sense that termination is too intense to be processed and should be avoided. Some co-leaders may feel it is unnecessary to process termination issues because they are going to co-lead again in the future. Despite the continuation of the relationship, it is important to be aware that this chapter of the relationship is coming to a close. Group is ending and it is important to say good-bye to this experience.

Co-leaders may also process the termination of the relationship too much in group and take up the time the group needs for its own termination discussion. To achieve balance, co-leaders are encouraged to use pre- or post-group meetings to process relationship termination while using group time to mainly focus on group termination. It may be appropriate to model comfort with termination by having each co-leader share a process observation of the co-leader relationship with the group.

Using the Reflective Process to Tie the Concepts Together

This chapter is designed to illuminate the co-leadership relationship as the clinical rationale for choosing this modality of leadership. You have been exposed to the benefits and disadvantages of using a co-leader and the developmental stages of the relationship have been outlined. The last piece of the puzzle helps illustrate how one can consistently attend to the importance of the developing relationship through a process of reflective practice.

Okech (2003) applied this process of reflective practice to co-leadership and, along with other authors, noted the advantages of those co-leader teams that engaged in reflective practice versus the consequences of those that did not routinely pay attention to the relationship dynamics (Miller 2005; Okech & Kline 2005). Reflective practice as applied to the co-leadership is characterized by co-leaders who routinely and systematically discuss and explore how the relationship impacts the group and each leader's own perception of self, the other leader, and the group as a whole (Okech & Kline 2005).

The application of reflective process provides an excellent structure for attending to the co-leader relationship. As Okech (2008: 239) observed, the process allows each leader to "simultaneously engage in intrapersonal and interpersonal processes, develop insights, which in turn inform their choices on how to engage with each other and group members to promote group member and group objectives" (see Figure 6.1).

Summary

Co-leadership is a leadership modality that uses the relationship of the co-leaders as a therapeutic tool. Prospective leaders considering co-leading group should understand that although co-leadership is widely practiced, it is also not well researched. Anecdotal evidence suggests that co-leadership is effective and can benefit both group members and the co-leaders. However, there are also pitfalls to the process that must be attended to for co-leadership effectiveness. Consulting developmental models of co-leadership development to assess functioning, careful selection procedures, and ongoing supervision and consultation can increase the chance of productive co-leadership teams.

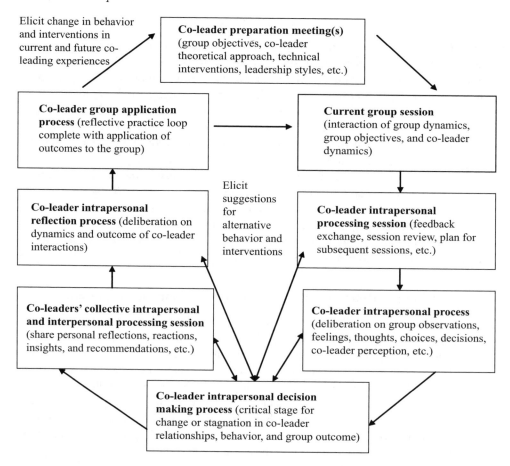

Figure 6.1 The intersection between co-leaders' intrapersonal and interpersonal reflective processes and group dynamics (Okech 2008)

Source: Okech, J. A. (2008), Reflective practice in group co-leadership. *Journal for Specialists in Group Work*, 33(3) 236–253.

References

Bernard, H. S. (1995). The dynamics of the cotherapy relationship. *Group*, 19, 67–70.

Bernard, H. S., Drob, S. L., & Lifshutz, H. (1987). Compatibility between cotherapists: An empirical report. *Psychotherapy*, 24, 96–104.

Breeskin, J. (2010). The co-therapist model in groups. *The Group Psychologist*, 20, 5–6.

Brent, D. A., & Marine, E. (1982). Developmental aspects of the cotherapy relationship. *Journal of Marital and Family Therapy*, 4, 69–75.

Bridbord, K. & DeLucia-Waack, J. (2011). Personality, leadership style and theoretical orientation as predictors of group co-leadership satisfaction. *The Journal for Specialists in Group Work*, 36, 202–221.

Dreikurs, R., Shulman, B. H., & Mosak, H. H. (1984). *Multiple psychotherapy: The use of two therapists with one patient*. Chicago, IL: Adler Institute of Chicago.

Dugo, J. M., & Beck, A. P. (1991). Phases of co-therapy team development. In B. Roller & V. Nelson (Eds.), *The art of co-therapy: How therapists work together* (pp. 155–188). New York: Guilford.

Fall, K. A., & Menendez, M. (2002). Seventy years of co-leadership: Where are we now? *Texas Counseling Association Journal*, 30, 24–33.

Fall, K. A., & Wejnert, T. J. (2005). Co-leader stages of development: An application of Tuckman and Jensen (1977). *Journal for Specialists in Group Work*, 30, 309–327.

Gafni, S. & Hoffman, S. (1991). Teaching cotherapy: Instructional and supervisory processes. *Journal of Contemporary Psychotherapy*, 21, 285–289.

Gallogly, V., & Levine, B. (1979). Co-therapy. In B. Levine (Ed.), *Group psychotherapy: Practice and development* (pp. 296–305). Prospect Heights, IL: Waveland.

Hadden, S. B. (1947). The utilization of a therapy group in teaching psychotherapy. *American Journal of Psychiatry*, 103, 644–648.

Kivlighan, D. M., London, K., & Miles, J. R. (2011). Are two heads better than one? The relationship between number of group leaders and group members, and group climate and group member benefit from therapy. *Group Dynamics: Theory, Research and Practice*, 16, 1–13.

Lundin, W. H., & Aronov, B. M. (1952). Use of co-therapists in group psychotherapy. *Journal of Consulting Psychology*, 16, 76–80.

McMahon, N., & Links, P. S. (1984). Cotherapy: The need for positive pairing. *Canadian Journal of Psychiatry*, 29, 385–389.

Miller, S. (2005). What it's like being the "holder of the space": A narrative on working with reflective practice in groups. *Reflective Practice*, 6, 367–377.

Nelson-Jones, R. (1992). *Group leadership: A training approach*. Belmont, CA: Brooks Cole.

Okech, J. E. A. (2003). A grounded theory of group co-leadership relationships. Doctoral dissertation, Idaho State University. *Dissertation Abstracts International*, 64, 409.

—— (2008). Reflective practice in group co-leadership. *The Journal for Specialists in Group Work*, 33, 236–252.

Okech, J. E. A., & Kline, W. B. (2005). A qualitative exploration of group co-leader relationships. *The Journal for Specialists in Group Work*, 30, 173–190.

Roller, B., & Nelson, V. (1991). *The art of co-therapy: How therapists work together*. New York: Guilford.

Winter, S. K. (1976). Developmental stages in the roles and concerns of group co-leaders. *Small Group Behavior*, 7, 349–362.

7

INITIATING A COUNSELING GROUP

I begin with an idea and then it becomes something else.

Pablo Picasso

Why do counselors seem so anxious about leading a group? Why are they apparently so resistant to trying a group approach? Here are some common reservations that we have heard from both students and practitioners:

> MARY (second-year graduate student): Group just makes me nervous. I am beginning to hit my stride with individual counseling and I have even begun to enjoy the different pace of marriage and family counseling. Group is too fast. There is so much going on that I am afraid that I am always missing something important.

> RILEY (private practice): Getting a group together seems more difficult than recruiting individual clients. I also think part of my hesitancy to do groups is that I never really observed too many examples of actual group leadership. In my training program, we participated in a personal growth group and that was the extent of my group experience. Maybe I just don't feel competent to lead a group. Where would I start?

Both Mary and Riley are experiencing internal resistances to leading groups. Although their specific reasons are different, a common theme is apparent. A primary reason for the high degree of apprehension is that counselors have seldom been taught precisely what to do and how to do it in a group setting. Effective group facilitation is much more than the application of individual counseling skills to a group setting.

Although theoreticians and researchers in group counseling have long demonstrated the efficacy of group procedures in many settings (Gerrity & DeLucia-Waack 2007; Westheimer et al. 2009; Thompson 2011), a continuing puzzlement to many counselor trainers, particularly those involved in group training, is that practicing counselors are not more involved in counseling groups. Many counselors have had specific group counseling training, and others would have little difficulty in transferring their individual skills to a group setting. Nevertheless, some hesitancy seems to exist about taking the initial step. Many counselors seem unwilling to risk beginning a group program. In private conversation, many counselors express themselves as accepting on an intellectual level that groups provide a therapeutic situation that cannot otherwise be achieved. At the same time, a hesitancy exists on the part of the counselor to begin such a program. Typical of the concerns raised are "I'm not sure what to expect from a group" and "I'm not sure what my role should be in a group." Reluctance to attend to the myriad of details involved in getting a group program started also seems to be a major factor.

Those counselors who have begun group programs consistently report that they become committed to groups as a potent counseling vehicle, and in many cases it becomes their preferred intervention mode. Our hypothesis is that not unlike a client who is viewing a number of options with anxiety and trepidation, some counselors never begin group programs simply because too many potential roadblocks and details need to be attended to.

With the available fund of knowledge relating to positive outcomes, procedures, and process, the practicing counselor must take the initial plunge into a first experience with group leadership. If the first group experience is a positive one, both for the members and the leader, more likelihood exists that the counselor will continue to use groups as an intervention method.

Most experienced group leaders report that the time spent attending to what might be considered minor details enhances the chance of a successful first experience. From numerous discussions with practicing counselors and trainers, the following guidelines were developed that conceivably could be used by the counselor as a checklist of activities to follow in getting a group started.

A Step Model for Creating Any Group

Step 1: Genesis

Every group starts with an idea quickly followed by a decision. The idea looks like this: "I have quite a few female clients seeking help for anxiety. How should I see them within my practice?" or " I have always wanted to work with parenting issues. How should I get started?" The decision that each clinician must face after getting the "group idea" inferred in these questions is whether or not to form a group or to see these clients on an individual basis. Creating a group can be much different than seeing individual clients, but in many ways it is similar. Much as with individual counseling, group counselors must decide what type of clientele they would enjoy working with and are competent to treat. Sometimes the decision to work with a certain population comes from desire; at other times, it comes from a need expressed in your work environment. Many groups die at this stage of the planning process because clinicians do not know what to do next or believe that setting up groups is much more work than seeing clients individually. Because the research and decision-making process is the largest obstacle you will face when trying to facilitate groups in the "real world," we are going to explore each step. We will follow a school counselor, Virginia, in her struggle to set up a group for adolescent girls in her school.

As mentioned earlier, the genesis of the idea can come from self or it can arise from a need in your environment. In this case, Virginia has noticed that many of the sixth-grade girls in her school are not taking advantage of the counseling services at the school and yet many are struggling academically and socially. She has always wanted to work with the girl-specific groups but has not made any concerted effort to formulate counseling services specific to the needs of girls (this indicates a desire coming from self). She has also been approached by a number of teachers and parents asking about services for some of the female students (this indicates a need arising from the environment). From these two sources, an idea is formulated: "I would like to create a group for adolescent girls." Once you have your idea, you can proceed to the next step of researching your idea.

Step 2: Research

The genesis step produces a raw idea for a group that must be refined before the group can begin. There is no need to reinvent the wheel when it comes to creating groups, and it should be of some relief to know that there is a large amount of literature covering the application of group to a wide variety of populations. To refine your idea, you must consult the existing literature for ideas. In our example, Virginia could either visit a local university or access almost any university's library website. There she could search databases such as PsychInfo and ERIC for journal articles related to her topic using the search terms *adolescent girls* and *groups*. She could also search online bookstores such as Amazon.com and BarnesandNoble.com for books on the subject. As you consult the literature, you can get ideas about how to set up and facilitate your group. In some cases, you may find ready-made manuals for your particular group, complete with handouts and other media aids. With all the information out there, it is highly unlikely that you will find nothing related to your group idea. The completion of this step arms you with an arsenal of information about how to approach the group. It is your job to sift through the ideas and move to the next step in the planning.

Step 3: Organizing the Specifics

By the time you reach this step, you may be overwhelmed by all the information about your one group idea. Who knew there would be so many different directions and themes to explore?! Instead of being paralyzed by the anxiety surrounding the information overload, we encourage you to see it as an opportunity. You do not have to cover all the themes for any given topic; you get to choose what will work best for you and your population. For example, Virginia was surprised to find that groups for adolescent girls were a widely explored area. She could focus on female bullying, self-esteem, dating violence, female culture, friendships, relationships with parents, relationships with other authority figures, and sports and competition, and the list went on. Instead of giving up with the "There is too much to do. I could never cover it all" attitude, she surveyed the information and found that the theme "Issues for young females" seemed perfect for her group. It was general enough to allow for inclusion of a variety of topics that could be flexible depending on the makeup of the group and specific enough to attract members of her chosen population.

To further organize the theme, she needs to decide on some other specifics about the group: duration and time for each session. Because Virginia is in a school setting, she will need to consult with administrators and teachers about time periods that would fit best with the school community. Weekly or semiweekly sessions from one and a half to two hours in length over a specified period of time is preferred. Sessions of less than one and a half hours are too short for adult groups due to warm-up and transition periods. Longer sessions, unless planned for in the prearranged context of an extended session or marathon, can be counterproductive if they become tiring for the members. For children's groups, a thirty- to forty-five-minute session is probably all they will endure before their concentration begins to wander. For her chosen population, Virginia consults the literature and her administrators and settles on a forty-five-minute group during morning assembly time.

In most school and agency settings, specified beginning and ending sessions are preferable to open-ended groups. This can range anywhere from ten to twenty-five sessions but should have a definite duration. Just as in the fifty-minute hour, duration tends to set up a series of expectations on the part of group members. If, at the end of the specified time, work is still to be done, the group should be formally dissolved and reorganized. Most likely, not all of the members will want to continue.

An extended session, ranging from eight to fifteen hours, is a possible option for an ongoing group. A marathon is recommended as an extended session that is part of the total group experience, rather than a freestanding, one-shot occasion. The extended session is usually scheduled after the group has had several regular sessions and has developed its own style. The extended session is best placed about three-quarters of the way through the life of the group so that adequate follow-up time is available if necessary.

Some groups also can be compacted into daily or twice-daily sessions over a short period of time to increase impact. This "total impact" approach is best used in a distraction-free setting where participants are in residence for a specified period of time and the group is used in conjunction with didactic training. This particular schema is popular with school personnel, organizational development units, inpatient setting, and other intact organizations where retreat-type workshops are administratively convenient. After considering all the options, Virginia decides that eight sessions would be a good length for this group. It allows her to cover five or six topics and leave one session for introductions and one for termination. After the completion of this group, she can assess whether or not the time and duration were adequate for this group.

One must also consider where the group will take place. The group setting should be a comfortable, attractive, inviting room that is small enough for intimacy without being crowded. Preferably, the room should be carpeted and provided with low, comfortable chairs and floor pillows so that group members can choose where and how they wish to sit. Low, soft, indirect lighting is preferred over harsh ceiling lights.

Freedom from outside distractions and complete privacy are essential. Coffee and soft drinks are acceptable, but food can be distracting. For extended sessions when eating is required, the preferred procedure is to take a formal break for eating rather than incorporating the meal into group time.

When the group is meeting for many separate sessions, the same meeting room is recommended as a consistent home base for security purposes. This does not rule out an occasional variation when appropriate or even necessary in order to change a set or introduce new stimulation.

Finally, group members should sit in a circle so that each member can view everyone fully. No obstructions should exist between members such as a table or a desk. Members should be close enough to reach out and touch each other if they choose, but at the same time not so close that they cannot shift body position without bumping someone. The aim of paying attention to these physical arrangements is to provide options for the integration of both intimacy and privacy. Virginia finds a classroom that is not in use during morning assembly. It has no windows, and although the door does not lock, she can place a "Do Not Disturb" sign on the door to discourage interruptions.

One issue that must be considered along with group setting is group size. To promote maximal interaction effectiveness in the group, the number of members should not exceed nine or ten for adolescent and adult groups. Groups for children would normally include five or six members. Also, the minimum number for adults should not be fewer than five members. This number provides enough people to tap the resources of the group dynamic while at the same time keeps the group small enough to allow closeness and intimacy. With numbers larger than ten, the group leader has difficulty in attending to all group members. Many transactions will be lost simply because time is not sufficient for all to become involved. An unrealistically small number in the group can create unwanted artificial pressures to respond and participate. Virginia is unsure how many girls will be interested in her group. She decides that she will aim for eight members but will hold the group with a minimum of four.

An effective configuration in a workshop or training setting is for large groups to be brought together in one assembly for the didactic or instructional phases of the program and then disbursed into small groups with an individual group leader for intra- and interpersonal development.

In addition to these concerns, if you are in private practice or in an agency, you will also have to consider cost of the group. You will also need to decide what type of group fits best with your plan (psychoeducational, counseling, etc.) and what leadership style and format (one leader or co-leader) you will use for your group.

Step 4: Marketing and Recruiting

The specifics that were organized in Step 3 allow you to begin marketing and recruiting for your group. Your setting largely dictates your strategy for this step. For example, Virginia might create bulletins asking for participation in her group and hand them out to female students. She might personally approach students who she feels would work well within the group. She could also ask for teacher referrals to the group. Counselors in private practice may solicit from other practitioners in agencies, schools, or hospitals, or cull clients from their own individual practices. We encourage counselors to develop brochures that advertise the group in an attractive manner. For one author (KAF), the skill of making a brochure was so overwhelming that many group ideas died on the vine at the marketing stage. With the excellent software programs available, this step has become much easier. In fact, I even require my graduate group students to work through these four steps as a class assignment (complete with brochure!).

Good recruiting and marketing allow you to reap the rewards of the hard work you have done in the previous steps. As a result of this work, you will begin to get calls from clients interested in your group. Your instinct will be to instantly begin group, to take whomever walks through the door. Caution! Your work has only begun, and we encourage you not to let excitement interfere with good judgment. The next phase, the pre-group interview, is just as important, if not more so, than any other activity you will do in the life of your group.

Step 5: Pre-Group Interview

Group processes, as such, are not automatically therapeutic. Just as in individual, one-to-one relationships, the group can be for better or for worse. One of the major variables, perhaps the most crucial, is the group leader. The leader is primarily responsible for structuring the group and engineering the dynamics in such a way as to promote positive growth in group members. Any group leader who has taken the time to hone interpersonal skills so that he or she is a constructive helper has the right and responsibility to create the conditions before and during the group that will maximize the potential for a constructive, growing experience. Group leaders owe it to themselves to do everything they can to ensure a successful outcome. Several things can be done or attended to before the group meets for the first time. The following are some of the considerations that can be classified as pre-group activities.

Selection and Composition of Group Members

Until young adulthood (college age and beyond) is reached, group members within a rather narrow age range is best. Throughout the school years, grade level seems to be a practical and sound method of selecting group members.

During the high school years, grouping ninth and tenth graders and grouping eleventh and twelfth graders will work well. The developmental concerns common to ninth graders, however, are vastly different from those of twelfth graders, and maturity levels will have an impact on group interaction.

Less need exists to be concerned about age homogeneity at college level and beyond. Usually by this age a sufficient level of maturity is available to foster an appreciation for the developmental concerns of those different than self. Differences and varied concerns can enhance an adult group and provide a wider range of opportunities to experience and facilitate new learning.

Pre-selection of group members is not always possible. When possible, however, it is the preferred condition. It may be necessary to work in groups with intact populations, for example, or time considerations may interfere with pre-selection procedures. Although a pre-group screening interview is preferred, the group leader will not always be able to afford this luxury, so he or she should sharpen assessment skills and implement procedures to screen during the initial group meeting. Following is a list of essential tasks that should be accomplished either in a pre-group interview or during the initial meeting.

1. **Assess the potential member's readiness for a group experience.** The potential group member should have good motivation for change and an expectation of success.
2. **Select as group members persons who are maintaining at least one minimal primary interpersonal relationship.** This reservoir of successful experience will aid the group member in dealing with the impact of multiple relationships in the group.
3. **Select only persons who have relative absence of pathology or problems too extreme for group members to deal with.** This factor, combined with No. 2, would indicate the need for a referral to individual therapy until such time as the potential member could profit from a group experience. Even in cases where the group is specific to the treatment of certain diagnoses (i.e. groups that focus on major depression or schizophrenia), the members will benefit the most from group through a team-based approach that includes individual, group, and family therapies combined with psychiatric assessments and medication maintenance. Specifically, personality characteristics that impede interpersonal connection, such as intense hostility, low frustration tolerance, and paranoia, are commonly screened out of most groups (Riva et al. 2000).
4. **Determine the potential member's "fit" in the group.** Ideally, the total group would be fairly heterogeneous in terms of personality dynamics. This will allow for greater creativity in problem solving and provide a wider range of interactional possibilities. This is especially important when groups are organized around common problems such as traffic violations, alcoholism, divorce, spousal abuse, or substance abuse.

Establishing Ground Rules and Primary Expectations

Unnecessarily rigid rules for groups should be used only to provide guidelines for members and to ensure protection and safety while maintaining maximum freedom to explore and test new behaviors.

In a pre-group interview, a helpful procedure is to review some of the primary expectations with prospective group members. An efficient way to do this is to simply print a statement or list on a single sheet of paper so that the group member can look them over before the first meeting. Where an interview is not possible, this should be a primary agenda at the first meeting. Minimal rules and expectations would include the following:

- **Attend sessions regularly and on time.** When accepting membership, the new group member should respect the time of the leader and the other group members by observing time frames carefully. The group leader also will find advantages in starting and stopping each group session promptly. This helps create an atmosphere of work and also allows the members to plan their out-of-group time efficiently.
- **Maintain confidentiality.** This is absolutely crucial to group development, and a concrete understanding needs to be obtained on the part of each group member. Talking outside the group in any form should be discouraged, and talking about the group and its members to nongroup participants should not be allowed. With this requirement, group members can at least have an assurance of bureaucratic-type trust that opens the possibility of developing psychological trust at deeper levels.
- **Listen carefully to other group members.** In order to earn the right to share oneself with the group, each member has the responsibility to tend carefully to other members while they are the focus of attention. This increases respect and allows for practice of tending skills.
- **Be honest, concrete, and open in discussing problems.** The group member can expect to get back from the group about what he or she is willing to invest in it. All groups offer the opportunity for members to function as both helpers and members. Groups tend to develop most helpfulness when a commitment is present on the part of members to be as genuine and frank as possible.
- **Set concrete goals for self-growth.** The group members should demonstrate a willingness to profit from the group experience by actively seeking clearer focus on solutions to problems. These should be stated in terms of goals for self. Work toward growth increases dramatically, within and without the group, when individuals have set obtainable goals.
- **Make a commitment to attend the first four meetings.** This expectation is based on the idea that it takes a minimum of four sessions for the individual member to do a realistic assessment of the group, the members, the leader, and the possible gains available for self. If, at that time, the member decides that his or her needs are not being met, he or she has fulfilled the initial obligation and is free to terminate.

Procedural Group Rules

Although informal group rules and norms will grow out of the unique life of any group, some minimal procedural rules are sometimes helpful to assist the group in getting started. If the procedural rules are distributed by the leader to each member during the intake interview, members will have an opportunity to read and reflect upon them before the first meeting. These rules then can be used as a method of beginning the initial session. Discussion can ensue regarding the rules, and additions or deletions can be made according to the needs of the particular group.

Group counseling is a learning experience, and members must learn how to work together to maximize the learning possibilities. The assumption cannot be made that group members already know how to work together as a group. Because the group counseling experience will be new to most members, an often helpful procedure is to provide a list in the first session of general guidelines of expected or suggested behaviors that other groups have found to be facilitative.

The following list of rules for the group could be copied and distributed to group members with instructions to select the rule they think they will have the most difficulty following. Members could then be encouraged to share the rule they selected and why they think it will be difficult for them. Other members could then offer suggestions about how they could help or what that person might do to help him- or herself.

- **Let others know what your ideas are**. What every member has to say is important. Sharing your thoughts and reactions with the group will stimulate other members and will help them to share what they are thinking.
- **Ask your questions**. If you have a question or you want to know more about something, ask. No such thing as a stupid question exists in this group. Several other members probably want to know the same thing.
- **Do not do all the talking**. Others want to participate also, and they cannot if you take too long to express your ideas.
- **Help other members to participate**. If someone looks as though he or she wants to say something but hasn't, encourage that person to do so. You could say, "Karla, you look as though you'd like to say something." Silent members may especially need your support and encouragement to participate verbally. Don't overdo it, though. A member doesn't have to talk to be involved in what is happening.
- **Listen carefully to other members**. Try to listen so intently that you could repeat what the other member has said to his or her satisfaction. You aren't listening effectively if you are thinking about what you are going to say when you get the chance. Give the other person's ideas a chance, and try to understand what he or she is saying. Listen to other members in the way you would want them to listen to you.
- **Group members are here to help**. Problems can be solved by working cooperatively together. In the process of helping others, you can help yourself. The information you have can be helpful to others. Suggesting alternatives or causes can help other members to make better decisions.
- **Be willing to accept another point of view**. Don't insist that you are right and everyone else is wrong. The other person just might be thinking the same thing. Try to help other members to understand rather than trying to make them understand.
- **Keep up with the discussion**. If the discussion is confusing to you, say so.
- **In this group, to talk about your feelings and reactions is acceptable**.

The Curative Factors

Yalom (2005) addressed what he termed *therapeutic factors* that operate in every type of therapy group. These curative factors are divided into eleven primary categories. As group leaders begin the group process, it is important to keep these dynamics in mind as they will be forces that will create change within the group. Each factor is explained below and you are encouraged to think about each as you read about the stages of group work in the next chapter.

1. **Imparting of information**. Included in this function is didactic instruction by the counselor, as well as advice, suggestions, or direct guidance about life problems offered by either the counselor or other group members.
2. **Instillation of hope**. Pre-group high expectations for success, and hope and faith in the treatment mode, have been demonstrated to be related to positive outcomes in groups.
3. **Universality**. The participation in a group experience often teaches people that they are not alone or isolated with the "uniqueness" of their problems, which are shared by others. This knowledge frequently produces a sense of relief.
4. **Altruism**. Group members help one another by offering support, suggestions, reassurance, and insights, and by sharing similar problems with one another. It is often important to group members' self-image that they begin to see themselves as capable of mutual help.

5. **The corrective recapitulation of the primary family group**. Groups resemble families in several significant ways. Many group members have had unsatisfactory experiences in their original families; the group offers an opportunity to work through and restructure important family relationships in a more encouraging environment.

6. **Development of socializing techniques**. Although methods may vary greatly with the type of group, from direct skill practice to incidental acquisition, social learning takes place in all groups. The development of basic social or interpersonal skills is a product of the group counseling process that is encouraged by member-to-member feedback.

7. **Imitative behavior**. A group member often observes the work of another member with similar problems. Through "vicarious" therapy, the group member can incorporate or try out new behaviors suggested or modeled by the group leader or other members.

8. **Interpersonal learning**. People are social animals living in communities. The group functions as a social microcosm providing the necessary therapeutic factors to allow corrective emotional experiences. Group members, through validation and self-observation, become aware of their interpersonal behavior. The group, through feedback and encouragement, helps the member see maladaptive social/interpersonal behavior and provides the primary supportive environment for change.

9. **Group cohesiveness**. Cohesiveness is defined as the attractiveness a group has for its members. More simply, it is we-ness, groupness, or togetherness. Cohesiveness in a group is analogous to the rapport or relationship between individual counselor and client. The acceptance and support demonstrated by the group, after a member has shared significant emotional experiences, can be a potent healing force.

10. **Catharsis**. The group provides members with a safe place to ventilate their feelings rather than holding them inside. The process encourages learning how to express feelings toward the leader and other group members. It is important to note that there are two vital aspects of catharsis: ventilation of emotion and acceptance by the group. It is the leader's role to facilitate the emotional release, while also ensuring that the group create a safe container for the processing of that emotion.

11. **Existential factors**. The givens of existence (meaninglessness, death, freedom and isolation) occur in all facets of life so it makes sense that they would operate in group as well. Group leaders are aware of the anxiety that is produced when confronting any of the givens and works with each member within the group to explore how the anxiety is being used in healthy or unhealthy, paralyzing ways.

Summary

Creating a group from scratch can be a daunting process that paralyzes many practitioners. This chapter provides a step-by-step model for the process needed to initiate a group while attending to all of the elements necessary to increase the probability that your group will be a success for you and your members. The last step in the process, the pre-group interview, was discussed as a vital step to ensure the group members you have in your group are a good fit. Careful attention to each step in the process will have you and your group members well prepared to address the issues of process and development outlined in the next chapter.

References

Gazda, G. M. (Ed.). (1982). *Basic approaches to group psychotherapy and group counseling* (3rd ed.). Springfield, IL: Thomas.

Gerrity, D. A., & DeLucia-Waack, J. L. (2007). Effectiveness of groups in the schools. *The Journal for Specialists in Group Work*, 32, 97–106.

Riva, M. T., Lippert, L., & Tackett, M. J. (2000). Selection practices of group leaders: A national survey. *The Journal for Specialists in Group Work*, 25, 157–169.

Thompson, E. H. (2011). The evolution of a children's domestic violence counseling group: Stages and processes. *The Journal for Specialists in Group Work*, 36, 178–201.

Westheimer, J. M., Capello, J., McCarthy, C., & Denny, N. (2009). Employing a group medical intervention for hypertensive male veterans: An exploratory analysis. *The Journal for Specialists in Group Work*, 34, 151–174.

Yalom, I. D. (2005). *The theory and practice of group psychotherapy* (5th ed.). New York: Basic Books.

8

MAINTAINING A GROUP
Process and Development

Few can foresee whither their road will lead them, till they come to its end.

J. R. R. Tolkien

After the group leader has attended to the details involved in getting a group started, attention can be turned to providing constructive leadership for the group. Our position is that no single leadership style automatically ensures successful group outcomes. Leaders approach the group with many different personality types and theoretical orientations. Seemingly, the leader's ability to integrate his or her leadership skills into a consistent personal style provides the most benefit for the group and its members.

The group leader needs to be in a continuing process of personal actualization and integration, which is behaviorally demonstrated through a calm self-confidence and self-acceptance. The leader must be able to communicate to group members high levels of acceptance, empathy, and warmth, and to take calculated risks in disclosing self behaviorally and vertically through interpersonal immediacy.

This chapter explores common stages of group development. These stages provide group leaders with a somewhat predictable backdrop for the formation of group dynamics, a rough road map of where the group "should" be headed if things are going well. We also explore various methods of evaluating leadership skills and group progress.

Stages of Group Development

Developmental phases within a group are rarely autonomous and freestanding but tend to overlap with boundaries that frequently are fuzzy. Most writers in the field of group counseling and group psychotherapy have identified stages of group development, but they tend to grow from observation and clinical experience rather than hard data. Because of the number of variables involved and the difficulty in controlling the variations, the number of systematic research studies involving group development is small.

What evidence we do have seems to suggest that groups develop in a cyclical fashion, that is, issues are reexamined in the group but at progressively deeper levels of perspective. Yalom (1995) provided a good overview of prevailing clinical descriptions of group sequences, and yet, because individual group members have an enormous impact on group development, the portrayal of developmental sequences in any group is highly theoretical. General developmental stages can be thought of as major themes which are complicated by the unpredictability of interpersonal interaction.

Although bearing in mind the circular nature of group development, we generally see groups sequence through three major stages that encompass several minor phases. Also good to remember is that not all members will be at the same stage at the same time, and because each phase represents mastery over individual and group developmental tasks, some members, and some groups, will never progress through the entire sequence. In general, however, healthy and cohesive groups tend to follow a similar developmental scheme to the one presented here.

Precommitment Stage

Initial Testing of Group Limits

In the beginning stages of a new group, members can be expected to experience a certain amount of anticipatory anxiety. Although some group anxiety can be helpful because it can lead to productivity, high degrees of unspecified anxiety can be counterproductive to the group. The more "group naive" the new members are, the more likely that anxiety will be present because of a general uncertainty of direction and purpose. At deeper levels, group members may be questioning their own ability to handle intensified interpersonal relationships. Initially, most group members will experience some degree of unspecified anxiety that usually relates to an uncertainty about the present and future.

Behaviorally, members will tend to fall back upon learned social behaviors that have worked well for them in the world in general. They will tend to activate their own prejudices, stereotypes, categorizations, and statuses in an attempt to bring some kind of cognitive order to the group. Some members will become very verbally active, and others will be silent and withdrawn. This period of becoming acquainted is characterized by covert testing of the leader, other members, and the group in general.

Confusion, uncertainty, and ambiguity may typify the group in the beginning as members attempt to adjust to a new and strange situation. Irrelevant topics and issues and avoidance of sustained work can be characteristic of the group as members become accustomed to being together.

The major issues in this initial stage involve the resolution of purpose and boundaries.

Precommitment Stage and the Question of Structure

Probably the chief concerns of the beginning group counselor are:

*   How do I start the first session?
*   What should I say?
*   What will we talk about?
*   Should I offer the group a topic to discuss?
*   What group techniques can I use?

These are questions counselors often ask themselves again and again as that first group counseling session draws near.

Most experienced group counselors have discovered that the question of how to structure the first session, and succeeding sessions as well, is more of a concern to the counselor than to the members. Such questions also suggest that the counselor may be accepting too much responsibility for the group and thus depriving members of the opportunity to struggle with the responsibility of creating a group in which they are willing to invest themselves in the process of exploring what is of primary concern to each member. This is not to suggest, however, that complete absence of structure must or should exist.

Counselors often avoid what they perceive to be structuring in order to adhere to a particular counseling approach. What is frequently overlooked is the fact that some structuring is evident in all groups. When the counselor explains to the group what group counseling is, he or she is structuring. The topic of discussion in group counseling is also structured to an extent, in that most group counselors are more likely to respond to the feelings they sense in members rather than the expressed verbal content. Likewise, determining when the group will meet, what general topics will be discussed, the importance of keeping confidences, and the setting of limits when necessary are all examples of structuring found in most groups. Appropriate structuring can be facilitative to a group; overstructuring, whereby the counselor becomes the teacher, or adherence to rigid rules, can interfere with the therapeutic developmental process inherent in groups. Recognition, therefore, that some degree of structuring exists in all groups results in a shift of focus. The question becomes not whether to structure but how to select the kind of structuring that will be most appropriate to the group.

One position on structuring is that greater responsibility for self, a goal of most group-counseling experiences, can be facilitated by allowing group members to contend with previous questions and to make some decisions for themselves. Another position on structuring is that some groups may not be ready to assume such complete responsibility. Possibly the members may need some assistance in learning how to work together and to conduct productive group discussions if they have had no previous group-counseling experience or have not been exposed to small-group discussions in other settings such as their classrooms. For example, students do not immediately become effective group members simply because they are placed in a counseling group. Some structuring, therefore, may be helpful in the initial session. Structuring does not necessarily imply a "takeover" role for the counselor. Structuring may be helpful in assisting the group to get started in those typically awkward first few minutes of the initial session. In addition, structuring also may help the counselor to approach the experience with more self-confidence, which is a prerequisite to the development of a cohesive group. High anxiety levels on the part of the counselor often contribute directly to the dysfunctioning of a group. This is especially true of groups where the counselor is reluctant to confront and reveal his or her own anxiety to the group. Failure to do so may be perceived by members as the counselor saying to the group, "In here, we don't talk about feelings," that is, structuring the relationship whether or not the counselor intended to do so.

Structuring for Members

The initial structuring in the first session might go something like the following excerpt from a school counselor's comments during the first few minutes of a new group:

> Well, everyone is here so we can get started. We all know each other, and we all know why we're here. Each one of you is concerned about your progress in school. Your grades aren't what you would like them to be, and you decided to come to this group because you want to work on that problem. There may be other problems or concerns we all share or that you feel the group can help you with. If there are, it is your responsibility to let us know about what you are concerned. It is our responsibility to work together to help each other and ourselves find out some of the reasons for the difficulty, and what we can do.
>
> We'll be meeting in this room every Tuesday at this time for the next ten weeks. While we're together in this group, you can say anything you want. Whatever is said is just for us and is not to be told to anyone outside the group. I will not talk to your teachers, parents, or the principal or anyone about what goes on here. I'm here to work with you. I don't have a lot of answers to give

you, but together perhaps we can work something out that will be helpful to all of us.

At least three alternatives exist at this point in the process of structuring:

1. The counselor may ask, "How do you feel about talking about yourself in this group?"
2. The counselor may ask, "Is there anything else we need to get cleared up, or does anyone have a question?" and then move on to the first question.
3. The counselor could say, "Other groups have found it helpful to go around the circle and have each person tell the group what they are concerned about, and how they think the group can help. Who would like to begin?"

Counselor Self-Structuring

The beginning group counselor might find some self-structuring such as the following reminders helpful in his or her efforts to facilitate group interaction.

- Be patient. Wait for responses to questions. Members need time to think about what they want to say.
- Help members to interact with each other by clarifying similarities and differences in what members are saying.
- If a member or several members seem to be confused, ask another member of the group to summarize what he or she thinks the speaker has been saying.
- Recognize that you, as the counselor, are not the authority. You don't have all the "right" answers. Help members to respond to each other. "Mark, you're talking to Ruth, but you're looking at me. Can you tell her?"
- Avoid being the answer source. If the counselor is asked for an opinion, refer the question to the whole group by saying, "What do the rest of you think?"
- Determine who is doing the most talking. If it is the counselor, he or she may be trying too hard to teach everyone something.
- Try to determine what the central theme of the discussion is and respond to that.
- Pull things together for the group by verbally linking what one member says with what another member has said if it seems to fit or be related.
- Listen to the feeling tones behind the words and respond to this inner depth rather than just to the words you hear.

If the counselor attempts to jump the group ahead in order to avoid the initial process of struggling together, the group may never feel safe enough with each other to relate the awkward and confused feeling many members experience. The experience of struggling together provides a degree of equality among members in that as they figure out what to do with the uncertainty. They are in the same boat of anxiety as they try to develop a sense of relating to one another. Individuals want to look up at the other faces but cannot. Something will not let them. For the counselor to remain completely inactive at this point would seem to provide an absence of structure but may in fact be structuring to such an extent as to be perceived by members as an indication that such feelings are inappropriate. Responding to such feelings, however, conveys to the group that this is a place where talking about self and feelings is acceptable. Such a move on the part of the counselor also says to the group, "I'm a person who is sensitive to what you feel, and I'm willing to face those feelings openly with you." For most members, this kind of structuring is a profound experience: "Hey, she really hears me."

The kind of structuring discussed here allows a great deal of freedom permissiveness within the group and at the same time provides a framework within which the group can begin to function. If structuring is handled properly, a facilitative relationship will be established that provides the freedom and security necessary for growth-promoting self-exploration.

Structure as a Freeing Agent

Although structuring in group guidance and group counseling is usually thought of as an aid to the group, benefits to the counselor should not be overlooked. Many counselors are hesitant to attempt group work because they may have little specific training in utilizing a group approach. Even those with some training may still be unsure of just how to approach the group or what they should do first. Leader anxiety resulting from unsureness about how to facilitate the group or how members will function is easily detected by most group members. Consequently, they may be reluctant to become involved in the group because "even the leader feels this whole thing is a bit shaky." When the counselor feels unsure, members usually don't feel safe.

The counselor's own feelings about self and the group have a definite impact on the functioning of the group. What is needed by many counselors is structure that provides a framework within which they can feel more sure of themselves and the group. The addition of structure, therefore, can free the counselor to utilize his or her skills more efficiently while gaining the necessary experience to function more effectively.

Too often, groups flounder because the counselor assumes members are knowledgeable about group dynamics and process. In reality, the majority of individuals, especially school-age youngsters, may indeed know very little, if anything, about the skills necessary to function as effective and contributing members of a group. Structuring, especially in the early stages of the group, can help members to learn how to be effective group contributors. As the sessions progress and members become more skillful, less structuring will be needed.

Structure provides direction, concreteness, and security for both the leader and the members. And this can be a source of maturation and growth in a group situation. Highly structured techniques tend to provide both the group leader and group members maximal amounts of direction and security with the possible consequence of a reduction in personal responsibility. Such structuring techniques typically rely primarily upon structuring by verbal means utilizing a predetermined sequence of questions or instructions. Accompanying pictures or puppets may be utilized in some highly structured approaches.

Moderately structured techniques tend to provide less specific direction and rely upon the group leader and group members to establish some degree of direction related to the initial focus of the structure. Consequently, a higher degree of personal responsibility is required. The vehicle for structuring the focus is usually a combination of some form of media presentation and open-end verbal responses that organize the focus of the group topically but still allow a wide range of member responses. Structure typically helps group members move from a discussion of what happened there and then to an exploration of self in similar situations here and now.

A limited structure approach allows group members to originate the topic of focus and is assisted by the specific verbal and nonverbal activity of the counselor. Although structuring by counselors is often based on verbal activity, in a school setting nonverbal structuring through the use of carefully selected media materials including pictures, filmstrips, films, and transparencies that promote visual stimulation may be at least as helpful, if not more so, than verbal structuring.

Structure can promote group cohesion as members more quickly begin to interact and focus on common problems. A significant benefit is that the frustration of not knowing what is expected can be largely avoided.

Limitations of Structuring

Structuring may initially prevent group members from experiencing the responsibility of determining what content will be important in the group. Also, experientially learning how to cope with the anxiety and frustration of ambiguous situations is precluded. An additional concern is that the introduction of new topics or areas of focus for each meeting, as is recommended when strictly following some structural programs, may break the continuity of the discussions from meeting to meeting or prevent group members from introducing their own immediate concerns. However, our experience has been that group members, regardless of initial structuring, will move quickly to assert their own needs for determining purpose and what is to be discussed. This usually occurs within three to five sessions and seems largely a result of group members having learned how to function together, which in turn promotes a feeling of self-confidence and trust in the group. Therefore, it is essential that the group facilitator be sensitive to the group's movement away from the structured focus and remain open as the group explores areas of spontaneous concern.

Kinds of Structuring

The following is a brief discussion of some of the kinds of prepackaged structured activities available for use with group members at various age levels. No attempt has been made to be all-inclusive, but rather the materials discussed are used as illustrations of the types of activities available to counselors. In general, they progress from highly structured to less structured in an attempt to adjust materials to the developmental level of the group members.

Moderately structured techniques also allow the introduction of a topic or "theme" but typically do not deal with it in such great specificity. Such a technique allows the group leader to formulate questions or leads depending upon the needs of the particular group. Specific examples of moderately structured techniques for children are structured exercise books and curricula by Landy (1992), Lane (1991), and Devencenzi and Pendergast (1988). Exercises are provided with directions for the leader and worksheets for the members. The exercises can be used to facilitate work on a number of issues such as motivation, self-esteem, belonging, peer pressure, and families. Any exercise used should be designed for the individual students and for the specific group with whom the counselor is working and should be formulated to aid students to begin talking about themselves, their feelings, and their behavior. Huss (2001) created specific sessions and activities for bereaved children, and Crutchfield and Garrett (2001) utilized Native American ideas to create a structured group model for children.

Corder (1994) discussed an extensive program for structuring adolescent groups. Corder developed her process through focusing on facilitating the curative factors reported as most important to adolescents and on decreasing high levels of anxiety she saw as inherent in the groups. The program consisted of several structured exercises such as "The New Learning Game" and "Role Assignments" to promote adolescent growth within the group process. Fall and MacMahon (2001) outlined a detailed group protocol for working with fifth- and sixth-grade boys. This group included a flexible curriculum designed to explore typical male issues such as communication, trust, and relationships with parents.

For junior-high-school youth through adults, somewhat more verbally oriented structured activities are found in Drucker (2003), Carrell and Keenan (2000), and Walker (2000). The determining factors as to the complexity of the media and activities are more related to the verbal and concept abilities of the group members than to simple chronological age. Another factor to be considered in choosing structured activities is the relative interpersonal skill level of potential group members. In general, the fewer group experiences that members have had, the more appropriate will be activities that structure and help in skill development.

Essentially, all group members need skill in giving and receiving feedback in constructive ways, clarifying their feelings and ideas through self-exploration and opportunities for self-disclosure. In addition to modeling the behaviors, group leaders need to be creative in searching out any number of activities that can enhance these skills in a group.

Using dyads and triads to break the group into smaller components often adds a measure of security and gives group members more opportunity to participate. The use of stimulus sentences, open-ended questions, and focused feedback works well and promotes group-member involvement and commitment. Structured activity manuals are also available to promote social skills building in and outside of the group setting (Khalsa 1996).

Summary of Structuring

There is general agreement that structure is a significant dimension in the group counseling process. Although structured techniques can be used to stimulate, to motivate, to teach, and to promote trust, the use of structure should not be abused. The recommendation is that structured approaches be used sequentially beginning with highly structured verbal approaches, followed by moderately structured visual approaches, and concluding with an approach involving no externally imposed structured topic, thus enabling group members to establish their own speed, direction, and personality. When used sequentially, structured approaches become complementary and developmental and are thus compatible with the developmental lifecycle of the group.

Tentative Self-Disclosure and Exploration

In this second phase, members become increasingly sensitive to the power in the group for potential acceptance or rejection; members want to be known and accepted for the person they are but are faced with the prospect of having to risk sharing some part of themselves (usually a feeling, unexpected personal data, or a reaction to a member) in order to ascertain the level of acceptance. Therefore, self-disclosures at this stage are rather tentative and exploratory in nature. In ambiguous situations, members will seek self-definition and personal status within the group. Leadership struggles are common at this stage as members explore power alliances and attempt to control and influence group direction. Personal attitudes and values, after an initial suspension, begin to emerge and crystallize. Although the verbal rate may be high, with some members attempting to keep interaction going smoothly and continuously, the content remains relatively superficial and issue-oriented.

A general tendency is present to protect the leader and other group members from criticism and attack coupled with a generalized anxiety related to the prospect of increased intimacy with others. Mini-affiliations tend to occur here in an attempt to form mutual support subgroups. At this point, real differences in interpersonal styles become apparent, particularly between those who are assertive and independent as opposed to those who project an image of dependency and passivity. Members' typical interpersonal styles will surface in accordance with the ambiguity of the situation and will become a valuable source of information for the leader. Feelings, behaviors, and styles that members have learned in other relationships and in families of origin are often the modes used in relating to the group.

Also, at this point, group members adopt roles that tend to set up a series of expectations by other group members. The chronic rescuer, resident comedian, and hostile attacker, to name but a few, have an opportunity to display their behavioral preferences to the group. These roles and labels can be comfortable initially because they give the group definition and expectations, whereas at later stages they obviously can hinder individual growth if group members covertly "force" a member to remain in the formerly defined role.

Through the primary self-disclosures and behavioral expressions associated with this developmental stage, members begin to learn more about each other, the leader, and themselves, and, using data available, make some initial commitment to a personal level of involvement in the group.

It is during this stage of group development that cohesion begins to be important. As the group members begin to share more intimate aspects of self, a connection often forms among the members. This connection, known as *cohesion*, acts as a facilitating force to help the group continue on its developmental journey. The interpersonal bonding or attraction that takes place in a healthy group is one of the few extensively researched process variables. Despite past research, cohesiveness remains a vague and complicated group factor to operationalize, and studies that have attempted to clarify the dynamic have met with little or conflicting success (Braaten 1990; Budman et al. 1993; Dion 2000). In 1989, Mudrack advised the group community to bury the term *cohesiveness* and to work on the forces that make up cohesion. Despite the confusion, cohesiveness as a sense of "we-ness" continues to be a group function that is directly related to positive outcomes in the literature.

Although too high a level of cohesiveness or "togetherness" can sometimes lead to low levels of group production, research indicates that members of cohesive groups are

- more productive;
- more resistant to negative external influences;
- more open to influence by other group members;
- able to experience more security;
- more able to express negative feelings and follow group norms;
- more willing to attempt to influence others;
- able to continue memberships in group longer.

If a high level of interpersonal freedom is a desired atmosphere in the group, seemingly the group leader should give the development of cohesiveness, rapport, and trust a high priority, particularly in the initial stages of group development. Group leader-facilitated conditions of personal involvement in the group, a focus upon the expression of feelings, a safe and secure atmosphere in the group, and interaction among members appear to be the process variables that lead to solidarity and interpersonal trust.

Although we feel that no such thing as a totally unconditional relationship exists, group leaders are well advised to establish a free and permission-giving climate in the early phases of the group. The resultant core of cohesiveness serves as a building block or base of trust that allows increasing behavioral conditionality in later group stages when the primary focus moves from the establishment of an initial feeling of comfort to a more problem-solving orientation. Marmarosh et al. (2005) noted that cohesion's true value extends beyond the confines of the group session. Cohesive groups will internalize the group experience and carry the feelings of connection and the resultant changes outside of the group and into their everyday lives. The seeds of cohesion are sowed in the precommitment stage and may be fully realized as the group develops into the commitment stage.

Commitment Stage

Depth Self-Exploration and Understanding

As the group progresses through its life, a subtle but discernible movement takes place away from the initial concerns involving purpose and power to an increasing involvement with issues of interpersonal affiliation and intimacy. The issue of closeness will be, in some measure, a major focus for the remainder of the group life.

During this phase the pattern becomes clear that the group has resolved issues of rules and procedures, and is beginning to develop its own unique style. Standards and norms may become apparent that are unique to the group and may not conform to those outside of the group. An insider/outsider feeling may develop, and expressions and behaviors that reinforce we-ness are more prevalent.

More focus is on "here-and-now" transactions in the group and on concerns unique to the group with an increasing disregard for those outside of the group. Even low-status members of the group will be included in intimate exchanges so as to at least preserve the illusion of cohesiveness and solidarity.

Problems of power become more up-front and readable, and are dealt with in a more constructive, conscious, and immediate manner. The leader typically becomes more confrontational of behavior and serves as the person with a high reality orientation. Informal leaders within the group begin to reemerge without threat to the group.

Group members themselves begin to "check out" or test their perceptions and assumptions about self and others. A higher rate exists of interpersonal risk-taking and depth of self-exploration and disclosure not present earlier. Interactions between members become more intensive and feeling dominated.

Finally, at this stage, group members begin to demonstrate more helping skills as they become involved with each other as well as self.

Commitment to Change and Growth

At this level is an unspoken but more apparent commitment to mutual help and support. The atmosphere of the group takes on a more relaxed and informal tone. Evidence appears of a good deal more interpersonal acceptance and egalitarianism, while at the same time a tougher, more demanding orientation to reality becomes apparent. The leader, although not withdrawing, will be able to share more responsibility and facilitation with group members as they begin to exhibit less defensiveness and more helping skills. The leader will notice group members modeling empathic responses and attempting to generate new insights.

Working Toward Increased Personal Effectiveness

This is clearly the most productive stage in the life of the group. Most early concerns and developmental tasks have been resolved and mastered. Respect levels are high as group members engage in less "rescuing" behavior. Also apparent is a decrease in aggression and more willingness to compromise on issues concerning the entire group. Group interactions are typified by much more free association of feelings and thoughts, and more frequent, open, feeling statements and expressions.

More than an illusion of unity appears at this stage because group members become genuinely concerned about the welfare of each other. Missing members become a focal point because of an obvious change in group composition in their absence. The group begins to take on a life of its own that offers the necessary security for individual behavior change.

Group members at this level are approaching a self-therapist existence with increased self-awareness and insight. Self-confrontations are frequent because much more reliance upon self-evaluation and independence occurs. Group members now develop a personal autonomy, while at the same time the group itself is becoming interdependent.

Fantasies are discussed and shared, and group members become more demanding of others and themselves in a quest to discover unconscious motivators for behavior. Interpersonally, members begin to risk new ways of relating to one another.

Preparing to Leave the Group

Clearly, the group that progresses through the foregoing stages offers levels of support, behavioral reaffirmation, interdependence, and an intensification of feelings that are frequently missing, if not impossible to achieve, in the outside society. Equally clear is that the kind of natural high experienced in this setting can create problems of separation at termination.

A certain ambiguity of feelings can be anticipated that often approximates the grieving process. Leave-taking will produce denial and withdrawal in some and elation in others. Overriding these natural feelings of loss and anticipation should be a general optimism and a sense of completion. The group leader needs to take special care in dealing fully with feelings of anxiety associated with leaving the group.

Termination Stage

The ending phase or stage in the group counseling process is as potentially crucial to the growth and development of a group as is the beginning phase. It may seem contradictory to suggest that termination is a significant part of the group's development. However, development in human-potential terms implies growth, and the ability of the group members to cope with, accept, and effectively explore the ending of significant relationships is a higher order of group development. The dynamics of the process of termination, though, need not be limited to an exploration of the termination of relationship. To do so would restrict growth. According to Yalom (1995), termination is much more than an act signifying the end of the experience; it is an integral part of the group process and can be an important force in promoting change.

Perhaps the awareness of the ending of events, happenings, experiences, and relationships in the lives of individuals is what provides the substance for significance and meaning. The very fact that there is a beginning implies that there will be an ending. Human experience consists of a series of beginnings and endings, and beginning again. This chapter begins and ends, and another follows. The day starts and ends so that another can begin. Semesters begin and end, and a new semester commences. Relationships also begin and end and are replaced by new relationships. Termination, then, is a part of a vital process. It is an ending, but that ending can become a beginning.

When dealt with openly, the impending termination of the group provides members with an opportunity to deal constructively with feelings of loss, to evaluate their own and each others' growth, to identify areas in need of continued work, and to develop plans and direction for continuing without the group. An exploration, then, of how each member can utilize what has been learned becomes equally as significant as learning to effectively cope with the ending of important relationships.

Determining When to Terminate

Closed Groups

Ordinarily, the majority of counseling groups in educational settings are closed groups; once begun, new members are not added. In such groups, the issue of when to terminate is usually not a problem because they typically meet for a predetermined number of sessions. Therefore, termination is a developmental phenomenon with which the whole group must deal. Some closed groups are formed without a fixed ending date, and members of the group are allowed to determine early in the group life how many sessions will be needed. Also, a closed group may begin with the understanding that they will meet for a determined number of times, usually six to eight sessions, and may at that time decide if additional sessions are needed.

Closed groups often conform to external circumstances such as the ending of the semester or school year, which dictate when the group will terminate. Such natural stopping places seem to work well in most instances. The counselor must recognize, however, that predetermined termination may not provide an opportunity for the group to meet the needs of all members and that individuals may be terminating with varying degrees of readiness. The counselor should be open to helping some members join a new group or continue in individual counseling.

Open Groups

An open group accepts new members as individuals terminate, thus maintaining a consistent size by replacing members as they leave. In such groups, the question of terminating the group is almost never the issue but rather when an individual member is ready to terminate. This is normally determined by the individual with the help of the counselor and the group. In open groups, termination is a recurring, extended, and comprehensive process. The exiting of members from the group and the assimilation of new members affect not only the dynamics of the group but also the process and level of cohesiveness. Therefore, the establishment of an open group is not recommended for inexperienced group counselors.

Additional variables affecting the group counseling process that the counselor must be aware of are readily apparent in the phases described by McGee et al. (1972) as typical of open groups:

- Questions arise about termination during the intake interview. Feelings emerge as other members leave the group.
- A member verbalizes a desire or intent to leave the group.
- A discussion ensues about the member's plan to terminate and the potential effect on the member and the rest of the group.
- Discussion regarding the terminating member will occur during the next several sessions, and the decision to terminate will be confirmed.
- The terminating member attends his or her last group session. Separation occurs.
- The member's leaving and the resulting implications are discussed periodically during the next few sessions.
- A new member enters the group.

Resistance to Termination

Reluctance to end a significant experience and to say good-bye to individuals who have become important is a natural reaction and one to be expected. Because individuals may for the first time have experienced this kind of close, intimate, caring relationship, they may face the ending of the group with a sense of loss and resistance. The continuing development of maturity, independence, and responsibility is hindered, though, when resistance is prolonged. A criterion of maturity is the ability to let go when relationships change or end. This willingness to turn loose fosters independence and self-responsibility in self and others. Therefore, the counselor may need to help group members explore feelings related to termination of the group and the resulting ending of meaningful relationships, and to engage in the process of turning loose.

The group counselor who anticipates resistance, anxiety, and dependence as probable reactions to termination will be better prepared to respond appropriately. Frequently, groups avoid termination by enthusiastically requesting additional sessions beyond the predetermined ending time. The counselor who is unaware of what is prompting the request may get trapped in such situations by his or her own need to be needed. In such situations, the counselor should respond to the underlying feelings rather than the specific requests. Another typical manifestation of reluctance to end is in the planning of reunions. These, too, should be discouraged because the group will not be able to achieve in a social setting that which has become so significant to them in a therapeutic setting. In our experience of working with well over 200 groups, we know of only two groups following through on their insistence that "we'll all get together again next semester."

As the date of termination approaches, group members are frequently reluctant to continue the process of working and exploring. Explorations may become less intense and discussions more superficial because members are reluctant to introduce new topics. The unverbalized attitude of the group seems to be a message of "Well, after all, we have only two more sessions." Our position is that an hour and a half in a counseling group can be profoundly productive, maximized far beyond the limits of time constraints by the intense nature of the therapeutic group. The counselor can help by verbalizing the reluctance sensed, raising the issue of termination, and stating his or her own expectations.

A crucial prerequisite to the effective facilitation of the termination process is the counselor's personal willingness to come to terms with his or her own reactions and feelings about the ending of relationships. The counselor also has shared in the pain and happiness inherent in the development of the group. He or she, too, has invested in the growth of the organism that has become a cohesive unit. The group leader frequently has felt cared for, liked, needed, and helpful. Such significant feelings are not easily given up. One of the most facilitative things the counselor can do at this point is to share openly with the group his or her feelings of reluctance to end the relationship. Confronting such feelings "opens the door" for group members to begin the process of turning loose and looking ahead to the possibility of new and equally meaningful relationships in their ongoing world.

Procedures for Termination

If the group members have not already indicated an awareness of the ending of the group counseling sessions, an important procedure is for the counselor to remind the group of the approaching last session at least two sessions prior to termination. Group members can then make their own decisions as to the investment needed to deal with unfinished business. Introducing the matter of termination too early in the life of the group may result in members focusing their energy on the ending of the group and thus avoiding continuing to work on areas of initial commitment.

Procedures for terminating a group range from allowing the members to decide how they are going to terminate, to the counselor initiating a discussion of feelings associated with the ending of the group, to structured exercises focusing on specific issues related to termination. Dies and Dies (1993) suggested that four tasks be addressed during termination:

1. Address any unfinished business.
2. Set goals for what to do once treatment ends.
3. Consider treatment alternatives such as continuing counseling.
4. Explore the personal meaning of the end of the group for each member.

A slightly different approach is taken by Corey and Corey (2005). During the closing session, they emphasized a focused type of feedback by asking:

1. how members have perceived themselves in the group;
2. what the group has meant to them;
3. what conflicts have become more clear;
4. what, if any, decisions have been made.

Other members then give feedback about how they have perceived and felt about that person. Many practitioners agree that the leader should focus on the fact of termination in advance of the last session by initiating a discussion of how members feel about the group coming to an end and how they can utilize later the things learned in the group (Posthuma 2002).

Communication exercises are useful in that they help members review and clarify experiences and changes that have been made and provide encouragement to action. However, a potential problem exists with such exercises in that members too often may give only positive feedback when responding to the above suggested questions, particularly if members have developed a deep, caring relationship. Some balance in what is shared can be structured by having members express additional feelings and reactions by responding to open-ended sentences having beginnings such as the following:

*   My greatest fear for you is:
*   My hope for you is:
*   I hope that you will seriously consider:
*   You block your strengths by:
*   Some things I hope you will think about doing for yourself are:

In groups where members have been unusually intense and constructively critical in their efforts to better understand themselves and to change, often no need will exist to be concerned about achieving balance in termination feedback. The crucial point seems to be that members utilize the last few sessions to continue the process of implementing what they have learned to do in previous sessions and that members continue to learn how to transfer these significant learnings to their daily lives outside the group.

Summary About Termination

What is needed by a given group approaching termination will be determined by the uniqueness of the group. No single termination exercise could possibly be appropriate for all groups. Therefore, the group counselor is encouraged to rely on his or her own sensitivity and creativity in determining how to help a group cope with the ending of the group counseling relationship.

Other Stage Theories and Concepts

Group practitioners and researchers have long espoused various models to explain group behavior. Stage models allow instructors to teach about common group dynamics, students to gain an understanding and apply structure to those dynamics, and practitioners to assess the progress of their groups. No single developmental model has been demonstrated to be superior to the others. In fact, most look strangely similar, with different names for the various dynamics. Although we have posited our own idea of what group development looks like, we also offer the following other developmental models for comparison (see Table 8.1).

Facilitating Responsibility

Assumption of responsibility for one's own behavior is not something that occurs automatically in group counseling. The group counselor must be able to facilitate the kind of climate that not only allows but also encourages group members to become involved in the process of determining what they will contribute and what they will get out of the group.

One of the major objectives of group counseling is to help members assume responsibility for themselves and their behavior. However, in initial group counseling experiences, counselors often feel they are solely responsible for almost everything that occurs in the group. Such an attitude may deprive group members of an opportunity to experience responsibility for many decisions they could make.

Table 8.1 Models of group development

	Corey (2004)	*Tuckman & Jensen (1977)*	*Trotzer (1999)*
Pre-group			
Precommitment stage			
1. Initial testing of limits	Initial stage	Forming	Security
2. Tentative self	Disclosure and exploration	Orientation and exploration	Acceptance
Commitment stage			
3. Depth self-exploration and understanding	Transition stage	Storming	Dealing with resistance
4. Commitment to change and growth	Working stage	Norming	Responsibility
5. Working toward increased personal effectiveness	Cohesion and productivity	Performing	Work
6. Preparing to leave group	Final stage: consolidation and termination Post-group	Adjourning	Closing

Depending upon the group counselor's theoretical and philosophical position, the perceived role is to initiate, motivate, encourage participation, or facilitate involvement. The counselor is not, however, responsible for "running the show." Group members need to share in the responsibility for what happens in the group. Therefore, the focus of attention in the group should be on the members.

Keeping the Focus on Group Members

Group members cannot be helped to learn about responsibility through observation alone. If group members are to assume responsibility, they must be allowed to experience the process of decision making. If the group counselor makes most of the decisions concerning the group, even the seemingly minor ones, dependency is much more likely to be fostered than responsibility. A better group counselor's approach would be to enable members to become more aware of their own strengths and the strengths of other members.

Allowing and helping group members to accept responsibility are especially crucial in the first few group counseling sessions because the tone is being set for succeeding sessions. Therefore, an important activity is for the group counselor to demonstrate in the early sessions that members can be responsible to each other and for themselves. The following points may be helpful in facilitating responsibility:

- Helping members learn how to work together effectively is a slow process and requires much patience on the part of the counselor.
- Group counseling is a new experience for most members. The counselor must remember that members may need time to learn how to work together effectively.
- Due to the nature of group process, the counselor may think very little is being accomplished in the first few sessions. The counselor should recognize this as a personal need rather than the members' need to "get something done."

In most groups, initially a tendency exists on the part of the members to give their responsibility to the counselor. Members may ask the counselor to tell them what to do and how to do it. To avoid this trap, the counselor could respond, "I know you have had people tell you what to do before, but in here, in this group, you can work things out for yourself. I'll try to help, but I won't decide what you want to talk about."

The group counselor has a responsibility to help members to respond to each other. In most groups, members tend at the beginning to direct their responses to the counselor even when talking to another member. The counselor could respond, "Robert, you are talking to Jack, but you seem to be telling me. Could you tell Jack?"

The counselor must be careful so as to avoid implying what answers should be. Often, implications are given by tone of voice or facial expression.

By answering all questions with direct answers, the group counselor quickly becomes the answer source and thus deprives members of the responsibility for deriving solutions. Members do not always want an answer from the counselor, even though they have asked. The counselor could reflect some questions to the whole group by asking, "What do the rest of you think?" When the counselor allows the group to "set members straight," the group experiences the responsibility of their behavior.

Patience: A Prerequisite

At times, group counselors may experience difficulty in restraining themselves in the group. This seems to be especially true during those moments when the counselor is experiencing a need to "get things going" or when the counselor suddenly "sees" what no one else in the group is perceiving. Group counseling requires patience and a willingness to allow members to discover for themselves. Patience is indeed a basic prerequisite to the developing of responsibility in a group. Grady Nutt (1971: 78) has written of patience: "Mushrooms grow to maturity overnight. Orchids take seven to twelve years to bloom. Your relationships can be mushrooms or orchids. The mature person waits for orchids but is patient with mushrooms!"

Through waiting to see what will happen or restraining a response for a few seconds, the counselor provides the members of the group with an opportunity to take responsibility for "getting things going" or helping other members. Group members thus come to realize that "this is our group," and the counselor learns that other helpers are in the group.

Group Member Responsibility

Acceptance of responsibility to help another person and experiencing the process of being helpful are for group members profoundly positive and self-enhancing encounters. The extension of responsibility outward to touch the lives of others in a helpful way adds a unique, depth dimension quality to the life of the helper. After just such an experience, a group member once wrote, "Working in this group has helped me to form a stronger self-concept, and I'm liking myself better with each session. I really can be helpful to people. That's important to know. I'm thinking of myself in a new light now."

Group members are more likely to experience personal change when they are allowed to be responsible for that change. Members tend to resist even the possibility of new behaviors when the atmosphere is one of attempting to force change. The potential for change is greatly enhanced when group members are granted the freedom to be and at the same time are helped to accept responsibility for resulting behavior. The impact of this willingness to allow rather than force change is perhaps best expressed by a group member who wrote,

> One of your ways of helping me is letting me change. I trust that. I'm not afraid of exploring something or making a change. You let me grow. If I were to come up against something and be immensely afraid, you'd let me be afraid even though you and I both would know plenty of good reasons not to be.

When members experience the opportunity to accept responsibility, they discover that they trust themselves more fully and as a result are more willing to risk and to explore the inner depth that they possess. Personal growth, then, is facilitated by members' responsible involvement in their own behavioral change.

Achieving Group Stability in Group Counseling

Groups are inevitable and ubiquitous. People being social animals, the very omnipresence of the group setting is what is so appealing. Persons tend naturally and spontaneously to form groups. The counselor in an educational setting is in an advantageous position to make use of this principle for the formation of counseling or "growth" groups.

Membership and Group Stability

Any counselor who initiates a group has an obligation to create the kinds of conditions most conducive to success. Evidence seems to point to the fact that voluntary membership is preferable to involuntary or counselor-contrived groups. This does not necessarily doom involuntary groups to failure, however, because even more important than initial membership is the atmosphere or growth climate that the leader is able to facilitate once the group is underway.

Group stability, or the desire of the group to remain together and work toward commonly accepted goals, is related to the attractiveness the group holds for its members. In other words, the group will achieve its goals in direct proportion to the extent to which members perceive the group in a positive way. If a group is to become attractive to its members, it must attempt to imitate the structural makeup of society in general. Single-sex or "single-problem" groups do not do this. The attractiveness necessary in achieving group stability probably is more attainable with heterogeneity. Barker et al. (2000) supported heterogeneity of groups by noting that heterogeneous groups were generally more productive than their homogeneous counterparts.

Leadership and Group Stability

The primary function of the leader is to facilitate interaction between group members and to assist in clarifying situations that group members see as being problematic. Unstructured group leaders will operate from a democratic base rather than as authoritarian types of leaders. They will not allow their own status needs to interfere as the group process produces emergent leaders. They will tend to see themselves as a member of the group but at the same time as a member who is capable of sensitivity to changing and evolving group needs and to those individuals who comprise the group.

The leadership variable that is so important to effective group interaction seems limited only by the degree of personal flexibility of the leader. Perhaps another way of expressing this concept is by saying that the leader needs to remain open to the content and the process of the group as it manifests itself. The group leader, to an even greater degree than in an individual setting, must remain in tune and be sensitive to the total dynamics of the group. The number of possible interactions is multiplied greatly in a group setting, thus offering fertile ground for exploring new areas of concern and affording new avenues for testing behaviors.

Progress and Learning in Groups

The learning that takes place in the group is again relative to the individual members' perception of the attractiveness of the group. If the climate of the group is such that individuals are overly concerned with protection and maintenance of the self, the learning process will be inhibited.

The leader has the responsibility for being sensitive to and adjusting group and personal motivational factors that enhance the learning situation. The nonthreatening, accepting, and empathic atmosphere will ease the need for self-protection and maintenance, and thus free the individual for new learning, exploratory, and self-enhancing behavior.

Group togetherness develops and grows through participation and sharing by group members and the leader. Each group member has an opportunity to share responsibility, thereby providing a feeling of true involvement and emergent leadership. Many writers have examined and continue to explore the concepts of group trust, interrelationships, dominance or power, and emotionality as they relate to total group progress and task accomplishment.

Lack of attractiveness or group stability will quickly lead to the dissolution of the group. On the other hand, a group that is attractive and meaningful to its members will have a powerful holding ability. This attractiveness, facilitated through meaningful interaction, should lead to group stability and its atmosphere of growth.

Attractiveness will not be consistently uniform among group members. This will account for feelings of dissatisfaction that are expressed at different points as the group progresses. The leader will need to work with these dissatisfactions as they are presented and at all times will need to be attentive to the expressed needs of the group along these lines. Groups are intuitive about progress, and the leader should be aware that groups will "run their course" at varying levels. If a climate of acceptance has been established, the group will be free to express their feelings with regard to perceived progress. In the unstructured setting, of course, the group will make the determination as to when it has fulfilled its function and should disband.

The group also will recognize when things begin to "bog down." At these points, the leader will want to help clarify the reasons for slowdowns in group progress.

Bringing It All Together: A Group Example

This counseling group protocol features one of the authors (RCB) working with an initial group of college undergraduates. The original group was two hours in length. This protocol has been edited to include some instructional transactions and focuses on a few of the group members.

LEADER: Thank you for all coming. We're all acquainted and have met before. I'm not aware of the reasons why each of you chose to participate in this experience, but that might be something you can think about for a minute. I would like for each of you to state briefly what you would like to work on this afternoon in the limited time we have available. Give that some thought. [*Looks around group.*]

The leader opens the group by welcoming the members, thanking them for their participation, and inviting them to participate in a brief go-around. This method encourages each member to become verbally involved in the group. When a person verbalizes in the initial session, there is a greater chance that the person will affiliate with the group in a positive way. It helps prevent a person from becoming verbally isolated.

DONNA: I will. I've been real withdrawn the past couple of months. I've kept myself away from everything and everybody. The day the people came around and asked for volunteers for this group, I said to myself, "Do it!" This group is one way to . . . not really risk, but to just do something. I've been trying to motivate myself to get out and do things, but I always change my mind.

LEADER: So, for you, Donna, it's like if you commit yourself to the group, you're hopeful something good will come of it.

The leader reflects content and feeling to connect with each initial comment of the members.

DONNA: I'm using this as a form of personal therapy.

LEADER: Good. OK. Thanks for sharing.

MIKE: I'm like Donna. I just needed to force myself to take a risk. I needed to do something where I wasn't sure what to expect. I really like to know what's going to happen [*laughs*]. This group is a challenge to myself.

LEADER: You're testing some new behavior. This experience is different for you.

MIKE: Yeah. Exactly.

LEADER: Thanks, Mike. I appreciate you sharing that.

SCOTT: This semester is different for me because I'm not as busy as I usually make myself. I have more free time. This group is something that a year ago I would have said, "I don't have time for that." Now it's perfect because I do have time. Along with the changes that are different in my life. Some things that are going on aren't as safe or understandable as I'm used to. Maybe I was looking for a place to share some of that.

LEADER: Super. Having the time just to do something nice for yourself represents some growth. Thanks, Scott; I'm glad you're here.

SCOTT: [*Nods and smiles.*]

JULIE: The second I heard about the group, I thought, "Extra credit for class. Thank God!" [*Laughter erupts among the members.*] Then I started thinking about it and how it was going to be group therapy, and I figured it was great. I would get extra credit and a place to talk.

LEADER: At first, your motives were for yourself. [*Laughter and murmuring among the members.*] So it might be safe to say that you are here with some ambivalence, some mixed feelings.

JULIE: Not now! I had somewhere else to be, but I chose to commit to this. [*Looks away from leader.*]

LEADER: And you feel good about this.

JULIE: Yes.

LEADER: To "commit to this," to use your words. OK. Thanks, Julie.

JILL: My situation is similar to Mike's in that I wanted to test myself and risk again. Once I finished my last group, my risk-taking ended. I just wanted to make myself get back out and see what I could do. I like things to be very straightforward and certain [laughs], so to do this was to test that even though I didn't know what was going to happen.

Notice that each person has the opportunity to express some issue or reason for attending the group. The leader will make a mental note of this while also paying attention to problems or situations that may require immediate group attention.

LEADER: OK. I sense that although this experience is a little scary, it's almost something you think you should do or need to do.

JILL: It's very similar to that. This experience may start the adrenaline going again [*laughs*].

LEADER: It's exciting—or can be. [*Pause.*] Jill, what's missing in your life right now?

Leader probes a little deeper, which gives other members an opportunity to experience differing levels of focus.

JILL: I guess a little excitement and finding things to do that are fun for me. That may be why I'm here.

LEADER: Yes. That may very well be true. Kind of like Scott—just doing together something good for yourself. A few of you seem uncomfortable being selfish and just doing something for yourself. [*Nods among the members.*] Thanks, Jill; I'm glad you're here.

Connects group members—universality.

NANCY: I have several reasons for being here. One reason is that the group I was in was different. I wanted to see what group felt like with another group of people. A lot of this is risk-taking. It makes me feel stronger. I was the type of child who would hide in the corner because I didn't want to play. It was safer to be in the corner. Little did I realize that by hiding in the corner, people bugged me more.

LEADER: So by hiding, you actually drew more attention to yourself.

Although the leader agenda might be to encourage everyone to become verbally involved in the group, he or she also needs to remain sensitive to the possibility of a therapeutic moment presenting itself in the group. The leader senses that opportunity here with Curtis, who tends to be somewhat shy and withdrawn. The transaction with Curtis demonstrates how to bring behavior into the group in an immediate fashion. In this case, a behavioral contract is negotiated with Curtis, thereby involving the entire group in the process.

NANCY: Oh yeah!

LEADER: I'm glad you took the risk. My experience of you is that it would be easy for you to hold back and not volunteer, and you have to sort of push yourself.

NANCY: Yeah. [*Smiles and nods.*]

CURTIS: I guess the reason why I came was to try to do something different from the ordinary routine I'm always in.

LEADER: Is there anything special that you might want from this group this afternoon?

Notice the shift from external, outside-of-group experience to here-and-now experience.

CURTIS: Just to listen, I guess.

LEADER: OK. Who here knows you best, Curtis?

The leader does linking and encouragement to provide feedback.

CURTIS: I don't know.

DONNA: I think Curtis is one of the hardest people in class to know.

CURTIS: Yeah, I mean I know some people from in class, but not really.

LEADER: Did you catch what Donna said?

CURTIS: Yeah, that I was hard to get to know.

LEADER: Can you give Curtis some more feedback?

DONNA: Curtis is pleasant, but a little unapproachable.

LEADER: Talk to Curtis.

At this place, the leader encourages Donna to address her remarks directly to Curtis rather than talking "through" the leader.

DONNA: [*Laughs.*] OK. I mean we can talk, but maybe it's just in passing. Maybe we just don't have time where we can get to know each other. I guess I haven't had time to meet you. There are others I don't know well.

LEADER: So it's not just Curtis.

DONNA: No.

LEADER: And yet, at the same time, I heard you (Curtis) say that your style is to just hang back and be a listener. Underneath that style of being, what might be what you really want from people?

CURTIS: Just to listen, I think.

LEADER: So you are announcing to the group, "I'm where I want to be, don't approach me"?

CURTIS: No. I want to be approached.

DONNA: I don't understand when he says he just wants to listen. Does he mean he wants us to listen or he wants to listen to us?

LEADER: Ask Curtis. [*Group laughs.*]

CURTIS: In the past, it seems no one has wanted to listen to what I had to say. Now, I'm getting to where people actually want to listen. It's more comfortable for me. It's something I'm working on.

DONNA: Getting people to listen to you.

CURTIS: Yeah! Just to seem like they're interested in what I have to say.

DONNA: I feel like that too sometimes. Maybe it's not so much making people listen to me as it's that I can't control what other people do. I can only control myself.

CURTIS: Yeah, that's true.

LEADER: In what you just said, Donna, is there a message in that for Curtis?

DONNA: Maybe he's just doing what is not his responsibility to do.

LEADER: Yes, and at the same time I heard you (Curtis) say that "I'm kind of learning that people are listening to what I say." It's a new experience for you, so it feels different.

At this point, Donna's feedback seems to liberate some energy in the group and sends a cross-transaction to Nancy.

CURTIS: Yeah.

LEADER: So a risk for you would be to say things and see yourself on an equal footing with everyone else in the group and to just take the risk.

CURTIS: Yeah, OK.

DONNA: On the flipside, since you have been quiet, when you do say something, I listen. Maybe I tend to listen to people who don't talk that much.

NANCY: Yeah, when quiet people finally talk, I think it must be important.

SCOTT: [*to Nancy*] Yeah, that's what I think about you.

LEADER: OK. In a normal group, Curtis, for two hours, how many times might you talk in a group?

CURTIS: Not very much.

LEADER: Can you put a number on it?

CURTIS: Two to three times at the most.

LEADER: Well, that's not bad.

CURTIS: Well, that's like the best.

LEADER: So that's a good day! [*Group laughs.*] Just for today, would you be willing to contract with the group to respond at least five times while we are and light, together?

The contract negotiation takes on a somewhat lighter tone. The message is that this whole exercise can be fun and doesn't need to be ponderously hard work.

CURTIS: OK. [*Smiles; nervous laughter in group.*]

LEADER: You appear uncomfortable. Can you talk about your discomfort?

CURTIS: Sort of scared. Feel like going into new territory.

LEADER: OK, and when I said, "Five times," you seemed to be getting a mental picture of yourself doing it. What was that picture?

CURTIS: It felt good. I could see myself talking.

LEADER: So you're telling me it's scary, but good. Sort of like going to the dentist. [*Laughter.*] Is five times OK with the group? [*Looks at Holly.*]

HOLLY: I wanted to get back into a group because I had been going every week and all of a sudden it was over and I felt cut off. I missed group.

The go-around is continued with the final member.

LEADER: What was the loss? Do you recall what the loss feels like?

HOLLY: I just looked forward to it. Group helped me out.

LEADER: How did it help out? How do you feel now, thinking about the group?

HOLLY: If I had anything that was bothering me, I could talk about it or just sit and listen.

LEADER: Is that not in your life right now?

HOLLY: Kind of. But not really, no.

LEADER: So for you, this group is a reconnection and at least an opportunity to get involved.

HOLLY: Yes.

LEADER: Great. Thanks. Did I touch base with everyone? OK. We've all mentioned some areas for change. Would anyone like to jump in and do some work? [*Silence followed by nervous laughter and murmuring.*]

This is another transition point in the group, and the climate tenses slightly. The invitation to work signals a move to another level of interaction and disclosure.

DONNA: OK. This is good. That's why I came: because I am withdrawn from everyone in my life right now and these people won't let me.

LEADER: So "Thank you, Holly, for not letting me hide in the corner."

DONNA: A lot of people in class just know when I'm withdrawn.

HOLLY: Like the card?

DONNA: Yes! Can I share that? [*Touches Holly.*]

HOLLY: Sure!

DONNA: Holly sent me a little card that read, "I know something's bothering you and I'm here for you." No one at home in my family would have picked up on that.

LEADER: That must have been special.

DONNA: Yes. Very much so! [*Moderately long silence.*]

SCOTT: OK. I'll say something [*nervous laughter*]. Like I said, I'm going through a lot of changes. I'm not really looking for an answer because I don't know if there is one. For a few years now, I have been busy all the time. Group was the first place that challenged why I was that way. After doing some thinking, I realized I didn't enjoy being under pressure all the time. Maybe I did it to feel needed.

Scott uses some time to talk about the growth he is experiencing in the way that he structures his time. His sharing is somewhat halting, careful, and cognitive. Because he is a sociometrically high-status person in the group, other members attempt to provide feedback and assistance. He gets good group support, and this is an opportunity for various group members to contribute to the dialogue.

LEADER: A place for yourself.

SCOTT: Yeah. I took the risk this semester to say, "No," to things. It's been hard.

LEADER: Yeah, it's a change in the way you're structuring your time. How has it been difficult for you, Scott?

SCOTT: I'm used to people calling me, asking for advice. Now that doesn't happen.

LEADER: Are you aware of any feelings with that situation?

SCOTT: Sure. I guess lonely, but every time I think that I say how stupid I am for thinking it.

LEADER: Oh, so you get to beat up on yourself too. [*Laughter in group.*]

SCOTT: Yeah, I think of all the people I counsel who are really lonely. I have so many good things in my life. But the other night, I was sitting there and I just felt sad. I couldn't pinpoint why. I usually don't let myself feel that way. I wanted to talk to some people, but I didn't want to blow my image by talking about my problems.

LEADER: So you're not ready to get into that issue yet.

Leader, through accurate reflections, begins to help Scott define his level of comfortable self-disclosure in the group.

SCOTT: Yeah [*looks down*].

LEADER: But you were willing to let yourself experience the sadness, and you survived it.

SCOTT: Yeah, I did. [*Smiles.*]

LEADER: And that's new for you. Do you think that by making your schedule so busy, you created a way to avoid dealing with some sadness?

SCOTT: Maybe, I guess, but not on purpose. I know the free time is good, but I still feel the urge to be constantly busy.

LEADER: You are still not sure what it's about.

SCOTT: Yeah. I don't know if there's an answer

LEADER: Does anyone have some insights into this . . . or observations?

Leader encourages feedback to foster cohesion within the group.

CURTIS: Yeah, I always need something to do. I never make time for myself. I know where you're coming from.

SCOTT: Thanks. [*Silence.*]

LEADER: What happens when you're alone?

SCOTT: I think about what I should be doing. [*Laughs.*] I'm just talking about structure. Sometimes I just feel guilty if I just sit around.

LEADER: What does it mean for you, Scott, to just do nothing, to just relax or not accomplish anything? What pops into your mind?

SCOTT: Just there are a lot of people hurting and a lot of good that could be done. I can't do that if I'm sitting around.

LEADER: Do you think that some of that need to help comes from your own pain?

SCOTT: Sure. Yeah.

LEADER: Have you looked at that?

SCOTT: I don't know. Maybe I've tried to identify it. I don't know why I do it. I guess it's just the way I am. [*Laughs and looks out window.*]

LEADER: Right now you're feeling awkward and uncomfortable. You've taken some steps into some areas that you are not sure you want to get into.

Leader utilizes here-and-now group feedback as a confrontation.

SCOTT: Yeah. I don't know.

LEADER: Can you talk about how you feel right now? That would be awful.

SCOTT: [*Deep sigh.*] I really feel that [*silence*] maybe I'm wasting people's time. [*Laughs.*] Yeah. The whole time I'm talking, I'm telling myself that it's not that bad, and I feel stupid for spending so much time.

JULIE: Surely someone has some real problems [*laughs*].

LEADER: So to feel like you're worth it is a big risk for you. I think you're worth it, but you might want to check it out with others.

GROUP: You're worth it.

LEADER: I think the sad part is that sometimes the rest of us are more convinced you are worthwhile than you are.

Leader utilizes here-and-now group feedback as a confrontation.

JILL: Maybe one thing you could do is to try to see where you fit in all of your activities. Where are you?

SCOTT: Somewhere, I guess. [*Silence.*]

HOLLY: I can see a change from last semester. You seem more relaxed.

LEADER: How does that look to you, Holly?

Encourages personal feedback.

HOLLY: I feel more comfortable around him because he made me feel guilty for hanging out. [*Laughs.*] He made it seem like I didn't do anything.

LEADER: So your experience is that when Scott is relaxed, he's more comfortable for you to be around.

HOLLY: Yes.

LEADER: You're getting some feedback, and you are aware of some changes. These changes have been very conscious on your part, and I applaud you for that because I don't think it's been easy. Do you feel more in control, a little bit better?

It is becoming clear that Scott is not ready to delve into this issue at a deeper level, and the leader senses that it's time to let it go for a while.

SCOTT: Yeah!

LEADER: More comfortable now that you are out of the spotlight. I like to work with people at their pace. If you are not ready today, that's OK. I feel people work best when they want to and when they are ready; all you have to do is say so.

SCOTT: Thanks.

NANCY: Yeah! I always think someone else has something more important to say.

LEADER: I don't believe that.

NANCY: Well, yeah, I tell myself it's silly but . . .

LEADER: What are you aware of needing in order to take risks? If you could construct a safe situation, what would it be like?

At this point, Nancy's posture and expressions seem to indicate a willingness to do some tentative self-exploration. Notice how Nancy uses short, clipped sentences and questions to stay in personal control and attempt to shape the transactions.

NANCY: A lot of it is mental talk. You tell yourself you are going to trust these people and you're not going to get anything unless you take the chance. So it's basically convincing myself . . .

LEADER: That . . .

NANCY: That it's OK.

LEADER: You said, "trusting these people," so that would be part . . .

Trust and safety are continuous issues in any group. At this point, the leader uses the moment in the group to help Nancy work on her trust issues while encouraging group movement into more immediate, here-and-now changes.

NANCY: Yeah! Trust would be a big part of feeling safe.

LEADER: How do you feel about your trust of this group right here and now?

NANCY: In this situation?

LEADER: Yes. On a scale of 1 to 10, 10 being "I trust this group completely" and 1 being no trust at all.

Bring the issue "into" the group and quantify it. This helps the issue become real and concrete.

SCOTT: Honestly.

NANCY: My mind tells me 9, but emotionally I don't feel that safe. Probably a 6.

LEADER: Is it safe to say that when you feel emotionally at 6, it has to do less with these people . . .

NANCY: Oh yes! It's all in me.

LEADER: Can you talk about the scary part, the 6 part? "I have trouble trusting sometimes because . . ."

NANCY: I have trouble trusting a lot of times because . . . well, it's a lot of times really, because of my past. You could say I've been kicked in the teeth a lot [*deep breath*] when I've tried to trust.

Nancy attempts to take the issue into the past, but the leader facilitates an emphasis on current experiences of the issue.

LEADER: You're still feeling that pain. Still close to the surface.

NANCY: Yeah. Comes and goes. [*Brief silence.*]

LEADER: Nancy, in your life right now, what are you missing because of that pain? What's the price tag?

NANCY: Close relationships. It keeps me from getting close to some people.

LEADER: OK. Some people you could potentially get close to.

NANCY: Right.

LEADER: The lack of trust keeps you from those relationships.

NANCY: Yeah. [*Silence.*]

LEADER: Who's the easiest person in this room right now for you to trust?

Linking Nancy and Jill in an immediate encounter helps solidify what has been somewhat abstract.

NANCY: Probably Jill. We've been in group together and have seen each other open up.

LEADER: Jill, does that feel right to you?

JILL: Yeah, it really does. We have shared outside of group as well. I also feel we have some things in common, like holding on to our hurts.

LEADER: You're holding on to some past hurts, too, so you can relate to what she's saying. Would you like to help her with her hurts?

JILL: [*Nervous laugh.*] I don't know how to go about it.

LEADER: Well, maybe just being willing to encounter her pain and build on your relationship with Nancy.

JILL: [*Nods.*]

LEADER: Nancy, on that same 1-to-10 scale, would you look at Jill and tell her where you are in that relationship with her and the level of trust you feel with her?

Leader is consistent in use to scale to explore experience.

NANCY: About an 8.

LEADER: Do you feel the potential is there for it to even reach a 10?

NANCY: Yes.

LEADER: Is the 8 because of Jill or because of you?

NANCY: Me.

LEADER: OK. Would you look at Jill again, tell her she's an 8, and that you take responsibility for that and why?

NANCY: [*Smiling.*] You're an 8 on my scale of trust. I take responsibility for that rating. I think some of it is my unwillingness to take a risk.

LEADER: Jill, would you like to respond to that?

JILL: Well, after knowing you, I really feel lucky to have an 8 with you. I appreciate that you can trust me so much.

LEADER: Nice risk. Thank you both. The other part of that is who is the scariest person for you in here to trust? [*Nancy looks down, plays with ear.*] I'm not going to ask you to take that risk now, but it's something to think about, OK? I appreciate you talking about trust because it's such a vital part of group. Thanks.

CURTIS: As I've listened to people talk, I've realized it's not that I don't trust others, but I don't trust myself. There are some issues I won't talk about because I don't trust myself to share them.

It is quite clear that Curtis has taken a good deal of encouragement from Nancy's disclosure and has decided to open himself up for some processing. In the process, he is quickly affirmed by the leader and the group.

LEADER: OK. Some of that is wise. How does your level of trust fit into this room today?

CURTIS: I feel really comfortable today. Maybe it's because of the people here. Maybe I'm ready to work on some issues.

DONNA: I looked at the names on the sign-up sheet to make sure I trusted the people coming. [*Laughs. Silence.*]

CURTIS: One thing is I often feel like if I share, people will blow me off and laugh at me.

LEADER: Well, I'm real proud of you, Curtis, for risking today and sharing in group.

GROUP: Yes. [*Clapping; Curtis smiles.*]

LEADER: You hold back because you are afraid others will laugh or disrespect you. Do you have any idea of where that comes from?

The leader senses that Curtis's interpersonal shyness may be related to some early painful experiences. He attempts to gently but specifically guide him into remembered hurts and wounds from the past.

CURTIS: From when I was growing up. I would get made fun of a lot.

LEADER: And you're still in touch with that pain. About how old were you?

CURTIS: Yeah. About sixth grade.

LEADER: Can you recall a specific incident?

CURTIS: In PE, I was always chosen last. In sixth grade.

LEADER: Do you remember the teacher or kids?

CURTIS: Not the teacher, but the kids were always the ones who were popular and thought they were hot stuff.

LEADER: Where are you in the mental picture of this class?

CURTIS: Outside. Ready to play softball or something.

LEADER: And they have captains. They are choosing sides, and it's down to the last few people and you're not picked yet. What are you feeling?

CURTIS: Sad, upset. I'm the last one.

LEADER: Sure. You're the last person. Any other sentences? [*Short silence.*]

LEADER: [*Notices Jill's discomfort.*] Does this ring any bells with you?

At this point, there is an opportunity to link Curtis and Jill around the "ugly duckling" issue. Many people carry slights and hurts forward from that important adolescent developmental period.

JILL: Oh yeah. I feel the same. Kids harassing me. Being left by myself continuously.

LEADER: Feeling different from the other kids.

JILL: Yes.

LEADER: Left out. Lonely. Kind of scared.

DONNA: Very embarrassing. I've felt that too.

JILL: I always wondered why they were picking on me. There were goofier kids, stupider kids. Why me? What's wrong with me?

CURTIS: Yeah.

JILL: What did I do to deserve this? I finally just decided I must be doing something wrong.

LEADER: So the inclination was to blame yourself. If you do that enough, pretty soon you convince yourself. What sentences did you say to yourself back then?

Notice the shift from external blame to internal blame and associated feelings. This facilitates a deeper level because members are able to focus on themselves.

JILL: I'm too ugly. I'm too tall. I walk funny. I can't get along with people. Just bashing myself. My mother would say, "Just ignore them, ignore them all."

LEADER: Don't have feelings.

JILL: [*Loud voice.*] "You don't need to get upset!"

LEADER: Your message at home was "Don't feel."

JILL: Right.

LEADER: So you learned to distance yourself from your feelings?

JILL: Yeah. Sure, I guess I did. When I finally let myself feel, I was sure something was wrong with me. Then I would get upset and I really couldn't get along with people! It was like a circle.

LEADER: Curtis, by your reactions, I can see you have had many of the same experiences.

Leader links members, encourages cohesion.

CURTIS: Oh, yeah.

LEADER: Did you have any idea that Jill had shared similar experiences as you had in the past?

CURTIS: No, not a clue.

LEADER: Why?

CURTIS: I don't know.

LEADER: Well, what do you think about Jill? You've heard her story.

Leader attempts to facilitate learning through the sharing that has been done.

CURTIS: Nothing different, but I'm not the only one out there. I know that now.

LEADER: What kind of sentences did you tell yourself when you were chosen last?

CURTIS: I'm no good. I can't play. I'm bad.

LEADER: And you remember feeling . . .

CURTIS: Sad. Angry.

LEADER: That was your world then, and you felt left out. What did you do in response to that? Not just you, but can anyone relate to what has been shared? [*Many members nod.*]

CURTIS: I just got through it. Endured it. Ignored it.

JILL: I withdrew. I didn't want to get hurt again.

LEADER: I appreciate the way you have all shared. I think the feeling of being different has been experienced by many here. [*Nods among members . . . moderate silence.*]

LEADER: Is there anything left over?

As it becomes time to close the group, the leader offers the opportunity for any member to get closure if they need it. In this case, Donna and Curtis seem to verbalize the feelings of many in the group as they symbolically bring the session to conclusion.

DONNA: Anything we need to close up?

LEADER: Anything anyone needs from this group or from anyone in this group right now? [*Silence.*] I'm just glad everyone took the time to come and not be too busy. I feel helped. Thank you. I heard that as a thank you to the group.

CURTIS: I feel great [*laughs*]. I am glad I came.

LEADER: I'm glad you came, too. Maybe one thing you have learned is that when you take a risk, you have the chance to gain. I think you took the risk today, and that's something you decided. We've talked about trust and our difficulties with it. Today I have experienced you as a trusting group and trustworthy. I appreciated your warmth and honesty and your time. [*Group members say thanks.*]

The leader briefly summarizes.

References

Barker, V. E., Abrams, J. R., Tiyaamornwong, V., Siebold, D., Duggan, A., Sun Park, H., et al. (2000). New contexts for relational communication in groups. *Small Group Research*, 31, 470–503.

Braaten, L. J. (1990). The different patterns of group climate critical incidents in high and low cohesion sessions of group psychotherapy. *International Journal of Group Psychotherapy*, 40 (4), 477–493.

Budman, S. H., Soldz, S., Demby, A., & Davis, M. S. (1993). What is cohesiveness? An empirical investigation. *Small Group Research*, 24, 199–216.

Carrell, S., & Keenan, T. (2000). *Group exercises for adolescents*. Thousand Oaks, CA: Sage.

Corder, B. F. (1994). *Structured adolescent psychotherapy groups*. Sarasota, FL: Professional Resource Press.

Corey, G. (2004). *Theory and practice of group counseling* (6th ed.). Belmont, CA: Brooks/Cole.

Corey, G., & Corey, M. S. (2005). *Groups: process and practice* (7th ed.). Pacific Grove, CA: Brooks/Cole.

Crutchfield, L., & Garrett, M. T. (2001). Unity circle: A model of group work with children. In K. A. Fall and J. E. Levitov (Eds.), *Modern application to group work* (pp. 3–18). Huntington, NY: Nova Science.

Devencenzi, J., & Pendergast, S. (1988). *Belonging: Self and social discovery for children of all ages*. San Luis Obispo, CA: Belonging.

Dies, K. R., & Dies, R. R. (1993). Directive facilitation: A model for short-term group treatments, Part 2. *The Independent Practitioner*, 13, 177–184.

Dion, K. L. (2000). Group cohesion from "field of forces" to multidimensional construct. *Group Dynamics: Theory Research and Practice*, 4, 7–26.

Drucker, C. (2003). Group counseling in the middle and junior high school. In K. R. Greenberg (Ed.), *Group counseling in K–12 schools*. New York: Allyn & Bacon.

Fall, K. A., & McMahon, H. G. (2001). Engaging adolescent males: A group approach. In K. A. Fall and J. E. Levitov (Eds.), *Modern applications to group work* (pp. 43–68). Huntington, NY: Nova Science.

Huss, S. (2001). Groups for bereaved children. In K. A. Fall and J. E. Levitov (Eds.), *Modern application to group work* (pp. 19–42). Huntington, NY: Nova Science.

Khalsa, S. S. (1996). *Group exercises for enhancing social skills and self-esteem*. Sarasota, FL: Professional Resource.

Landy, L. (1992). *Child support through small group counseling*. Charlotte, NC: Kidsrights.

Lane, K. (1991). *Feelings are real: Group activities for children*. Muncie, IN: Accelerated Development.

McGee, T., Schuman, B., & Racusen, F. (1972). Termination in group psychotherapy. *American Journal of Psychotherapy*, 26 (4), 521–532.

Marmarosh, C., Holtz, A., & Schottenbauer, M. (2005). Group cohesiveness, group derived collective self esteem, group derived hope, and the well being of group therapy members. *Group Dynamics*, 9, 32–34.

Mudrack, P. E. (1989). Defining group cohesiveness: A legacy of confusion? *Small Group Behavior*, 20, 37–49.

Nutt, G. (1971). *Being me*. Nashville, TN: Broadman Press.

Posthuma, B. W. (2002). *Small groups in counseling and therapy* (4th ed.). Boston, MA: Allyn & Bacon.

Trotzer, J. (1999). *The counselor and the group*. New York: Taylor & Francis.

Tuckman, B. W., & Jensen, M. C. (1977). Stages of small group development revisited. *Group and Organizational Studies*, 7, 419–427.

Walker, E. (2000). *Helping at-risk students: A group counseling approach for grades 6–9*. New York: Guilford.

Yalom, I. D. (1995). *The theory and practice of group psychotherapy* (4th ed.). New York: Basic Books.

9

WORKING EFFECTIVELY WITH RESISTANCE IN GROUPS

If you ever catch on fire, try to avoid seeing yourself in the mirror, because I bet that's what REALLY throws you into a panic.

Jack Handy

If things go wrong, don't go with them.

Elvis Presley

What Is Resistance?

The field of counseling has focused a considerable amount of thought on the dynamic of resistance in the therapeutic process. Although much of the literature frames resistance as a client issue, we prefer to view it as both a window into how each group member confronts change and the interplay between individual dynamics and those of the group. From this holistic perspective, resistance can be viewed and assessed as inter- and intrapersonal phenomena.

Most group leaders will encounter resistance in the group at one time or another. Groups will sometimes "agree" at an unconscious level to stay put or resist moving toward more intense interpersonal levels. This can occur with individuals in the group or among several group members simultaneously.

Group leaders need to look at their own feelings when a group becomes resistant. Leaders who have unrealistically high expectations for the group can become frustrated with the lack of progress and thereby lose objectivity. A point to remember is that some resistance can be expected in most groups at some time. If leaders are aware of this, they will be less inclined to personalize the resistance and accept too much responsibility for the group.

Remember that resistance typically is related to issues of trust and security. When several individuals are reluctant to take risks in self-disclosure and interpersonal encounter, usually an issue of lack of trust is at the base. Trying new and risky behaviors in the group can put members in touch with their basic feeling of insecurity. "If I disclose my most closely guarded secrets, who will be there to nurture and care for me? Will I still be acceptable to these people if they know what I'm really like? Can I trust these people to care for my personal issues in a gentle and caring way?"

The most effective strategies involve leaders sharing their own immediate observations as to behavior and causation. "The groups seems to be stuck on content issues at this point. I wonder if this means that we're feeling somewhat insecure and a little scared to move toward more honest confrontation—and maybe intimacy?"

Whatever the intervention choice is, remember that some resistance is natural and that issues of security and trust are usually the cause. When group members have an opportunity to deal with their individual and collective feelings of doubt and mistrust, the opportunity will exist for a quantum leap in group development. Kline (1990) noted that leaders respond best to resistance when they are clear about their own reactions and decisions to intervene and have some grounding intervention principles and objectives. A group leader who is comfortable with handling resistance can facilitate some of the most powerful opportunities for group progress.

Group leaders can effectively work with resistance by asking the following questions when encountering an impasse in the group:

- What is the nature of the resistance? In considering the nature of the resistance, the group leader attempts to identify the elements and characteristics of the behaviors and attitudes classified as *resistance*.
- Is the client actively disruptive to the group process, that is, monopolizing group time, constantly changing the subject of the group conversation, or cracking jokes during serious explorations, or is the resistance more personal in nature?

Otani (1989) classified forms of resistance into four main themes:

1. withholding communication: silence, vague responses, tangential stories;
2. restricting content: questioning and intellectualizing;
3. being manipulative: demeaning others, externalizing;
4. violating the rules: missing appointments or showing up late, not paying for counseling, inappropriate behavior such as sexual or aggressive acting out.

This general taxonomy might be helpful as you try to consider the specific characteristics of any given resistance in your groups.

- What does this resistance say about the way this member handles change in other areas of his or her life?
- How are the other group members responding to the resistance? Is the behavior group supported (normed) or does the behavior violate the group norms?
- How am I responding to the resistance? Does the member's behavior reflect an interpersonal conflict between the leader and the member?

Group Process Obstacles

Our experience has been that many potential problems in group process can be minimized if the group leader will give careful attention to detail during the organizational stages of a group. Many of these administrative details, although somewhat time-consuming, can pay benefits when the group actually begins. Many of these activities, which we term *pre-group activities*, are covered in the chapter on getting a group started (Chapter 6). Group-member selection procedures, group composition, the use of structure in the group, formal operating rules, and guidelines are examples of decisions that can be made prior to the group starting that will have an impact on the eventual success of the group.

We feel that the leader needs to have a reasonably good grasp of what constitutes normal group development and stages through which a group can be expected to progress. Developmental stages in process groups are discussed more thoroughly in the chapter on maintaining a group (Chapter 7). In this section, we discuss some common group processes that can develop into patterns of resistance.

Meaning of Silence in Groups

Although much has been written to help the counselor understand the silent member in group counseling, total group silence is perhaps even more difficult to comprehend. This section is an attempt to help the group counselor anticipate and better understand what is happening when the counseling group experiences periods of silence.

Silence is a significant part of the group counseling process and can be as varied as the happenings and feelings experienced in the group. Each period of silence has a distinctive character. Silence can convey many different messages and seems almost like a contradiction of the word itself because the silences that occur in counseling groups typically "speak loudly" of what is happening. Each silence has its own unique purpose. Group silence is not silent; it is gestures, unspoken words, unverbalized feelings, facial expressions, and the group atmosphere.

Silence: Part of the Group Process

Silence in a group is a natural part of the group process. What occurs or is experienced during the silence is not necessarily different from those times when the group is not considered to be silent. Because only one member can be heard at a time, the group membership at any given time is usually silent with but one exception, the speaker. A time of silence, then, is but a slight departure from the typical setting in that only one more member than usual is silent. When silence is accepted as natural and productive, it becomes a means of growth and not a frustrating villain to be avoided.

That communication exists in silence is often evident in group sessions. At the start of a group session, members commonly visit with each other; then, as if by some signal, members become quiet as they shift gears and start up again within the context of the purpose of the group. This kind of silence reflects group communication of the need to change behaviors. The unspoken message is "We're ready to move to a deeper, more personal level." By their silence, the group indicates a readiness to work and grants permission for any member to begin.

Silence probably occurs most frequently in initial group counseling sessions and often conveys feelings of awkwardness and apprehension. Silence at this stage can serve many purposes. It could be due to the anxiety that members experience by being in a new situation, or it could be a generator of anxiety and thus motivate members to break the silence and attempt to make contact with others in the group. Nevertheless, silence does often happen in beginning stages of the group process and usually conveys a variety of feelings. After an initial group counseling session, one group member wrote in her group log,

> Silence . . . on and on and on. I scratched, swung my leg, doodled, and fervently wished that someone would say something, anything, so that I could look up and see the group instead of sneaking furtive glances at them from under downcast eyes. I searched vainly for a question to ask without appearing foolish. No question! What to do?—sneeze, cough loudly, fall out of the chair in a dead faint? Certainly not! Maybe if I smile crookedly everyone will think that I have all the answers and wish they had them too. No one said anything. There are lots of things I could say, but I'm not about to say anything. NOT A THING! Why don't I ask what I want to know? Can I trust this group? Well, test the water before you plunge headlong into a stump filled lake.

Working Silence

How long a period of silence in the group seems to last, not in actual passing of time but rather how long it feels, is often an indication of the amount of work going on in the group. The point here is not one of what is productive, for in terms of the developing group process a long and frustrating group silence can be productive. However, a working silence is usually experienced as being of short duration. Time seems to be condensed, and the silence is hardly noticed as members share through their own thoughts and feelings in the experience of the group. Indeed, the silence is not even experienced as silence. Often, silent periods become more acceptable and comfortable as members experience a growing sense of adequacy. A nonworking silence is felt, is noticed, does drag on, and seems to say, "We are being silent." Such a silence is characterized by darting glances around the group, shifting postures, busy hands or feet, nervous grins, avoidance of eye contact, and a feeling that everyone is waiting for someone to do something. This is especially true when the group is thinking that the other members in the group are "troubled" or "sick," and each member works doubly hard at reflecting and probing in order to keep the focus on any other member who happens to say something, whether personal or not. As if by some invisible signal, the members of the group will lapse into a period of silence in which each member seems determined not to be the one to break the silence. The sensitive group facilitator can almost feel the resistance, the pulling back, the holding in that says, "I'm not about to say anything and get put on the spot." At such a time, the group silence certainly communicates.

Silence in a group does not mean "nothing is going on." Quite the contrary: silence by the group may convey support for a member who is having difficulty expressing feelings or ideas. Such a silence is permeated with encouragement that the member seems to feel as much as sense. Support is also evident in the silence of togetherness that follows the sharing of hurt or sadness, when the group seems to know words would be inappropriate. Silence can be a time of experiencing deeply one's self when facilitated by an awareness of the support and acceptance of others. Following a fifteen-minute silence in a group, a member remarked, "This has just been the most profound period of deep introspection I have ever experienced. I was able to look closely at some parts of my life I've avoided for ten years." Silence in a group can be a warm blanket.

The silence that occurs in a group after an outburst of anger is certainly not silent. The atmosphere in the group is "charged" and "crackles" with the electrical impulses of emotion. This kind of silence is felt as members experience the weight of the silence. The silence may be alive with the hundreds of unspoken words generated inside each member as they try to understand the reason for the angry outburst. Or the group silence may be reflecting stunned awkwardness that says, "Now what do we do? How do we get going again?"

Silence may be used for thoughtful resolution of conflict, gaining insights, and recognizing ideational relationships. In other situations, it expresses hostility, confusion, discouragement, or withdrawal. Many authors have suggested that some silences communicate togetherness and cooperation, whereas at times the group may seek relaxation and relief in silence following the exploration of deep feelings and the ventilation of emotions or following an especially meaningful "peak" experience where members seem to know something meaningful has happened and will sit for long periods of silence feeling quite comfortable and "alive" (Donigian & Molnati 1997; Jacobs et al. 2006; Kottler 2001).

Responding to Silence

Just as no single kind of silence exists, no single way for the counselor to respond to silence is apparent. However, the group facilitator may find help by keeping in mind the following process-oriented questions:

- Am I uncomfortable with the silence? Why?
- Is the group uncomfortable with the silence? How do I know?
- Are the members really not participating because they are silent?
- What does silence mean to the group?
- What nonverbal behaviors are present to reflect and process?

Silence can provide the stepping stone to further interaction in the group, and yet the silence often is interaction. How the counselor responds can determine whether or not group silence is facilitative to the group process or individual introspection. Probably the most helpful thing the counselor can do is to examine his or her own feelings about group silence and try to resolve any anxieties that would interfere with sensitivity to the meaning of group silence. The counselor then can be more facilitative by responding to the meaning rather than the silence.

Silence that conveys acceptance and support, and that seems to be encouraging to members working through their own thoughts and feelings, is constructive and generally needs no response by the counselor. However, the counselor must be sensitive to those times when silence indicates a nonworking relationship, is not constructive, or has meaning that should be verbalized. At such times, the counselor can be facilitative by sharing with the group personal perceptions of the meaning of the silence or personal feelings or reactions to the silence. The counselor also could facilitate members sharing with a response such as "It could be helpful to the group if some of you would share what you have been feeling or thinking during this silence" or by asking, "Susan, could you share with us what you think has been going on in the silence or what it means?" Some counselors might prefer to develop the meaning of the silence through a structured activity. The important thing is that group silence does have meaning and needs to be recognized. Because silence can emerge due to normal feelings of anxiety related to the beginning of a new experience, the following are a few things the leader can do to explore that anxiety and facilitate connection among members.

Introducing a Discussion of Group Rules or Guidelines

The leader will definitely want to reinforce the confidentiality aspects of the group. A good idea is to get a public concurrence with this rule. It begins to reassure members that they can disclose themselves in relative safety.

LEADER: Confidentiality means that what is said in here stays in here. It's something that is common in counseling, but pretty rare in other relationships. Confidentiality is not just my job; it's the responsibility of everyone here. What are some of the ways that confidentiality will help our group?

GEORGE: Well, I don't trust a lot of people, so if I'm going to open up in here, it might make me feel better if I knew everyone was going to keep my stuff secret.

PETER: Yeah, I agree. I can't talk in here if I think everyone is going to be blabbing my business outside of group.

Other group guidelines also can be discussed if necessary. This has the advantage of providing content about which the group can verbalize. A goal of the leader would be to get as many members as possible involved verbally. Verbal involvement can signal commitment.

Modeling Appropriate Self-Disclosure

Frequently, members are reluctant to begin to participate simply because they're not sure how to start or about what to talk. We have had a good deal of success with starting groups by sharing with members our own affective states at the particular time. A slight case of anticipation anxiety is usually something with which most members can identify, and this disclosure frequently sets the tone for talking about one's feelings. Members tend to feel less isolated and unique, and frequently will say, "Yes, I'm kind of nervous too. My stomach has butterflies—'cause I don't know these people." This has the added benefit of usually eliciting empathic responses from some group members. Most usually, this kind of beginning is followed by one or several members coming forth with some problem or aspect of themselves that they are willing to share and work on.

Using Some Low-Threat Interpersonal Exercise

These activities or techniques are frequently called ice-breakers and, when used judiciously, can help ease the transition to group productivity, particularly for group members with little prior group experience. A number of these activities are available whose primary goal is to get members interacting with each other (Khalsa 1999; Radd 2003). Activities that focus on personality characteristics, attitudes, values, beliefs, and perceptions tend to be better than those that are content-, topic-, or data-oriented. Exercises designed to work with first impressions tend to break the ice.

Subgroups

What quickly becomes apparent in the initial stages of a group is that verbal participation will be unequal. Several of the more verbally powerful members may unconsciously form an alliance that excludes some of the more passive members. They can quickly monopolize group time as resentment builds among the less assertive members. Structured activities and in some cases a timer can be used to prevent this. As the group becomes more trusting and self-responsible, these issues can be dealt with directly in the group.

The leader will want to remain sensitive to the possibility of subgroups developing around verbal skill, personality dominance, value differences, attitude variances, and so on. Although some of this is inevitable in heterogeneous groups, when splinter groups are allowed to simply run their course they can be destructive to the group as a whole. Conflict within the group can be helpful and growth-producing if the leader is prepared to deal with it openly and fairly. All participants should be encouraged to present their opinions and points of view. An atmosphere of respect can develop between all members when conflict and differences are viewed as natural, healthy, and to be expected. The leader can model this behavior by facilitating the exploration, acceptance, and resolution of conflict and differences.

Power Struggles

Power struggles will occur in the group just as they do in individual relationships. A certain amount of this can be considered natural. Just as in a family, members will jockey for position and a recognizable spot in the pecking order. In the normal course of things, this issue is usually quickly resolved. The leader needs to guard against promoting power struggles by equally sharing his or her time and attempting not to show favoritism. In a healthy group, the issue of power is shared and the group remains flexible with expertise available as issues emerge. Only when a subgroup remains outside of the mainstream is group growth retarded. This requires direct intervention on the part of the leader if the total group is to be salvaged. Further growth and cohesiveness are impossible if competitive subgroups are allowed to function. Although power struggles often occur between members, it is also common for group members to attempt to engage the leader in power struggles, as the example below illustrates.

RUSTY: Who are you to be telling us how to run our lives? You aren't any older than my son! I know as much about living as you do. Maybe I should run the group!

LEADER: Tell me about what you would like to do differently in group.

RUSTY: I don't know. I guess I just feel like you don't understand us all the time. You are just like everyone else out there . . . judgmental.

LEADER: I can tell that you feel frustrated about not being understood. Susan, you have also spoken in group about feeling misunderstood in your marriage. Does that happen for you in group as well?

SUSAN: Sometimes, but it's nice in here because people seem genuinely interested in what I have to say.

In the example, note how the leader does not try to convince Rusty that he is incorrect. The leader does not enter into the power struggle by debating Rusty's assertion. Instead, the leader encourages Rusty to delve deeper into his feelings and then validates the feelings. The leader then links Rusty's feelings to those of another member, thereby dissipating the power struggle. The leader can continue to process this theme without the power struggle.

Group Cohesiveness

Cohesiveness in a counseling group refers to the feeling of togetherness experienced by some groups. It is frequently talked about as the "glue" of a group—that difficult-to-define quality that results from an overall interpersonal attractiveness. In a constructive sense, it is related to the chemistry of a group and the overall good, supportive, and respectful attitudes that members have for each other and the group as a whole. Cohesiveness is evidenced when members begin to assign some priority to the group experience, value and equality to other members, a willingness to give as well as to receive, and a certain "we-ness" than can be exclusive of persons not in the group.

Although this cohesiveness is a desirable group goal because of its benefits to members in terms of support, what is also possible is for some groups to unconsciously unite and become "too cohesive." This is a difficult process problem for the leader because the underlying motivation is usually anxiety or fear of disclosing, perceived loss of control, and lack of trust in the leader, the group, or the process. Groups like this can become "cousin" groups where what occurs are a lot of rescuing of individual members, denial of problems and conflict, and circular and superficial talk. Kurtz (1992) discussed too much cohesion as "group think," where members avoid conflict to maintain a warm atmosphere.

Probably the most effective leader intervention is to gently point out the problem and help the group to reexamine their goals and confront their anxieties.

LEADER: I am having some mixed feelings about the group and our progress. On one hand, I am impressed with the connections you have built in such a short amount of time. There is a feeling of respect and closeness in here that is very comforting. On the other hand, I am wondering if that comfort might be holding us back a bit. You know, maybe we are worried that if we get any deeper, we might lose the good feelings.

MOIRA: I don't understand. I think we are doing some pretty good work in here. I really like the people in here a lot.

LEADER: Yes, you have built some very nice connections here. I guess I'm wondering if there is more to be gained. Have any of you had something you really wanted to say in here, but didn't because you didn't want to disturb the peace? [*Heads nodding.*] Would anyone like to take a risk and share that moment?

According to Slavin (1993), the best time to promote cohesion, even with resistant clients, is with immediacy through confronting issues in the here and now. Leaders need to guard against becoming personally frustrated when the group refuses to move. All the leader can do is create the conditions for growth. He or she cannot force a group to grow. Taking too much responsibility for the progress of the group is a frequent trap for inexperienced leaders. If all else fails and the group seems committed to staying in one place, the idea of dissolution is a possibility. No guarantee can be given that every collection of individuals will become an effective group.

Problems Encountered with Group Members

Control and Controlling

When the group leader encounters various individual member styles and resistances, it can almost invariably be assumed that the issues are related to group members' needs for personal control and, by extension, a need to control the situation. Experience has taught us that members who have a high need for situational control typically feel threatened and anxious about exploring their personal issues too carefully for fear that they will "lose control of self" and be overwhelmed by feelings of insecurity and worthlessness. Fear of the unknown or of ambiguous, unstructured, and confusing situations pose a real threat to these individuals.

Our observation has been that members will call upon their basic personality orientation in attempts to bring order and understanding to these perceived fearful situations in the group. Much of the behavior that might be viewed objectively as rigid or resistant seems to occur outside of all conscious awareness of the controlling or controlled member. Within this framework, controlling behavior can be viewed as a purposeful, although in many cases extreme and maladaptive, attempt on the part of a member or members to bring reason, stability, and comfort to an unsettling situation.

Naturally, at the deepest intrapsychic levels, needs for control can be viewed as core personality issues that are related to trust in oneself and others. Vague and sometimes highly specific fears need to be treated gently and with much of the reassurance and support that were probably missing in that person's life at an early and impressionable developmental stage. No quick fixes exist for a person's resistance to vulnerability and trust. Empathy and gentle compassion coupled with focus on the behavior tend to lessen the anxiety.

We have also found that a useful procedure is to briefly explain to group members that all normal human beings seek a certain measure of personal control, and when monitored and kept within non-neurotic boundaries, the control is useful and is related to a powerful sense of self. The polar opposite or extreme would be "out of control" and the implication of impotence, helplessness, and total dependence. Nobody wants to experience those feelings. Within this general framework of control, we can proceed to a discussion of various individual members' styles or roles that surface in the group as an attempt to maintain intrapsychic homeostasis. In general, these members' behaviors center around avoidant behaviors, dependent behaviors, and aggressive and power behaviors.

Avoidance

Avoiding the encounter with others and self is considered by some group leaders to be among the most difficult member behaviors to impact constructively. The member who uses some form of avoidance is choosing an isolated position in the group and can quickly become a frustration to other group members. Behaviors associated with avoidance can range on a continuum from absence from the group to somewhat more active avoidances such as the Pollyanna or naive role. Of course, a member who is habitually *absent* from the group becomes an overt management problem for the leaders. Some members will attend a session, sometimes becoming the focus of attention, only to go AWOL for the next three meetings. Naturally, the leader needs to intervene with this behavior and discuss the implications of this "hit and run" behavior for the members and for the group as a whole. Generally, if a member cannot make a concrete commitment to regular attendance, he or she needs to consider exit from the group.

Distancing behavior in the group begins with the habitually silent member. This extreme form of continual reluctance to participate verbally can set up the member either as a "group project" or as a scapegoat—depending upon the member's overall attractiveness to the group. Either outcome has serious implications for the group. The group might unconsciously join the silent member in offering inappropriate advice and reassurances in order to enlist the member's participation. A person with a low level of attractiveness might become the target of group discontent and even hostility. The group leader needs to heed warning signs that a member is withdrawing by focusing on the behavior and helping the member to risk and develop trust in the process.

A chronically *withdrawn* member might be depressed, and the group leader may well suspect depression with any member who is choosing avoidance as a coping mechanism. Social withdrawal is a common symptom of depression and, coupled with other observable signs such as crying spells, depressed facial expressions, and lack of animation, needs to be checked out by the group leader. Psychological indicators of depression include feelings of worthlessness and guilt, anxiety, and loss of energy. Physical signals associated with depressive states might be an increase in sleep disturbances and changes in appetites and sexual interest.

The leader must suspect depressive states with any of the avoidance behaviors because they may be early indicators of suicidal intentions. When depression is suspected, the group leader needs to consult with a psychiatrist because some form of psychopharmacological treatment may be indicated as an adjunct to psychotherapy.

The *alienated* member may couple his or her withdrawal with active fault-finding and negative assertions in the group. This type of behavior, although disconcerting to some members, is actually easier to deal with because the person at least gives some responsiveness to current events. The anger base that alienated members often come from can be linked to early experiences as a way of helping the individual open up and trust.

Finally, avoidant behavior is sometimes manifested by *naive* or *Pollyanna-type* personalities. Although they are somewhat related, the naive member may truly lack some essential life problem-solving skills. This is one of the few group member types who can in some instances truly profit from concrete and specific advice from other helping members. Because the naive member's experience base is typically limited, other group members can help increase his or her awareness by sharing their own experiences and ideas. Sometimes, group members will share specific verbatim sentences for the naive member to use. When the sentences work (and they often do) and the naive member begins to perceive constructive changes in his or her environment, a change in attitude or perspective often trails along. Naive members typically need a lot of encouragement and reassurance.

The *Pollyanna* has become convinced that the world is Disneyland with a perpetual silver lining. This is an active denial of all things unpleasant—the *rose-colored glasses syndrome.* This behavior in group is most often observed in response to another member's problems where the indication is to gloss over and deny pain. The skillful group leader will spend some time instructing the Pollyanna members, and others in the group, of the benefits of experiencing the fullness of an event. Frequently, out of pain, grief, and hurt is when we stretch and grow most.

Dependency

The next major group of resistances centers around *dependence* issues. Once again, the seeds of dependent personalities were probably planted early in a person's history. Overly socialized or compliant personalities often label themselves as people-pleasers when they become aware of the motivation for their behavior. In general, this personality type is quite responsive to the environment and is "sensitive" to others. They often are perceived as warm and nurturing, as accepting and nonjudgmental, and as people who listen well. Nice to be around, if not exciting, they often elevate others at the expense of their own denied wishes and desires. Acutely sensitive to power in relationships, they sometimes go to extreme lengths to avoid conflict and the arousal of displeasure in others.

Harmonizer

The *harmonizer* is one example of the dependent type. He or she will tend to gloss over potential growth-producing conflict in the group by distracting and changing subjects. Cooperative to a fault, the harmonizer will seek to avoid confrontation with his or her own fears by attempting to create an atmosphere free of tension in the group. Closely akin to the harmonizer is the coordinator.

Coordinator

The *coordinator* often takes harmonizing a step further and serves as the unofficial group coordinator. This is a more active defense and frequently involves "doing" things for the group and the members. The coordinator may volunteer for any number of tasks large and small in an attempt to ingratiate him or herself with the other members.

Group Clown

The *group clown* shares some of these needs but is also somewhat more exhibitionistic in pleasing others. When handled appropriately, the person with the great sense of humor can provide tension release and opportunities for therapeutic laughter in the group. Laughing, particularly at oneself and our own foibles and mistakes, can diffuse some of the deadly seriousness with which we approach our problems. Laughter and humor are signs of a healthy person and are excellent ways to share our humanness with each other.

The flipside is when the clowning is out of context or inappropriate. Although laughing and depression are incompatible responses, to think that we can laugh our troubles away is to be very naive. Laughter can provide perspective. When the clown uses jokes and silliness at the expense of a true and meaningful encounter, it has the potential to interfere with group progress. The clown needs to be reassured that he or she is OK and has a secure, stable, and valuable place in the group. The person needs to understand and internally recognize that winning the clown spot each week is not necessary.

Rescuer

Rescuers are probably guilty of projection in the group. When sensing the onset of conflict or discomfort for a particular member, the rescuer will often rush in to "save" the person who is perceived to be in the hot seat. Rescues can often be marked as subtle helping, so the leader needs to be alert to this phenomenon. A gentle intervention that confronts the behavior respectfully but directly helps not only the rescuer but also the person being rescued. Everyone gets to be an adult and take care of self. Much rescuing behavior happens outside of the rescuer's conscious awareness, so the problem is sometimes difficult to manage. Several "reminders" may be needed from the group leaders.

Problem-Solver

Problem-solvers also can pose a unique management situation in the group. People with this orientation are usually quite convinced that they have many helpful suggestions to remedy a person's problem. Persistent advice and problem-solving suggestions are most often offered from a "commonsense" experiential base, are highly specific, and frequently ignore many of the intrapsychic subtleties. This type of helping often comes from persons who have made their way themselves and have an abundance of ego strength. They often cannot understand why another person doesn't "just do it"! They tend to be cognitively oriented and action-directed and have a hard time relating to people who experience ambivalence. Subtle interventions typically don't work very well.

Strokes for listening well, attending, and supporting other members will sometimes get the desired behavior as the problem-solver gains an appreciation for some of life's complexities.

Poor Me

The *poor me* member has become accustomed to staying in self-pity, helplessness, and despair. They seemingly gain a good deal of personal control and power by having a lot of group attention focused on their problems. Members with codependent issues and "victim" personalities often fit this picture. Similar in style to naive members, the poor-me person seems much more invested in maintaining, albeit at unconscious levels, a one-down life position. In relationships, they are almost invariably clinging and overly dependent upon the other person for their own feeling of self-worth. They sometimes seem capable of enduring endless mistreatment.

This member needs enormous reinforcement and affirmation of OK-ness in order to counterbalance what is probably a lifetime full of diminished self-esteem. Naturally, this is a slow and patient process that hopefully will culminate in increased self-trust.

Compulsive Talker

Compulsive talkers present a somewhat unique problem for the group leader because, unmonitored, their behavior can become overly intrusive in the group. Also, because many members feel somewhat impotent in the face of rapid-fire verbals, the talker may set up him- or herself to become the group scapegoat—or at least a poorly favored member. We sometimes suspect the talker of having an unconscious fear of death. In many instances, although not all, compulsive talkers have a need to affirm their existence by hearing the sound of their own voice. This phenomenon usually has its roots in early developmental experiences, so awareness is usually deeply hidden. Talking can be a compensation for feelings of inferiority. "If I can talk and command attention, I must be important." This behavior needs to be confronted gently but firmly. Ignoring it can have detrimental effects on the group. Inferiority feelings in the compulsive talker are often linked to self-perceived intellectual deficiencies and sometimes are coupled with perfectionism, particularly in school matters and academic achievement in general. The person is usually well read and possesses a breadth of information.

The final major group of resistance has to do with issues of *aggression* and *power*.

Manipulator

This final category of individual member roles or styles distinguishes itself from the others, and the roles are grouped together because they tend to be more active resistances in the group. A person in this group could be labeled a *manipulator*. This person will tend to seek control in the group in order to accomplish his or her own internal agenda. Two general types of manipulative personalities are recognizable. The first one is relatively benign but still can have an impact on the group. We sometimes refer to Type 1 as the *Music Man*. Such a person frequently is relatively transparent in his or her needs for group control, may use clowning and a highly developed sense of humor, and is most often quite charming and attractive. These people have highly developed social skills, are accustomed to pleasing other people, and have almost a desperate need for approval. Their behavior is often designed to seek leader approval as the group's "favorite son or daughter." This person, with gentle persuasion, will often recognize this behavior and contract to modify it.

Type 2 manipulators are much more difficult to deal with and in some ways are not good candidates for group intervention. Their needs for power, control, and dominance are usually much more repressed and unconscious. This, coupled with a diminished level of social interest and underlying wounds that surface in anger, frequently results in group behavior that is emotionally detached and even hostile. These members often will be suspicious of nurturing and caring behavior in the group and not trust it because no history of that exists in their experiences. They view the world as a place that is unfriendly and to be guarded against, so supportive behaviors in the group tend to be mistrusted.

The double bind that this member puts on the group is that when group members become frustrated and begin to match the Type 2 behavior with detachment or overt disapproval, the manipulator can then view the group's behavior as further evidence that the world is "out to get him or her" and that he or she had better protect self.

Clearly, behavior that is rooted this deeply in a history of deprived significant relationships will not yield to quick or temporary fixes. This person will probably require ongoing therapy. The leader needs to be at once gentle but firm. Interestingly, once this type of personality is *enlisted* in the therapeutic process, and that is a key variable, they often become excellent group members. An important point is that they view the group leader as a strong and competent person.

Intellectualizers: Superhelpers and Special Interest Pleaders

These intellectual types are similar in their in-group behavior in that they rely heavily upon their cognitive abilities to seize and maintain control in the group. *Helpers* are usually well read in popular psychology and gain a certain amount of group attention by offering their interpretations of others' behaviors and problems. This can be seductive in the group because sometimes they can be very accurate and helpful. Most frequently, however, their interpretations address only part of the problem or are offered too quickly and at the expense of other group members' exploration. Again, they tend to be intellectual solutions based on the assumption that knowledge and information will surely change behavior. Reinforcing helpful suggestions and actively interfering with those that are not helpful seem the most appropriate leader interventions.

The *special interest pleader* is typically locked into a highly focused frame of reference that makes it difficult for him or her to see a large and complex picture. Whatever the special interest, the pleader has typically discovered "the truth" and is so involved in it that he or she will have an almost compulsive need to share experiences and ideas with others so that they too might have "the truth." We have seen this particular orientation surface in group members around religious and spiritual issues, drug and substance use, various kinds of intensive and excludatory "group" experiences, and exercise and diet regimes. The pleader is typically a recent convert to the cause and is practically obsessive in his or her interest.

In the early stages of the group, the leader needs to be accepting of the individual's point of view while also limiting long discourses on any special topics. Interventions need to be fairly direct because those with highly focused special interests often do not perceive and respond to normal social cues that group members might offer.

Attacker

The final difficult member can be labeled an *attacker*. This can often be the most frightening member for the inexperienced group leader because the grab for power is frequently very direct, aggressive, and even hostile. Because this person has probably never felt included, the group pressure to conform to social standards will often elicit responses that are rebellious and challenging—in effect, a resistance to becoming a part of the group. This grows out of a fear of being overwhelmed and incorporated with a loss of individuality and independence.

Attackers almost always stimulate and energize the group. Because of their assertive demands, they help other, more reticent members of the group get in touch with their own feelings about conflict and self-assertion. Consequently, reframes can accomplish two goals. This first is to reassure the attacker that his or her place is assured and that boundaries will be respected. The second is to demonstrate to the group that differences in behavioral styles are acceptable and can add to the richness of the group. As an example: "Thank you for pointing that out. We can always count on your honesty and directness in this group."

Once the attacker has attached him- or herself to the group therapy process, the leader will want to help investigate the underlying cause of the behavior that results in putting off people or keeping them at a distance.

A final caution with attackers. When the issue under attack has to do with content or depersonalized ideas, it can simply be an annoyance or perhaps an inhibitor to progress. If the attack is directed at a person and is abusive in nature, the group leader needs to take direct action in stopping the behavior. Abusive behavior should not be permitted in groups any more than it should in families or other social collections. For instance,

John, I appreciate your courage in confronting Mike with your feelings. It's clear that you have a lot of investment in this issue. At the same time, you'll need to find more appropriate ways to express your disagreement—your words feel abusive to me and that won't go in here.

Summary

This chapter provided a general introduction to forms of resistance commonly found group. A method for evaluating resistance was outlined, along with a discussion of important topics such as silence, subgroups power struggles, and the role of cohesiveness. Specific problem group member roles are addressed as they relate to a member's basic personality and their impact on the group.

References

Donigian, J., & Malnati, R. (1987). *Critical incidents in group therapy.* Pacific Grove, CA: Brooks/Cole.

Jacobs, E. E., Masson, R. L., Harvill, R. L., & Schimmel, C. J. (2011). *Group counseling: Strategies and skills* (7th ed.). Pacific Grove, CA: Brooks/Cole.

Khalsa, S. (1999). *Group exercises for enhancing social skills and self esteem*, vol. II. New York: Professional Resource Exchange.

Kline, W. B. (1990). Responding to problem members. *Journal for Specialists in Group Work*, 15 (4), 195–200.

Kottler, J. (2001). *Learning group leadership.* Boston, MA: Allyn & Bacon.

Kurtz, L. F. (1992). Group environment in self-help group for families. *Small Group Research*, 23, 199–215.

Otani, A. (1989). Client resistance in counseling: Its theoretical rationale and taxonomic classification. *Journal of Counseling and Development*, 67, 458–461.

Radd, T. (2003). *Classroom and small group activities for teachers, counselors and other helping professionals*, vol. II. New York: Grow With Guidance.

Slavin, R. L. (1993). The significance of here-and-now disclosure in promoting cohesion in group psychotherapy. *Group*, 17, 143–149.

10

EVALUATING THE LEADER
AND THE GROUP

A converse relationship seems to exist between evaluation and years of experience. For the counselor in training, everything done is evaluated, and then with increased experience, few, if any, supervisors insist on evaluating the counselor or what takes place in the counselor's groups. Evaluation can contribute to continued growth on the part of the counselor and group members. Therefore, the group facilitator has a continuing responsibility to assess and evaluate the effectiveness of his or her groups.

Leader Self-Evaluation

The first focus of evaluation by the facilitator should be on self. The leader needs to have a genuine concern and openness to learn about self and one's approach to groups. Co-leading a group can provide excellent opportunities for feedback from the co-leader about projected attitudes, blind spots, missed opportunities, and general facilitative approaches. Also, the opportunity always exists for self-critique through audiotapes or videotapes.

Following each group session, the facilitator might find that a helpful procedure is to examine the following questions:

- How did the group experience me?
- What feelings did I experience in this session? Did I express those feelings? Did I have some feelings with which I did not feel comfortable?
- What were my reactions to various group members? Did I feel "turned off" to some members, rejecting? Do all members know I care about them? Do they feel accepted by me?
- What did I communicate to each member? Did I say what I really wanted to say? Was my message clearly stated?
- How much time did I spend focused on the content of the discussion rather than on the interaction taking place or feelings and needs subtly expressed?
- What do I wish I had said or done? What would I do differently next time?
- Did I dominate? How willing was I for someone else to assume the leadership role?

In addition to the qualitative exploration leaders can implement to self-assess, Page et al. (2001) developed the Group Leader Self-efficacy Instrument (GLSI) to measure trainees' self-efficacy for performing group facilitation skills. This thirty-six-item, Likert scale instrument asks questions related to perceived confidence in a wide variety of leader skills, such as "I am confident I can make interventions based on theory" and "I am confident I can encourage expression of differences" (Page et al. 2001: 175). Although used primarily with beginning group workers, this measure could be used with all group leaders as a means to self-assess and find areas where growth can occur.

Leader Evaluation of Group

Developed by William F. Hill, the Hill Interaction Matrix (HIM) can serve as a particularly valuable tool for the group leader. It is one of the most useful measuring tools for the leader to use in conceptualizing group dynamics and process by examining verbal interaction between members. It is also one way to help determine objectively the extent to which a group is progressing toward meeting its goals.

Hill's matrix (see Figure 10.1) grew out of the clinical study of hundreds of hours of group observation. Interactions within the groups were intensively examined. A thorough discussion of the developmental process is available in Hill's *HIM: Hill Interaction Matrix* (1956). The HIM was developed in a clinical-therapeutic setting, and, consequently, most of the examples are related to mental health. The matrix is generalizable to virtually any group setting, however, because the principles of categorization remain the same.

Within the matrix, the categories are ordered in terms of assumed therapeutic benefit. The rankings are based on the following assumptions:

- **member centeredness**: the desirability of having a focus person in the group much of the time;
- **interpersonal risk taking**: the desirability for group members to give up the need for interpersonal security;
- **interpersonal feedback**: the desirability of all group members acting as both providers and receivers of immediate feedback.

Content Style

The HIM conceptualized verbal interaction in the group along two major dimensions. The first, across the top of the matrix, is the *content style*. Content categorizes what is being discussed in the group. The second axis has to do with member work styles and is related to the process of communication or how members relate to each other and the group.

The content dimension is concerned with categorizing the subject matter being discussed. Generally, Hill (1956) saw all verbal subject matter as falling into one of the four content categories. Following are some general descriptions of those categories and some points that may help distinguish among them.

Topic

Subjects fitting into this broad and general category include virtually any subject *other than* the group itself, a member of the group, or a relationship *within* the group. General-interest material fits here, and, by definition, so would conventional socializing conversation between members of the group. As a further example, most of the content of any discussion group would most probably fit into the topic category.

Group

In this context, verbal interaction is *about* the present group exclusively. It may involve an examination of the group's rules and procedures, formation, operation, and goals. The interaction is characterized by and limited to the present and immediate group.

Personal

This is almost always a focus person or one who is being discussed. Focus can be by the topic person himself or herself, or by other group members directed toward the topic person.

	Content				
	Style				
	Topic-centered		Member-centered		
	Topics	Group	Personal	Relationship	
	I	II	III	IV	
A	I A	II A	III A	IV A	Responsive
PRE-WORK WORK STYLE					
WORK					
B	I B (1)	II B (2)	III B (9)	IV B (10)	Conventional
C	I C (3)	II C (4)	III C (11)	IV C (12)	Assertive
D	I D (5)	II D (6)	III D (13)	IV D (14)	Speculative
E	I E (7)	II E (8)	III E (15)	IV E (16)	Confrontive

Figure 10.1 The Hill interaction matrix

The content of the interaction is upon an individual group member or his or her current status, personality characteristics, traits, behaviors, history, problems, and/or issues.

Relationship

This category is ranked highest of the content dimensions because it involves immediate or "here-and-now" transactions between present members of the group. It is not *about* relationships but rather gives evidence of a relationship within the group. It can speak to a relationship between group members or between a member and the group as a whole.

Work Style

The second axis, which involves *work style* or process categories, concerns itself with the *manner* in which members discuss any of the content possibilities. The critical determiner is how an individual group member initiates or responds to group content. Once again, following are some general descriptors that help distinguish the five process categories.

Responsive

This very basic style dimension indicates an unwillingness on the part of a group member to verbally participate. The member may limit interaction to a brief response to direct questions or encounters. This category is useful only with severely withdrawn members or those who may be highly defensive.

Conventional

Conversation may be about any number of general-interest topics, facts, or information and is conducted in a socially appropriate manner. A work orientation or context has not been established, and the level of interaction could best be termed as *descriptive* and *social* rather than *problem-solving*.

Assertive

Our opinion is that this category could more aptly be labeled *aggressive* in the context of our current understanding of those terms. This process category is frequently distinguished by a hostile or attacking tone. Statements are *often* argumentative but also may include passive modes of behavior. One of the most valuable clues to watch for in this category is that the tone of the interaction tends to close down discussion rather than enhance it. Speakers tend to be finalistic in their pronouncements and do not appear to be open to another point of view, and exchanges tend to be one-way rather than two-way.

Speculative

The tone changes to a discussion of information or problems that are task-oriented and contains an implicit invitation to further examine two-way, open, and continuing communication. Speculative interaction is characterized by a cooperative desire for understanding of the problem or context.

Confrontive

One of the key words to characterize this category might well be *clarify*. Confrontive statements tend to draw upon what has already been said in an attempt to clarify, evaluate, and resolve issues. Confrontive statements are typically backed up with some form of concrete documentation. The speaker supports his or her opinion. The encounter involved in this style of communication may frequently be as therapeutic for the speaker as it is for the topic or focus person.

We refer to the lower right-hand section of the HIM as the *power quadrant*. The assumption is that the more time a group spends in speculative-personal, speculative-relationship, confrontive-personal, and confrontive-relationship interaction patterns, the greater will be the gain for individuals and the group.

Member Evaluation of Group and Facilitator

We have found that the following open-ended sentence or short-paragraph beginnings provide an excellent structure for member evaluation feedback. The group facilitator can take a few minutes at the conclusion of the last session or send a response form home to be mailed back. Members are more likely to be honest if they are not required to identify themselves on the form.

Instructions

Write your first reactions to the following sentence beginnings. Please be as open and honest as you possibly can. You may want to view these as short paragraph beginnings. It is not necessary for you to write your name on this page. The sentence beginnings are as follows:

This group . . .

This group leader . . .

I best liked. . .

I least liked. . .

I feel . . .

For more specific feedback from members about their reactions to the group facilitator, use the rating scale shown in Figure 10.2.

Whether or not questionnaires are administered in the last session or mailed to group members after the group ends, consideration should be given to the length of the questionnaire. Group members may feel overwhelmed by a twenty- to thirty-item questionnaire requiring lengthy responses to each item. Figure 10.3 is an example of a more specific questionnaire.

The experience of writing about the group and self can help members clarify and substantiate for themselves meaningful changes that need to be supported and encouraged.

Member Self-Evaluation

Evaluation often seems to be a natural part of the last stages of maturation of the group-counseling experience and results from the need members have to feel successful, that is, that something worthwhile has been accomplished. This evaluation process will seldom take the form of members relating specific defined goals but will usually occur in the last few sessions as members share their perceptions of how they have changed, what the experience has meant to them, or changes they observe in other members. A synthesis of what has gone on before may be described in light of specific group experiences. This is a natural approach to evaluation and should be recognized as such by the group facilitator.

Because groups have a life of their own, members may redefine their goals and expectations as a natural process of changes experienced during the course of the experience. Therefore, in some instances, to evaluate the group or changes in members on the basis of initially defined purposes or by contracts established may not be appropriate. Evaluation should always allow for and take into consideration the dynamics of the process of change inherent in counseling groups. In light of such experiences, members may redefine their expectations of self or may set new goals.

Group counselor rating scale

Counselor's Name _____

Instructions: Rate your group counselor as you see her/him functioning in your group.

Respect: Shows a real respect for the group members by attentiveness, warmth, efforts to understand and freedom of personal expression.

5.0	4.5	4.0	3.5	3.0	2.5	2.0	1.5	1.0
very high		high		moderate		low		very low

Empathy: Communicates an accurate understanding of the group members' feelings and experiences. The group members know the counselor understands how they feel.

5.0	4.5	4.0	3.5	3.0	2.5	2.0	1.5	1.0
very high		high		moderate		low		very low

Genuineness: Realness. Everything he/she does seems to be real. That's the way he/she really is. This person doesn't put up a front.

5.0	4.5	4.0	3.5	3.0	2.5	2.0	1.5	1.0
very high		high		moderate		low		very low

Concreteness: "Tunes in" and responds to specific feelings or experiences of group members. Avoids responding in generalities.

5.0	4.5	4.0	3.5	3.0	2.5	2.0	1.5	1.0
very high		high		moderate		low		very low

Self-Disclosure: Lets group know about relevant immediate personal feelings. Open, rather than guarded.

5.0	4.5	4.0	3.5	3.0	2.5	2.0	1.5	1.0
very high		high		moderate		low		very low

Spontaneity: Can respond without having to "stop and think." Words and actions seem to flow easily.

5.0	4.5	4.0	3.5	3.0	2.5	2.0	1.5	1.0
very high		high		moderate		low		very low

Flexibility: Adapts to a wide range of conditions without losing his/her composure. Can adapt to meet the needs of the moment.

5.0	4.5	4.0	3.5	3.0	2.5	2.0	1.5	1.0
very high		high		moderate		low		very low

Confidence: Trusts his/her abilities. Acts with directness and self-assurance.

5.0	4.5	4.0	3.5	3.0	2.5	2.0	1.5	1.0
very high		high		moderate		low		very low

Figure 10.2 Group counselor rating scale

Of what changes have you become aware in your attitudes, feelings about yourself, and relationships with other people?

How did the group experience help these changes to come about?

What did the group leader do that was most helpful and least helpful to you?

Was the group experience hurtful to you in any way, or did it have any negative effect on you?

Briefly identify any group exercises you especially liked or disliked.

In what ways do you wish you had been different in the group?

How are you most different as a result of the group experience?

Figure 10.3 Group member evaluation of facilitator

The Self-Assessment Scale shown below is a semantic differential type procedure that allows an individual to make a personal evaluation of where he or she sees self now and where he or she would like to be. This scale and others like it can be valuable to both group members and group leaders.

This instrument is designed to help determine how you see yourself in relation to the words and concepts listed. It will be used to work with you in developing programs of self-growth in those aspects of self you choose to emphasize.

In completing this instrument, you are asked to indicate your position in terms of what the scale items *mean to you.* Do not be concerned about different ways the descriptive items can be interpreted. Here is how you are to complete the first part of the assessment process:

Directions: Step 1

If you see yourself as *very* like one or the other descriptive terms at each end of a line, you should place an X as follows:

Strong __:__:__:__:__:__:__: x Weak

Strong x :__:__:__:__:__:__:__ Weak

If you see yourself as *quite* like one or the other descriptive terms at each end of a scale, you should place an X as follows:

Fair   __:__:__:__:__:__: x :__ Unfair

Fair   __: x :__:__:__:__:__:__ Unfair

If you see yourself as *rather* like one or the other end term of a scale, you should place an X as follows:

Wise   __:__:__:__:__: x :__:__ Foolish

Wise   __:__: x :__:__:__:__:__ Foolish

If you see yourself as only *somewhat* like one or the other descriptive terms of a scale, you should place an X as follows:

Complex __:__ __:__:__: x :__:__:__ Simple

Complex __:__:__: x :__:__:__:__ Simple

Important: (1) Place your marks in the middle of spaces, not on the boundaries. (2) Be sure you place an X mark on every scale. Do not omit any.

Work fairly quickly through this part of the process. Do not puzzle or worry over individual scale items—just give your first impression, your immediate "feelings" about each item.

Self-Assessment Scale

leader	__:__:__:__:__:__:__	follower
sloppy	__:__:__:__:__:__:__	neat
angry	__:__:__:__:__:__:__	peaceful
dull	__:__:__:__:__:__:__	bright
dogmatic	__:__:__:__:__:__:__	tolerant
open	__:__:__:__:__:__:__	closed
active	__:__:__:__:__:__:__	passive
out of style	__:__:__:__:__:__:__	in style
sad	__:__:__:__:__:__:__	joyful
good vocabulary	__:__:__:__:__:__:__	poor vocabulary
insensitive	__:__:__:__:__:__:__	sensitive
warm	__:__:__:__:__:__:__	cold, aloof
confident	__:__:__:__:__:__:__	unsure
clumsy	__:__:__:__:__:__:__	graceful
depressed	__:__:__:__:__:__:__	optimistic
read slowly	__:__:__:__:__:__:__	read fast
insincere	__:__:__:__:__:__:__	genuine
talk a lot	__:__:__:__:__:__:__	talk infrequently
independent	__:__:__:__:__:__:__	dependent
out of shape	__:__:__:__:__:__:__	in shape
helpee	__:__:__:__:__:__:__	helper
understand	__:__:__:__:__:__:__	don't understand
flexible	__:__:__:__:__:__:__	rigid
self-directed	__:__:__:__:__:__:__	other-directed

feminine	__:__:__:__:__:__:__	masculine
shaky	__:__:__:__:__:__:__	stable
write well	__:__:__:__:__:__:__	write poorly
specific	__:__:__:__:__:__:__	vague
poor figure	__:__:__:__:__:__:__	good figure
loner	__:__:__:__:__:__:__	activity-oriented
poor researcher	__:__:__:__:__:__:__	good researcher
neutral	__:__:__:__:__:__:__	sexy
accept ideas	__:__:__:__:__:__:__	challenge ideas
listen well	__:__:__:__:__:__:__	listen poorly
verbal	__:__:__:__:__:__:__	nonverbal

Step 2

In the first part of the self-assessment process you have just completed, you indicated how you see yourself in terms of the series of descriptive scales on the preceding page. The second part of the process will consist of going back through each of the scales, and placing an O at the point on each scale you would like yourself to be.

Important: (1) Place your marks in the middle of the spaces, not on the boundaries. (2) Be sure you place an O on every line. Do not omit any. (3) On a few scales, you may see yourself as being now where you would like to be. In that case, draw a circle around the X mark you entered on that line in the first place.

Step 3

When you have finished marking your Xs and Os, look back over the descriptive scales, and pick out the four or five items which seem the most important to you in terms of your self-growth. You should select those four or five descriptive items which, to you, seem to represent aspects of yourself on which you most want to work to change. Draw a line in the margin to the left of each of the items you feel are most important and indicate on that line the priority ranking (1, 2, 3, 4, 5) you wish to assign to that concept, in terms of change.

For example:

1 (2, 3, etc.) Fair __: x :__:__:__:__: o :__ Unfair

Walters (1975)

Daybooks as a Therapeutic Self-Exploration Tool

If group members are asked to keep a daybook, this can provide the group facilitator with ongoing insight into the member's experiential evaluation of the personal impact of the group. Daybook entries also provide an excellent overview of the ongoing process of the group and afford members the opportunity to assess changes in a nonevaluative manner. Thus, the daybook is a nonthreatening source of member self-evaluation.

Because most of the work by individuals in group counseling takes place between sessions, the group facilitator may want to consider avenues for encouraging continuation of the process that has been initiated during the session. The use of a diary or daybook by group members to record their feelings and reactions can significantly facilitate continued self-exploration outside the group sessions. Because in any group only a limited amount of time is available to any individual member, the daybook can be viewed as an opportunity to express and explore thoughts and reactions for which there was not an opportunity in the group.

Riordan (1996) reviewed what he termed "scriptotherapy" in counseling and cited several benefits to using writing in counseling. Some researchers have linked writing about personal issues to improved health and psychological functioning (Pennebaker 1997; Wright 2002). Doxsee and Kauligham (1994) noted that writing about therapeutic experiences can ease both interpersonal and intrapersonal confusion. The impact has also been noted in the research literature related to the positive effects in group work (Falco & Bauman 2004; Hall & Hawley 2004). Haberstroh et al. (2006) expanded journaling beyond the "hard copy" and demonstrated the utility of using e-journals as a complement to group work.

Daybooks are seldom used with groups younger than high-school age, and even at this level with considerable caution, because school-age adolescents may view writing in the daybook as homework or an assignment. In such cases, unnecessary resistance to the total group process may develop. A very simple approach to the daybook utilizing a list of feeling objectives and self-descriptive phrases from which to choose could be quite effective with elementary-school-age children. Children also could be asked to draw pictures depicting what they learned in the group that day, how they felt, or something they experienced between sessions.

For members who find it difficult to express very personal feelings and reactions in the group, the daybook can be a safe place to begin. Our experience has been that such members then are better able to verbalize those same feelings and reactions in the group and usually in a more direct manner. Although it is possible that writing in a daybook could "drain off" or detract from the spontaneity of the expression, this is not usually the case.

The daybook also affords the group facilitator an opportunity to know and understand group members more fully. These additional insights can greatly enhance the facilitator's sensitivity, understanding, and effectiveness in the group. A caution seems appropriate at this point, though. Material revealed through journalism should not be introduced into the group by the facilitator. This is the responsibility of the group member. Premature introduction by the facilitator could be viewed as a violation of confidentiality by the member, or at least it could create dependency on the facilitator to "bring it up" and then deprive the member of the opportunity to learn from taking a risk.

The purpose and structure of the daybook should be discussed fully with the group and their wishes honored. The following two examples of structured guidelines for writing in the daybook could be utilized separately, or parts of each combined, to meet the needs of your particular group.

Example 1: Guide to Writing in the Daybook

The daybook is like a diary but different in that it is not a simple chronicle of events and situations that occur in the laboratory group. Rather than summarizing what happened, your focus in writing should be upon your own feelings as you experienced them in the group. You may have feelings regarding other people in the group, the leader, yourself, or the "group" in general.

The following are some guidelines:

* Write in the daybook as soon as you can following each group experience. This will make your recollection as current as possible.
* Focus on your own affect, rather than upon other people or group process.
* Be specific and concrete.
* Try to make the daybook an extension of the group experience rather than a summary. It should be an exercise in deep self-exploration.
* The logical extension of "getting in touch" with your current feelings is to inspect them for motivation.
* Treat the daybook as you would any professional material that is highly confidential in nature. The daybook will be read by your group facilitator.

The following four excerpts from daybooks illustrate the kind of material that is most helpful to the writer.

Excerpt 1

Perhaps that's why I'm so interested in __ as an individual. I'm also wondering if significant people for me develop because of their approval, trust and liking—it has a big part to do with it. I have enjoyed very few people who gave me negative feedback. Criticism is difficult for me to accept—but I find a deeper respect and eventually high regard for those who give me criticism in a building way.

Excerpt 2

When Marilyn said we weren't totally strangers, it really hit me that that's exactly what I felt—a stranger, separate, and alone. While I was talking about myself the first time, I was glad because I wanted almost to be forced to be open, to reveal myself although it scared hell out of me to do it. I wanted the group to focus on me because I wanted to be reassured that they wouldn't let me get by with being phony, that they wouldn't just leave me as I was.

Excerpt 3

So a woman is good, kind, open, and honest, and really has some basic strong points. But these are not selling points in today's market. Is what I am asking too much? I really can't believe that it is. But I find myself doubting me and even the strong points when I face the everyday world I live in. I almost want to shout "I have played the game fair and done everything I was taught to do and still it isn't enough. Why! Why! Why!"

Excerpt 4

I winced a little as Frank suggested that Jim was not being open. It was obvious that Jim felt great pain at such a charge. I too felt the pain because even though I would like very much to be open, I don't seem to know how.

Example 2: Structure for Daybook Entries

Group Goals

Were the group goals defined? Do they change from session to session?

Personal Goals

Are your own goals well defined, unclear, or in the process of development? Do they change from session to session? Are they specific or general?

Group Process

What was the level of interaction: intellectual, feeling oriented, additive? Is the group stuck or moving? Are there subgroups? What is the emotional climate of the group in general?

Personal/Individual

(Names are OK, but not necessary.) What are the attitudes, feelings, beliefs, and reactions/behaviors of individual group members? How do I feel, respond, and behave? Did anything get triggered in me? What avenue of self-exploration can I pursue to learn more about myself?

Session

What did this session accomplish (a) for the group, and (b) for me?

Entries in the daybook often are quite creative, as is shown in the following poem written by a graduate student enrolled in the master's level group-counseling course.

Group
Persons thrown together
At random;
By chance.
The luck of the draw
Bringing people together
To communicate with others
To communicate with others
About what's important.
We share hopes for marriage,
The pain of broken relationships,
Frustration caused by overload.
We want to know how others
See things important to us.
Like God and family and work
And dissertation topics.
Sometimes our progress
Isn't impressive or dramatic;
Not easily measured
Or apparent to a casual observer.
When the intruder came by
To sell miracle cleanser,
He was politely informed:
"You will have to come back later. I'm involved in something
important right now."

Gunn (1988)

Follow-Up Sessions

Scheduling a follow-up session two to three months after the group's termination and apprising members of such can provide an impetus for members to continue to work on growth-promoting areas of change. For short-term, intensive, time-limited groups, a follow-up session is essential to afford members the opportunity to deal with unresolved issues and to receive support and encouragement from the group. A major criticism of short-term, intensive groups is the failure of the facilitator to provide for such follow-up sessions. Facilitators of short-term groups should

- plan a follow-up session;
- develop a referral source of professionals to whom they can refer group members when continued professional involvement by the facilitator is not possible;
- inform group members of other sources of assistance.

The follow-up session can provide an excellent opportunity for group members to identify new goals for themselves, to explore sources for continued growth toward these new goals, and as to work on any unresolved issues. This is typically not a time when major issues are resolved. After being "on their own" for several weeks, members seem to need emotional support and affirmation more than they need answers or advice. Perceptions of changes are shared, gains solidified, and areas of concern for self and others shared.

Summary

Evaluation and follow-up are crucial steps in the total group-counseling process and should not be viewed as appendages to be added on to the group experience. Evaluation is a necessary and significant factor in the group facilitator's effort to provide effective help to group members. The group facilitator should engage in a process of developing self-awareness and be open to feedback from group members. A systematic and effective evaluation procedure can greatly enhance the facilitative efforts of the group leader.

Follow-up sessions can be a means of providing an impetus for members to continue to work on growth-promoting areas of change. Therefore, group facilitators are encouraged to plan ahead for follow-up sessions.

References

Doxsee, D. J., & Kauligham, D. M. (1994). Hindering events in interpersonal relationship groups for counselor trainees. *Journal of Counseling and Development*, 72, 621–626.

Falco, L. D., & Bauman, S. (2004). The use of process notes in the experiential component of training group workers. *The Journal for Specialists in Group Work*, 29, 185–192.

Gunn, P. W. (1988). Group. Unpublished poem. Denton, TX: University of North Texas.

Haberstroh, S., Parr, G., Gee, R., & Trepal, H. (2006). Interactive e-journaling in group work: Perspectives from counselor trainees. *The Journal for Specialists in Group Work*, 31, 327–337.

Hall, J., & Hawley, L. (2004). Interactive process notes: An innovative tool in counseling groups. *The Journal for Specialists in Group Work*, 29, 207–224.

Hill, W. F. (1956). *HIM, Hill Interaction Matrix*. Los Angeles, CA: University of Southern California, Youth Studies Center.

Page, B. J., Pietrzak, D. R., & Lewis, T. F. (2001). Development of the group leader self-efficacy instrument. *The Journal for Specialists in Group Work*, 26, 168–184.

Pennebaker, J. W. (1997). Writing about emotional experiences as a therapeutic process. *Psychological Science*, 8, 162–165.

Riordan, R. J. (1996). Scriptotherapy: Therapeutic writing as a counseling adjunct. *Journal of Counseling and Development*, 74, 263–269.

Walters, R. H. (1975). A factor analytic study of the EPIC self-assessment scales. Unpublished doctoral dissertation. Denton, TX: North Texas State University.

Wright, J. (2002). Online counseling: Learning from writing therapy. *British Journal of Guidance and Counseling*, 30, 285–298.

11

GROUP COUNSELING OF CHILDREN

I must take issue with the term "a mere child," for it has been my invariable experience that the company of a mere child is infinitely preferable to that of a mere adult.

Fran Lebowitz

Children and adolescents need and want assistance. Group counseling is an excellent means to assist in their development, to help them learn about themselves, and how to prevent negative and increase positive interpersonal relationships, and to help them explore the here and now while considering implications for the future.

Group Counseling with Children

As an age group, children are probably the least understood and the most difficult to work with for most counselors. Children do not communicate in the customary ways familiar to most adults. They often fail to follow the usual rules of courtesy in groups and are not inclined to be turned on by insight-inducing self-exploration as are most adults. They can be blatantly disruptive and may even ignore the best facilitation moves the counselor has to offer. Although these points are typically true of children's groups, they can also be the most alive, active, sensitively caring, and rewarding groups. Greater group-facilitation skill may actually be required for working with children's groups because they are developmentally more diverse and more likely to stimulate the subjective values of the facilitator. It may be quite difficult for many group facilitators to refrain from reacting as a typical parent to disruptive behavior in a children's group, something that almost never happens in most adult groups.

Goals and Purposes

In group-counseling relationships, children experience the therapeutic releasing qualities of (a) discovering that their peers have problems too, and (b) a diminishing of the barriers of feeling all alone. A feeling of belonging develops, and new interpersonal skills are attempted in a "real-life" encounter where children learn more effective ways of relating to people through the process of trial and error. The group, then, is a microcosm of children's everyday world. In this setting, children are afforded the opportunity for immediate reactions from peers as well as the opportunity for vicarious learning. Children also develop a sensitivity to others and receive a tremendous boost to their self-concept through being helpful to someone else. For abused children who have poor self-concepts and a life history of experiencing failure, discovering that they can be helpful to someone else may be the most profound therapeutic quality possible. In the counseling group, children also discover that they are worthy of respect and that their worth is not dependent on what they *do* or what they *produce* but rather on who they are.

As in group counseling for adolescents and adults, group counseling for children is basically a psychological and social process in which children learn about themselves and others and the dynamics of interacting in ways that are mutually satisfying and basically encouraging. When children experience difficulty in developing appropriate social relationships, lack self-discipline in controlling their own behavior, have poor self-esteem, experience a lack of motivation, or in general have difficulty in developing coping behaviors that enable them to make adequate and self-enhancing adjustments, group counseling can be considered a significant intervention process (Homeyer and Sweeney 1999). Emphasis on succeeding coupled with a high incidence of divorce, alcoholic parents, physical abuse, sexual abuse, financially stressed parents, and parents who abuse drugs are all factors that may contribute to stressed children who have difficulty coping or succeeding, especially in classrooms. We believe group-counseling experiences should be provided for children before they begin to experience the consistent and cumulative failure that often leads to an unhealthy self-concept.

Special Considerations

Although the basic principles of group counseling apply to working with children in groups, some additional essential considerations are needed regarding the structuring of sessions. A basic rule of thumb is the younger the children the shorter the attention span and thus the shorter the session. The most effective time frame for preschool and primary-grade children seems to be thirty- to forty-five-minute sessions, with some groups meeting twice a week.

A second rule of thumb is the younger the children, the greater the degree of physical activity and thus the smaller the group. Groups of five to six children are usually recommended up to age nine. Play-therapy groups might have only two or three children depending on the needs of the children and the size of the playroom or play area.

If the therapeutic group approach is based primarily on verbal discussion, then the third rule of thumb is: the younger the children the less they know about how to function in a group and thus the more structure is needed. Our own experience has shown that as children learn how to assume responsibility for their behavior in the group, less emphasis is needed on structure.

The same ethical codes of professional conduct required for working with adults apply when working with children. The counselor employed in an agency or private practice must obtain approval from the parent or legal guardian. By law, parents are responsible for children and therefore must be informed about the nature of the group-counseling procedure, and consent must be secured. Because of the high incidence of divorce in our society, the counselor must ensure that permission is obtained from the adult who has legal custody of the child. In most public schools, obtaining parental permission is not an issue because the counseling program is considered to be an extension of the educational program of the school. However, this is not the case in all public schools, so the counselor is well advised to be acquainted with local school policy.

An appropriate procedure in most children's groups is to review basic group rules during the first session. Children need to know what limits are in effect; therefore, reviewing rules for group interaction such as *one person talks at a time, remain seated,* and *listen to others* can be a way of helping children to learn how to function effectively as a group. Responsibility can be conveyed to the group by asking the children to share what rules they think are necessary to have a successful group. As will be discussed later, in play-therapy groups, limitations on behaviors are best stated at the time they are needed.

Group counseling with children is distinctly different to group counseling with adults. Children are not as capable of verbally expressing themselves as are adults. Their natural means of interaction are play and activity-oriented. Indeed, for children younger than nine or ten years of age, the natural means of communication is play. Therefore, counselors for children's groups must have had supervised training with children so they will know how to utilize this medium effectively to facilitate children's communication with each other and the counselor.

Formats

Formats for counseling with children in groups should take into consideration the developmental level of children and should be based on children's natural means of communicating their emotional and social needs. Because children's natural "language" is play, they are much more comfortable acting out their behavior than talking about their problems or concerns. Therefore, exclusive emphasis on the interview or discussion-type format of group counseling is not recommended for children younger than nine years of age. When children feel uncomfortable trying to conduct themselves appropriately with what is for them an awkward procedure, the relationship that is so crucial to the group counseling process is slow to develop. Depending on the age of the children, the formats for group counseling with children that are recommended are group play therapy, activity group therapy, and structured group counseling.

Group Play Therapy

Meaning of Play

Group play therapy is recommended for children to age nine and takes into consideration the developmental implications of abstract reasoning and thinking that are not fully developed until approximately age ten or eleven. Because much of our verbal language is communication based on abstract symbols, children younger than age nine experience difficulty using this medium to express feelings and explore relationships. A difference also exists between children's production and comprehension of language. The level of children's understanding typically surpasses the maturity of their speech. To restrict children to verbal expression imposes unnecessary limitations on the communication that must take place between children and the counselor and within the group if the time together is to be a therapeutic experience. Play is to children what verbalization is to adults. It is a medium for expressing feelings, exploring relationships, describing experiences, disclosing wishes, and achieving self-fulfillment.

According to Landreth (2012), play is the child's symbolic language of self-expression and can reveal (a) what the child has experienced; (b) reactions to what was experienced; (c) feelings about what was experienced; (d) what the child wishes, wants, or needs; and (e) the child's perception of self. An understanding of children's play behavior provides cues to help the therapist to enter more fully into the inner life of the child. Because the child's world is a world of action and activity, play therapy provides the therapist with an opportunity to enter the child's world. The selection of a variety of appropriate toys by the therapist can facilitate a wide range of feeling-oriented expressions by children. Thus, children are not restricted to discussing what happened; rather, they live out at the moment of the play the past experiences and associated feelings. Therefore, the therapist is allowed to experience and participate in the emotional lives of children rather than reliving situational happenings. Because children thrust their total being into their play, expressions and feelings are experienced by children as being specific, concrete, and current, thus allowing the therapist to respond to their present activities, statements, feelings, and emotions rather than past circumstances.

For children, play is their voice, and group can become the social learning laboratory for change. Homeyer and Sweeney (2001: 98) noted, "Children learn about themselves in group play therapy. They learn because they are permitted to communicate in their own language. They learn as they hear and observe the perceptions of the therapist and the other members." The group becomes a social microcosm of their everyday world, yet it is a world where everyday anxieties can be worked through using play as the medium, a medium that the child finds comfortable.

Play Process

In the natural course of interacting with each other in the playroom, children learn not only about other children but also about themselves. Ginott (1994) suggested that the presence of several children in the playroom helps to anchor the experience to the world of reality. In the process of interacting, children help each other assume responsibility in interpersonal relationships. Children then are able to naturally and immediately extend these interactions with peers outside the setting of group play therapy. Unlike most other approaches to group counseling, in group play therapy no group goals exist and group cohesion is not an essential part of the developing process.

Playroom and Toys

The physical setting for group play therapy can be either a playroom designated for that purpose or a part of a larger room with toys and materials appropriately displayed. A major consideration is a setting that affords privacy and is large enough to afford a certain degree of freedom within the context of limitations on destructiveness. A room that is too small restricts children's expressions and may promote frustration. Likewise, a room that is too large may encourage too much activity and inhibits the development of a relationship with the counselor or other children because too little contact and interaction occur.

Because toys and materials are used by children to communicate their personal world, Landreth (2012) recommended selecting toys and materials that facilitate the following goals:

- establishment of a positive relationship with a child;
- expression of a wide range of feelings;
- exploration of real-life experiences;
- testing of limits;
- development of a positive image;
- development of a self-understanding; and
- opportunity to redirect behaviors unacceptable to others.

He recommended toys that represent the three broad categories of

1. *real-life toys*, such as a doll, a bendable doll family, a dollhouse and furniture, a nursing bottle, play dishes, a small car, an airplane, and a telephone;
2. *acting-out or aggressive-release toys*, such as handcuffs, a dart gun, toy soldiers, a pounding bench, a rubber knife, and inflatable punching toys; and

3. *toys for creative expression and emotional release,* such as crayons, newsprint, blunt scissors, pipe cleaners, popsicle sticks, Play-Doh, hand puppets, a Nerf ball, Gumby Scotch tape, and nontoxic glue or paste.

Activity Group Counseling

Activity group therapy is recommended for children aged nine to thirteen, who are still developmentally play- and activity-oriented but also to whom the group and team activities are extremely important.

Meaning of Activity

At this age, children generally feel more comfortable in and thus prefer same-sex groups. They are not comfortable talking about their problems and are much more likely to act out their emotional reactions. As Slavson (1945: 202), one of the pioneers of the activity group-therapy approach, has stated,

> What little children gain through play and acting out, young children in their latency period and early adolescents achieve through manual activity, creative expression, and free play interaction with one another. Older adolescents and adults require verbal expression and insight to gain the same results.

Slavson viewed the acting-out behavior of children in the therapeutic process as a primary form of communication.

Selection of Members

In activity group counseling, a great deal of attention is paid to member selection and the balancing of groups because there is very little counselor intervention. The activity and the interaction of the group members are viewed as the primary facilitators of change and growth. Ginott (1994) recommended that certain children not be placed in activity group counseling:

* sexually acting-out children;
* siblings exhibiting intense rivalry;
* sociopathic children (those who intentionally harm without remorse);
* extremely aggressive children;
* children with very low self-esteem;
* children who recently have been involved in a trauma or catastrophe.

Counselor Role

The role of the counselor is characterized as permissive and nonintervening.

S. R. Slavson has used the term "neutral" in describing the role of the worker in activity group therapy. He does not use it in the sense that the worker demonstrates fairness in conflict situations between children, which is also true, but rather as a quality of being available and meaningful to the children in terms of each child's unique need. Each child "makes" of the worker that which he requires (Schiffer 1969: 46–47).

Limits on behavior are introjected as suggestions for behavior rather than as attempts to stop behavior. For example, if a child began painting the leg of the easel, the counselor would take newspaper over and place it on the floor and offer the child a smock. This method is viewed as having a compressing effect on the behavior (Schiffer 1969).

Process

Schiffer (1969: 2–3) described the therapeutic process in the play group as being set in motion through the purposeful use of permissiveness by the counselor, which results in the following phases.

Preparatory Phase

- Introduction to the play group and the children's initial reactions to permissiveness.
- Testing the reality of the new experience.
- Discovery and relaxation.

Therapeutic Phase

- Development of transference on multiple levels—toward the worker and the other children.
- Regression.
- Aggression.
- Abatement of anxiety and guilt.
- Catharsis.

Reeducational Phase: Integrative, Maturational

- Increased frustration tolerance and capacity for delaying gratifications.
- Development of personal skills: expansion of interest areas.
- Improved self-image.
- Sublimation.

Success in Intragroup Participation: Recognition from the Group

- Group controls become more efficient; responsiveness of the individual to the group increases.
- Interaction resembles that of normal groups.
- Transference becomes diluted; identifications move closer to reality.
- Termination.
- Temporary regression in behavior resulting from separation anxiety.
- Acceptance and conclusion.

Activity Rooms and Materials

For activity group counseling, a designated activity room is a must. Usually a room of approximately 300 square feet is considered adequate for a group of six children. Schiffer (1969: 73) suggested the following materials for activity group counseling:

- objects representing significant persons and animals: dolls, puppets, a large inflatable plastic figure, face masks;
- objects which are identified with significant persons and their activities: adult "dress-up" clothing, crib, carriage, refrigerator, sink, toy-size house furniture;

- plastic, multifunctional media: poster paints, finger paints, Plasticine clay, self-hardening clay, blocks, water;
- manipulative skill and craft materials: lumber and basic woodworking tools, looms for weaving, leather craft, materials for sewing, knitting, crocheting;
- recreational supplies, toys and games: ring toss, a soft rubber ball, a simple boxed game which two or more children can play at one time, dominoes, checkers, pick-up sticks, Nok Hockey, truck, auto, airplane.
- Other standard furnishings are tables, chairs, easel, cabinets, bookshelves, sink, broom, dustpan, mop, pail, newspapers, and so on.

Length of Sessions

Sessions of an hour and a half to two hours once a week are generally recommended, with the last thirty minutes reserved for refreshment time. The refreshment time is usually the only time when the children come together as a group. The counselor sits with the group but is not the leader. This time usually becomes a time for planning outings and group activities.

Structured Group Counseling

Structured group counseling entails group-counseling experiences focused upon the limited ability of children to verbally discuss topics that have been predetermined by the group counselor. These groups include presentations through some form of structured media such as puppets, stories, role-playing, games, or activities, or a highly structured series of questions and discussion stimulus leads.

Structured groups meet specific needs of participants through skill acquisition, help the members adapt to a challenging life event or transition, or address specific issues or themes relevant to the lives of those who join the group. For example, a structured group around the issue of friendship may include the group leader reading the book *Making Friends* by Kate Petty (1991). After reading the book, the group members may talk or draw a picture about the story or answer questions posed by the group leader about friendship.

Activity-Interview Group Counseling

Although children lack the verbal facility to express themselves fully and possess inadequate group intervention skills, Gazda (1989) believed that appropriate structured and training activities can be utilized to help children learn how to function adequately in groups. In his format, games and activities are followed by discussion of the relevance of experiences or activities to the problem behavior in need of modification. After the first three or four free toy-play sessions, which are viewed as relationship-building experiences, the counselor structures the last half of each forty- to sixty-minute session through reading and telling stories and incorporates puppets in the process. Gazda recommended moving from puppets to dolls in structuring situations dealing with problems at hand. The children are asked to use dolls to work out solutions. In many instances, interpersonal problems that develop during the free-play part of the session become the focus of the structured problem-solving discussion. Free-play activities and games should be selected according to needs of group members and should be varied across sessions in order to accommodate interests of a variety of members. As the children learn how to function more effectively in a group, Gazda suggested moving toward structuring most of a given session.

A word of caution is offered: The completion of a game or planned activity should not supersede a meaningful and appropriate spontaneously generated discussion. Structure should be flexible.

Structured Games and Multimedia

Another approach to structuring is the utilization of simulation games and comprehensive multimedia programs. In simulation games, children face reality-oriented problems and must work out strategies for surmounting them. Such games teach knowledge and skills, and provide for the development of self-awareness.

Selection of Members

A perusal of the available resources indicates that one can find games and multimedia aids for a wide variety of ages and specific issues. Group leaders are encouraged to fully research any resources intended for group to ensure appropriateness for the chosen population.

Group Counseling for Abused Children

Of the many groups of children in our society who are at risk, none is perhaps any more needy or presents a wider range of problems than children who have been abused. Crosson-Tower (2004) outlined the immediate significant behavioral, emotional, cognitive, and interpersonal problems associated with abuse, and other researchers have demonstrated the long-term effects that abuse can have on children (Ater 2001; Strand 1999). Fall and Howard (2004) noted that the word "abuse" is used to broadly include a wide range of behaviors including physical violence, intimidation, emotional manipulation, and sexual exploitation. According to some estimates, as many as 3 million children may be abused each year in the USA. Every state has a child-abuse law requiring the reporting of child abuse.

Goals and Purposes

Because abusive parents are so inconsistent and unpredictable, children learn to distrust not only their parents but also other significant adults in their lives, including counselors. In addition, they have learned not to trust themselves or their environment. Consequently, abused children have internalized three significant messages: "Don't talk. Don't trust. Don't feel." To work with abused children is very difficult and requires great patience on the part of the counselor. Abused children may be aggressive, extremely withdrawn, and/or isolated; they may exhibit academic problems or socially maladaptive behavior. The first major goal with such children is the building of a relationship in which they will feel safe enough to risk trusting a new adult in their lives.

As in the case of other special population children, abused children need to be helped to discover that they are not alone in their experiences and feelings. Such children need opportunities to act out these intrusive experiences and in the process they experience a feeling of being in control. In addition, abused children need opportunities to express the full range of mixed and confusing feelings felt toward the perpetrator.

Selection of Members

Caution must be exercised in placing abused children in group-counseling experiences. The feelings associated with abuse are so potentially intense, especially in cases of sexual abuse, that individual counseling may be required initially or in conjunction with group counseling. In cases of recent traumatic sexual abuse, individual counseling would be recommended. Same-sex groups are recommended for children of all ages in cases of sexual abuse. This does not seem to be a necessary prerequisite for other forms of abuse.

Intervention Strategies

Group play therapy is the most preferred format for children younger than ten years of age because it affords children who are unable to verbalize an opportunity to express their feelings. Jones (2002) outlined strategies specific to helping with the common behavioral and psychological problems associated with abuse such as aggression, withdrawal, hyper-vigilance, and boundary problems. For older children, the structured group-counseling format could use focused discussion topics and simulated games to help children share and explore what they have experienced and their feelings and reactions.

Group Counseling for Children of Divorce

The incidence of divorce touches at least 50 percent of the children in the USA and leaves many of them feeling bewildered, confused, hurt, angry, rejected, or abandoned. Because children are egocentric, many feel guilty, believing that something they did caused the divorce. Some children experience serious problems in development as a result of the trauma of divorce. Younger children experience their world in a very concrete manner, and, therefore, many fear that if parents can "abandon" each other, they too can be abandoned. This fear may result in a developing distrust of any adult who seems to care.

Goals and Purposes

Children of divorce need opportunities to express their feelings and reactions in a safe and constructive environment that breaks down the barriers of isolation and provides experiential communication with which they feel comfortable. Groups exploring the dynamics of divorce help the child explore the feelings associated with this type of family loss, discuss the various ways the divorce will impact everyday life, help them become more assertive in asking for what they want and need from each parent, and help them understand that they are not alone in experiencing the divorce of one's parents.

Selection of Members

Eleven- and twelve-year-old children would seem to be best suited for the structured group-counseling format because of their abstract reasoning ability and their ability to generalize from the group experience to daily life. Group play therapy would provide younger children with constructive physical outlets for their anger and the opportunity through play to develop a feeling of control at a crucial time when their world seems to be out of control. Both formats would help children to discover they are not alone.

Intervention Strategies

Gilbert (2003) outlined an eight-session group for coping with divorce and separation. The group covers the topics of feelings, universality within the group to decrease feelings of isolation, practical issues related to coping with divorce, and life skills. The group utilizes process and structured activities, giving the group members opportunities to learn new skills and time to discuss their own individual perspectives. Some of the activities in the group include bibliotherapy (*Divorce Happens to the Nicest Kids* by Michael Prokop and *Dinosaurs Divorce* by Laurie and Marc Brown), a game with popsicle sticks, a board game (*My Two Homes*, from Child's Work Child's Play), and open discussion and play.

Filial Therapy

Parents in our society are experiencing increasing difficulty in maintaining the kind of family relationships and atmosphere that are conducive to the healthy development of each member of the family. How parents feel about themselves and their sense of adequacy as a person and a parent significantly affects their interaction with their children and thus their children's development. Parents need assistance in learning skills that encourage the development of positive parent–child relationships and that will in turn positively impact parents' perceptions of themselves as parents. To assume that most parents already know what these skills are and how to utilize them is not borne out by fact or experience. Relatively little effort has been put forth in our society to teach parents how to interact with their children in facilitative and therapeutic ways. According to Landreth (2012: 324), "Children need time for emotional sharing with their parents, and parents need to know how to respond in facilitative ways if the necessary relationship is to develop." Filial therapy, which trains parents in basic child-centered play-therapy skills, is unique among parent-training programs in that the objective of filial therapy is to train parents to become therapeutic agents in their children's lives.

Historical Development of Filial Therapy

Although filial therapy is a relatively recent development in the field of mental health, precedents for training parents to be therapeutic agents in their children's lives can be traced to the early part of the twentieth century.

Freud, in the early 1900s, served as the therapeutic consultant to the father of a five-year-old phobic child in the famous case of "Little Hans." Freud provided instruction to the father for having play sessions at home and would later interpret the child's play in sessions with the father (see Freud 1959). Baruch (1949) advocated parent–child play sessions at home for the purpose of enhancing communication and improving the parent–child relationship. Nancy Rogers-Fuchs (Fuchs 1957), with the counsel of her father, Carl Rogers, conducted home play sessions with her daughter based on the writings of Virginia Axline (1947). Fuchs reported positive changes in her daughter, who had been experiencing emotional difficulties related to toilet training. In addition, she noted positive changes within herself. Moustakas' description of home play sessions was one of the earliest: "Play therapy in the home . . . is a way through which the child opens himself to emotional expression and in this process releases tensions and repressed feelings" (1959: 275). These early experiences of parent–child play interactions differed from filial therapy in several ways: The parents (a) did not participate in regular training and supervision from a professional, and (b) did not share their experience in a support format (Landreth 2012).

In the early 1960s, Bernard Guerney recognized the burgeoning demand for and unavailability of mental-health services for children and families, and developed an innovative treatment methodology based on training parents in basic child-centered play-therapy skills to treat their own emotionally disturbed children (Guerney 1997). Landreth (2012) expanded on this concept, emphasizing that even parents whose children are not suffering from adjustment problems can benefit from learning how to relate more effectively to their children. The objective of this approach is to help the parent become the therapeutic agent in the child's life by utilizing the naturally existing bond between parent and child, thus the term *filial therapy* (Guerney et al. 1966). Typically, parents are trained in a small-group format to use child-centered play-therapy principles and skills as practiced by Axline (1969), Ginott (1965), Landreth (2012), and Moustakas (1959). These skills are implemented in special weekly home play sessions with their own children. Combining a support-group format with didactic instruction provides a dynamic process that sets filial-therapy training apart from other parent-training programs, the majority of which are exclusively educational in nature and behaviorally oriented.

Why Use Filial Therapy?

The primary source of children's maladjustment can presumably be attributed to interpersonal relationships within the family and to patterns of these relationships. The underlying rationale for the use of filial therapy is based on the hypothesis that if parents can be taught to assume the role of therapist, they can conceivably be more effective than a professional because the parent naturally has more emotional significance in the life of the child. The filial-therapy approach enlists the parent's participation as a key player in assisting the child, thus encouraging the parent's motivation to be helped and to be of help with his or her child. Unlike traditional therapy where parents may feel guilty as the cause of their child's problems and threatened by the therapist's relationship with their child, filial-therapy appeals to the parent as an ally, an essential partner in the child's improvement. When parents feel valued and supported, they are more likely to support a child's therapy rather than sabotaging it.

The difficulties parents experience in learning to utilize the therapeutic role and skills being taught may stimulate significant issues that may serve as a catalytic force for insight and personal growth for all members of the training group during the group discussion process. As parents improve their observational skills, develop a genuine interest in their child's needs, and become more sensitive to their child's emotional messages, they may gain a greater understanding of their child and more realistic expectations for the child.

As parents learn to communicate this enhanced genuine interest, attention, and sensitivity to their child, an improved self-concept, an increased sense of security, and a decrease in aggressiveness by the child may be expected. The parent's success in utilizing the prescribed therapeutic role should have an effect far greater than a therapist could achieve by doing the same thing. These therapeutic attitudes and interpersonal skills acquired by parents can be utilized by parents to help all their children fulfill their potentials and to maintain their progress long after the formal training has ended. Thus, the interpersonal dynamics of the entire family system are positively affected (Guerney 1969).

Unique Aspects of Filial Therapy

Filial therapy is unique among parent-training programs in focusing on developing and enhancing the parent–child relationship as opposed to correcting or changing behavior problems. The means by which to achieve these goals include the use of play, which is recognized in play therapy as the medium through which children communicate. This is in contrast to other parent-training programs, which are based entirely upon verbal communication. Filial therapy creates an opportunity for the child to be actively involved in the process rather than just having the parents apply new skills to the children.

The skills learned in filial-therapy training are employed by the parents in weekly thirty-minute structured play sessions with their children. Requiring the skills learned to be practiced only once a week avoids the usual parent-training approach of overwhelming the parent by requiring global parenting changes in all interactions with their children. The filial skills, however, are readily generalizable to parent–child relationships outside the special play times as the parent feels comfortable to do so. This helps to ensure a successful experience for the parent and is thus reinforcing to the utilization of the skills learned in the training sessions.

A major component of filial therapy is the supervision of the parent–child weekly special play sessions either through live demonstrations by the parents or via videotapes parents make of their home sessions. This supervision component of the training process also sets filial therapy apart from other parent-training programs. Supervision of counselors-in-training is considered crucial to the development of therapeutic skills and is likewise considered crucial for parents learning new skills in building relationships with their children. If parents are not able to demonstrate acquisition of the skills being taught, then additional training can be applied.

Objectives of Filial Therapy

The primary objective of filial therapy is to build and enhance the parent–child relationship. Van Fleet (2005a: 6) posited several overall aims of the filial therapy process: "(a) eliminate the presenting problems at their source, (b) develop positive interactions between parents and their children, and (c) increase families' communication, coping, and problem-solving skills so they are better able to handle future problems independently and successfully." Within the framework of these general objectives, there are goals or objectives for both children and parents within the process.

Landreth (2012) proposed several objectives for child-centered play therapy, which also apply to the filial-therapy process. Filial therapy helps the child

- develop a more positive self-concept;
- assume greater self-responsibility;
- become more self-directing;
- become more self-accepting;
- become more self-reliant;
- engage in self-determined decision-making;
- experience a feeling of control;
- become sensitive to the process of coping;
- develop an internal source of evaluation; and
- become more trusting of self.

(Landreth 2012: 84–85)

The fact that problem issues between the parent and child (as opposed to between a therapist and child) are being addressed may, in fact, reinforce the development and fulfillment of these objectives.

Equally important objectives of filial therapy are those pertaining to the parents. Parents are affirmed and empowered in filial therapy, which in turn creates an opportunity for their children to be affirmed and empowered. As children observe their parents' increased self-confidence in their efficacy as parents, they feel secure and empowered themselves. Filial therapy helps parents

- develop a more positive concept of self as parents;
- recognize the importance of play in the lives of their children;

- increase self-confidence in parenting abilities;
- decrease feelings of chaos and frustration;
- develop a wider array of parenting skills;
- assume a greater level of responsibility in the parenting of their children;
- experience a feeling of control;
- increase levels of empathy and acceptance of their children; and
- develop patience.

Structure

The structure of the filial-therapy training sessions and parent–child play session is to establish and enhance a therapeutic relationship. Although the relationship between the parent and child would not be considered "therapeutic" in a clinical sense, the intent is for the parent to serve as the therapeutic agent of change in the parent–child relationship.

An established structural component of the filial-therapy process is the training and qualification of the filial-therapy trainer. Because filial therapy is based upon the foundational skills of child-centered play therapy, the filial therapy trainer must be a trained and experienced play therapist. Van Fleet (1994) suggested several principles central to filial-therapy training. First, filial therapists must recognize the importance of play in child development. This includes a consideration of play as the primary means by which children communicate and through which children can be understood. Second, filial therapists must believe that parents are capable of learning the necessary skills to conduct child-centered play sessions with their own children. Third, filial therapists must have a preference for educational versus biological models of evaluation and treatment.

The filial-therapy training model was originally developed and designed for use with groups of parents. Although the specific skills learned in filial therapy can be taught on an individual basis, there is no substitute for the shared emotional experience and vicarious learning that occur within a group setting. It is imperative, therefore, for the filial-therapy trainer to be skilled in group therapy as well as play-therapy skills. A filial-therapy training group normally consists of six to eight individual parents or three to four couples. A larger number of parents interferes with group process and makes it difficult to provide the necessary supervision of the parents' play sessions.

The filial-therapy training model developed by Landreth (2012) meets weekly for two hours each session for ten weeks. This is considered to be the minimum amount of training necessary for parents to be trained and supervised adequately and for proper support to be extended to the parents, who may be dealing with emotionally charged issues with their children. Although ten sessions is a minimum for filial-therapy training, it is often difficult to get parents to commit for longer periods of time in today's busy lifestyle. The expense of participating in a longer training schedule is also a significant factor.

Because discussion and interaction are considered crucial to the training process, the facilitator should not cast him- or herself as the "expert," because this tends to inhibit parents from volunteering their own solutions. Questions are turned back to the group, and possible solutions are generated through lively discussion. Handouts and homework assignments are given at each session and are reviewed at the beginning of each subsequent meeting. Homework reinforces the training, and reviewing the homework reinforces the material covered in the assignments. The handouts include general information about play therapy and materials on limit setting, discipline, and other parenting subjects. Homework assignments include worksheets on recognizing and responding to feelings, employing reflective communication, engaging in appropriate limit setting, and so on, as well as assignments to put together the filial-therapy toy kit, to select and prepare a time and place for the play times, and to conduct the sessions. Parents should be encouraged to ask questions and take notes. A major focus of the training sessions is the supervision and feedback the parents receive. Although it is not possible to give a step-by-step delineation of each session here, the following is a summary of Landreth's (2012) session structure.

Session 1

Parents introduce themselves and the child of focus. Parents should be encouraged to conduct the special play times with the child who is most in need of an enhanced parent–child relationship (this will be, of course, the child exhibiting adjustment difficulties). All play sessions with each child should be conducted by the same parent, because alternating between parents sets up potential confusion and conflict. The purpose of the training is discussed, role-playing is employed, and homework is given. The focus is primarily upon sensitizing the parent to the child's emotions and the use of reflective listening, which is modeled in role-playing situations.

Session 2

Homework is reviewed, and role-playing continues, with the therapist modeling empathic responses. A videotape is generally shown of the therapist conducting play therapy (it is advisable to show a tape of yourself, not another therapist), or a live demonstration is done with a parent's child. Parents are given a list of toys to use for the special play times. The therapist demonstrates each toy and discusses the purpose for inclusion. The toy kit is essentially similar to the toy list in the section on play therapy in this text. Homework is assigned, which includes putting together a toy kit and selecting a place for the play session.

Session 3

Homework is reviewed (parents report on toys and session location selected). Another videotape of the therapist conducting a play therapy session is shown, or a live demonstration is given. The homework assignment is to make a "Do Not Disturb" sign with the child for use during the play session and to have the first play session. Parents are encouraged to adhere to the following rules during the play times:

Don't

1. Don't criticize any behavior.
2. Don't praise the child.
3. Don't ask leading questions.
4. Don't allow interruptions of the session.
5. Don't offer information or teach.
6. Don't preach.
7. Don't initiate new activities.

(These first seven are taken from Guerney 1972.)

8. Don't be passive or quiet.

Do

1. Do set the stage.
2. Do let the child lead.
3. Do track behavior.
4. Do reflect the child's feelings.
5. Do set limits.
6. Do salute the child's power and effort.
7. Do join in the play as a follower.
8. Do be verbally active.

Session 4

Parents give reports of the first play session with supervision and feedback from the therapist. The focus is on the parents' feelings about the experience. A videotape or live demonstration of a parent–child play session is viewed with feedback from the therapist and the rest of the group. Another parent is asked to videotape his or her next session. Every parent should have at least one session videotaped and reviewed in the group.

Sessions 5–9

Following approximately the same format, the parents report on their play sessions with supervision from the therapist and feedback from the group. Homework assignments and handouts are given at each session. Training and role-playing continue. The parents will begin to generalize their experiences and skills outside of the play time. Limit setting is discussed in more detail.

Session 10

Parents report on their play sessions, a videotape is reviewed, and the training process is reviewed and evaluated. The therapist shares notes from the first session of the parents' description of their child to reference the change that has occurred. Parents or children requiring additional intervention are scheduled for further assistance (Landreth 2012).

Clientele

An important aspect of the structure of filial therapy involves the selection of parents. Although it is advisable to screen out parents from filial-therapy training groups who have substantial emotional problems themselves (severe depression, psychosis, etc.), the training benefits parents from all situations. Likewise, filial therapy is appropriate for parents of all children, not just children who are experiencing emotional and behavioral difficulties. Successful filial-therapy training has included many parent and child populations, as noted below in the Research section, as well as grandparents, parents of teenagers, first-time pregnant parents, older siblings, and so on. It is clear that no families are exempt from occasional disruptions, such as the birth of a new child, change of employment, death of a friend or relative, and so on. Any of these experiences can cause some level of anxiety or depression in a child, which in turn leads the child to act out. A parent who has been trained in filial therapy will most likely look beyond the behavior to the emotional need being expressed as opposed to immediately seeking to eliminate the undesirable behavior.

Research

Considerable research has been conducted on the Guerneys' model (Guerney et al. 1966) and a shorter ten-week model developed by Landreth (2012) validating the efficacy of filial therapy with various populations of parents and with various populations of children. For a comprehensive review of filial therapy research, consult Van Fleet (2005b) and Baggerly et al. (2010).

One of the earliest studies on filial therapy was compiled by Oxman (1973). After a twelve-month treatment period, fifty-one mothers, whose children had been diagnosed as emotionally maladjusted, reported a decrease in the number of problem behaviors displayed by their children. These mothers also described their perception of an ideal child. Both results were significant as compared to a control group of seventy-one mothers, whose children displayed normal behavior with typical childhood problems, who did not participate in the training.

Glass (1987) found that filial therapy significantly increased the parents' feelings of unconditional love for their children and significantly decreased the parents' perception of expressed conflict in their family. In addition to the statistically significant results, there were some important trends that were mentioned as directional conclusions.

- Filial therapy may be a more effective treatment for increasing parents' self-esteem than children's self-esteem.
- Filial therapy may be effective treatment for increasing closeness of the parent–child relationship without altering the authority hierarchy.
- Filial therapy may influence the family environment, especially in the areas of expressiveness, conflict, independence, intellectual-cultural orientation, and control.
- Filial therapy may be an effective treatment for increasing parents' understanding of the meaning of the children's play.

In research involving single parents in a ten-week model of filial-therapy training, Bratton and Landreth (1995) measured significant increases in single parents' empathy toward their children, acceptance, allowing self-direction, and involvement. Significant increases in respect for a child's feelings, a child's unique makeup, a child's need for autonomy, and unconditional love were also measured. Overall parental stress as well as perceived problems of child behaviors decreased significantly.

Chau and Landreth (1996) investigated the effectiveness of filial therapy with Chinese parents. After a ten-week filial-therapy training program, the Chinese parents who received training had significant changes over the Chinese parents in the control group who did not receive training in the areas of increased level of empathic interactions with their children, increased attitudes of acceptance toward their children, and reduction in their level of stress related to parenting.

Landreth and Lobaugh (1998) conducted a study to determine the effectiveness of a ten-week filial-therapy model on increasing incarcerated fathers' acceptance of their children and reducing the stress they experienced as parents. The fathers in the filial-therapy group significantly increased their acceptance of their children on all four subscales of the Porter Parental Acceptance Scale and significantly reduced their stress as a result of the training. They reported significantly fewer problems in the post-test checklist. In addition, the children of the experimental-group parents significantly increased their self-concepts as a result of the training.

Glover and Landreth (2000) conducted a study to determine the effectiveness of a ten-week filial-therapy training model as an intervention for Native American parents and their children residing on the Flathead Reservation in Montana. Children who participated in filial-therapy special play sessions with their parents significantly increased their level of desirable play behaviors with their parents. Although the measures of parental acceptance, parental stress, and children's self-concepts did not show significant change, there were positive trends on all measures.

Tew et al. (2002) examined the effectiveness of a ten-week filial-therapy training group for parents of chronically ill children. Results indicated that parents in the experimental group significantly increased their attitude of acceptance toward their children and significantly reduced their level of stress as compared to parents in the control group. Children in the experimental group scored significantly lower than control-group children on total behavioral problems, anxiety, and depression.

Smith and Landreth (2003) conducted intensive filial training with parents of children who were witness to domestic violence. Results indicated that children in the experimental group significantly experienced reduced behavior problems and significantly increased their self-concept as compared to children in the nontreatment group. Results also demonstrated that mothers of the experimental group scored significantly higher after training on both their attitudes of acceptance and empathic behavior. Interestingly, comparative data revealed that intensive filial therapy facilitated by the children's mothers was as effective in reducing behavior problems as intensive individual play therapy and intensive sibling group play therapy facilitated by professionally trained therapists.

Lee and Landreth (2003) explored the effectiveness of a ten-week filial training with immigrant Korean parents in the USA. Results indicated that the Korean parents in the experimental group significantly increased their level of empathic interactions with their children and their attitude of acceptance toward their children while significantly reducing their stress level related to parenting as compared to the control group.

More recent research into filial therapy has expanded the application beyond parents and has examined the effectiveness of the approach with a wide variety of caregivers. For example, Robinson et al. (2007) trained fifth-grade mentors in filial therapy and found a significant increase in their empathic interactions with their kindergarten mentees. Helker and Ray (2009) trained teachers and their aides in filial concepts and found a significant increase in the use of relationship-building behaviors in the classroom, which decreased the frequency of externalizing behavior among the students. Morrison and Helker (2010) trained Head Start preschool teachers in filial and small-group play-therapy skills and found a significant decrease in externalizing behaviors in their students.

References

Ater, M. K. (2001). Play therapy behaviors of sexually abused children. In G. L. Landreth (Ed.), *Innovations in play therapy: Issues, process, and special populations* (pp. 119–130). New York: Brunner-Routledge.

Axline, V. (1947). *Play therapy: The inner dynamics of childhood.* Boston, MA: Houghton Mifflin.

—— (1969). *Play therapy.* New York: Ballantine.

Baggerly, J. N., Ray, D. C., & Bratton, S. C. (Eds.) (2010). *Child-centered play therapy research.* New York: Wiley.

Baruch, D. (1949). *New ways to discipline.* New York: McGraw-Hill.

Bratton, S. C., & Landreth, G. L. (1995). Filial therapy with single parents: Effects on parental empathic interactions, parental acceptance of child and parental stress. *International Journal of Play Therapy,* 4, 61–80.

Brown, L. K., & Brown, M. (1988). *Dinosaurs divorce.* Boston, MA: Little, Brown.

Chau, I., & Landreth, G. L. (1996). Filial therapy with Chinese parents: Effects on parental empathic interactions, parental acceptance of child and parental stress. *International Journal of Play Therapy,* 6, 75–92.

Crosson-Tower, C. (2004). *Understanding child abuse and neglect* (6th ed.). Boston, MA: Allyn & Bacon.

Fall, K. A., & Howard, S. (2004). *Alternatives to domestic violence* (2nd ed.). New York: Brunner-Routledge.

Freud, S. (1959). Analysis of a phobia in a five-year-old boy. In S. Freud, *Collected papers: Case histories*. New York: Basic Books.

Fuchs, N. (1957). Play therapy at home. *Merrill-Palmer Quarterly*, 3, 89–95.

Gazda, G. (1989). *Group counseling: A developmental approach*. Boston, MA: Allyn & Bacon.

Gilbert, A. (2003). Group counseling in an elementary school. In K. R. Greenberg (Ed.), *Group counseling in K–12 schools* (pp. 56–80). Boston, MA: Allyn & Bacon.

Ginott, H. G. (1965). *Between parent and child*. New York: Macmillan.

—— (1994). *Group psychotherapy with children: The theory and practice of play therapy*. Northvale, NJ: Jason Aronson.

Glass, N. M. (1987). Parents as therapeutic agents: A study of the effect of filial therapy (doctoral dissertation, University of North Texas, 1986). *Dissertation Abstracts International*, 47(07), A2457.

Glover, G., & Landreth, G. L. (2000). Filial therapy with Native Americans on the Flathead Reservation. *International Journal of Play Therapy*, 9, 57–80.

Guerney, B. G., Jr. (1969). *Psychotherapeutic agents: New roles for nonprofessionals, parents, and teachers*. New York: Holt, Rinehart & Winston.

Guerney, B. G., Jr., Guerney, L. F., & Andronico, M. P. (1966). Filial therapy. *Yale Scientific Magazine*, 40 (March), 6–14.

Guerney, L. F. (1972). Play therapy: A training manual for parents. Unpublished manuscript, Pennsylvania State University at State College.

—— (1997). Filial therapy. In K. O'Connor & L. M. Braverman (Eds.), *Play therapy theory and practice: A comparative presentation* (pp. 131–159). New York: Wiley.

Helker, W. P., & Ray, D. C. (2009). Impact of child-teacher relationship training on teachers' and aides' use of relationship building skills and the effects of student classroom behavior. *International Journal of Play Therapy*, 18, 70–83.

Homeyer, L. E., & Sweeney, D. S. (1999). *Group play therapy: How to do it, how it works, and whom it's best for*. New York: Routledge.

—— (2001). Group play therapy. In K. A. Fall and J. E. Levitov (Eds.), *Modern applications to group work* (pp. 95–114). Huntington, NY: Nova Science.

Jones, K. D. (2002). Group play therapy with sexually abused preschool children: Group behaviors and interventions. *The Journal for Specialists in Group Work*, 27, 377–389.

Landreth, G. L. (2012). *Play therapy: The art of the relationship* (3rd ed.). New York: Routledge.

Landreth, G. L., & Lobaugh, F. A. (1998). Filial therapy with incarcerated parents: Effects on parental acceptance of child, parental stress and child adjustment. *Journal of Counseling and Development*, 76, 157–165.

Lee, M., & Landreth, G. L. (2003). Filial therapy with immigrant Korean parents in the United States. *International Journal of Play Therapy*, 12, 67–85.

Morrison, M. O., & Helker, W. P. (2010). An early mental health intervention for disadvantaged preschool children. In J. N. Baggerly, D. C. Ray, and S. C. Bratton (Eds.) *Child-centered play therapy research* (pp. 427–446). New York: Wiley.

Moustakas, C. E. (1959). *Psychotherapy with children*. New York: Harper & Brothers.

Oxman, L. K. (1973). The effectiveness of filial therapy: A controlled study (Doctoral dissertation, Rutgers University, 1972). *Dissertation Abstracts International*, 32(11), B6656.

Petty, K. (1991). *Making friends*. New York: Barron's.

Prokop, M. S. (1996). *Divorce happens to the nicest kids* (rev. ed.). Warren, OH: Alegra House.

Robinson, J., Landreth, G. L., & Packman, J. (2007). Fifth grade students as emotional helpers with kindergartners: Using play therapy procedures and skills. *International Journal of Play Therapy*, 16, 20–35.

Schiffer, M. (1969). *The therapeutic play group*. New York: Grune & Stratton.

Slavson, S. (1945). Differential methods of group therapy in relation to age levels. *Nervous Child*, 4, 196–210.

Smith, N., & Landreth, G. L. (2003). Intensive filial therapy with child witnesses of domestic violence: A comparison with individual and sibling group play therapy. *International Journal of Play Therapy, 12,* 67–88.

Strand, V. C. (1999). The assessment and treatment of family sexual abuse. In N. B. Webb (Ed.), *Play therapy with children in crisis* (pp. 104–130). New York: Guilford.

Tew, K., Landreth, G. L., Joiner, K. D., & Solt, M. D. (2002). Filial therapy with parents of chronically ill children. *International Journal of Play Therapy, 11,* 79–100.

Van Fleet, R. (2005a). *Filial therapy: Strengthening parent-child relationships through play* (2nd ed.). Sarasota, FL: Professional Resources Press.

—— (2005b). Filial therapy: A critical review. In L. A. Reddy & C. E. Schaefer (Eds.), *Empirically based play interventions for children* (pp. 241–264). Washington, DC: APA.

12

GROUP COUNSELING WITH ADOLESCENTS

Adolescence is generally regarded as a period of great change. For many adolescents, this stage of development is characterized by conflict, questioning of values, a bewildering array of choices, confusing physiological changes, and an overwhelming need for approval by peers. Added to these stressors is an increased pressure to be responsible for one's own actions. During this stage of development, many adolescents feel they are alone in their mire of self-doubt. They seek approval from others, especially peers, and at the same time struggle with the issues of independence–dependence in relationships involving significant others. For most adolescents, this is a time of enormous peer pressure. Values and traditions are questioned in light of peer-group reaction and standards. The need for peer approval and acceptance may often be stronger than their own issues of self-respect. Adolescents often look to their peer group for self-identity. Therefore, this is an opportune time to utilize group counseling to deal with feelings of isolation and the overwhelming number of choices facing adolescents.

As Aronson and Scheidlinger (1996: 76) stated, "Adolescence and the concept of group life are inextricably woven together. A typical high school comprises a number of defined groups, each bound by its own structure." Because the everyday life of adolescents includes groups, group counseling often can provide a comfortable place to explore change. In addition to the commonsense fit, research also supports the use of group for a wide range of adolescent issues (Malott et al. 2010; Sanci 2011; and Schectman & Mor 2011).

General Considerations

When working with adolescents in group, the following should help you set up a physical environment conducive to processing.

Comfortable Setting

As with any group, the environment needs to be conducive to learning and sharing. Pick a space that is large enough to arrange the seats in circle format, allowing for enough room between seats not to feel cramped. Focusing the group seems to be more of an issue with adolescents than with adults, so minimize the number of distractions in the room. For example, while a window might be aesthetically pleasing, the squirrel in the tree might create competition for the attention of the group. It is also important to keep the room consistent. In a school setting, it might be necessary to move rooms from group to group, but try not to do this. Each time you move the group, you will sense the group "starting over" as they get used to the surroundings. Consistency adds to the atmosphere of safety which will produce greater group cohesion and focus.

Group Size and Duration

Groups with adolescents tend to work best with membership around five to ten members. The smaller group format allows for a feeling of intimacy and will differentiate the group from a class. The life of the group will largely depend on the type of group as well as the setting. If you are doing groups in a school, your group will probably need to fit within the school semester structure, with time considered for exams and holidays. In general, adolescent sessions will last between an hour and ninety minutes. Anything less than an hour makes it very difficult to process at a deep level. It will take the group about ten minutes to get settled and focused, another ten minutes to get ready to leave (the group members will sense it's almost time to leave and start getting distracted), so that leaves forty minutes to work in an hour-long group.

Purpose and Goals

Because adolescents have such a strong need for peer identification and approval, group counseling is especially appropriate because it provides a supportive atmosphere in which they feel safe enough to risk sharing their concerns. Through the interaction process in the group, they discover that other adolescents have similar problems and that they are not alone. Within the group-counseling structure, many adolescents experience for the first time that they can give as well as receive help. To receive help from another person or a group is a positive experience, but indeed a much more powerful experience is for adolescents to discover they can be helpful to another person. Out of such experiences comes a respect for self as adolescents experience a sense of usefulness and an acceptance of themselves as contributing persons in the lives of other members. Adolescents also learn that they are unique and special, and that they are genuinely accepted by a group of peers whom they have come to admire and respect. These therapeutic factors contribute to the development of a cohesive, growth-promotion group. Adolescents' perceptions of the therapeutic factors in group counseling provide helpful insight into the importance of such a group experience. The factors selected by adolescents as most helpful, according to Corder et al. (1981: 348), are as follows:

- "Learning to express my feelings."
- "Learning that I must take ultimate responsibility for the way I live my life."
- "Other members honestly telling me what they think of me."
- "Being in the group was in a sense like being in a big family, only this time a more accepting and understanding family."
- "Belonging to a group of people who understand and accept me."
- "The group giving me an opportunity to learn to approach others."
- "Seeing I was just as well off as others."
- "Helping others and being important in their lives."

These therapeutic factors could easily be translated into general goals for adolescent group members. As with any group, however, the adolescent group members must decide for themselves what specific goals are appropriate.

Intervention Strategies

Topics addressed in adolescent groups should be directly related to changes occurring in their lives. For example, junior-high students are generally concerned with socialization issues, whereas high-school students are more concerned with self. Other common topics or themes that arise in adolescent counseling groups are alcohol and drug abuse, relationships with parents, conflicts at school, making one's own decisions, feeling rejected and unloved, learning to repress feelings appropriately, and relating to the opposite sex.

Although to specify a topic or to develop a group theme is sometimes advisable for certain sessions, spontaneously generated problems or concerns of members not related to the topic should be encouraged. Such spontaneous discussions are often the most productive and usually touch areas of concern or feelings of other group members.

Adolescents are not as developmentally capable of coping with uncertainty as are most adults. Therefore, some structuring of sessions will help group members to feel more secure and thus more willing to risk sharing in keeping with the direction provided by the structure. Apparent disinterest by some adolescents in the group may mask their fear of being unable to express appropriately and comfortably their feelings and needs. Role-playing, one of the most easily utilized intervention strategies, is especially effective with adolescents because they are allowed to be someone else and thus are not as likely to be self-conscious.

Role-playing can be a means of gaining practical experience in expression of feelings. This informal here-and-now reality dramatization allows adolescents an opportunity to take on various roles and in the process to develop insight into how another person thinks, feels, and experiences. It is a learning-through-experiencing activity and thus can have a significant impact on experience-prone teenagers. Role-playing also affords teenagers the opportunity to practice human relations skills and is highly recommended for practicing communication with parents, teachers, peers, and employers. Role-playing fosters creative problem-solving, helps members express themselves more spontaneously, improves communication, increases involvement in the group interaction, increases feelings of empathy for others, and facilitates the development of new insights into self.

Other techniques or intervention strategies which have been found to be helpful in working with adolescents are *human potential lab exercises* for teaching adolescents how to give positive feedback, assertiveness training, decision-making training, and socialization skill-building exercises.

Resistance

Adolescents usually come into counseling as involuntary clients, that is, at the behest of teachers, parents or even the court system. As an involuntary client, the adolescent will initially view the group a consequence and the leader as a surrogate for the person who sent them to group. Obviously, this is not the most comfortable place to begin a therapeutic alliance, but as it is a reality, the group leader should be prepared to work through these issues. Below are a few tips for moving your adolescent group member from an involuntary to a voluntary client.

Make Use of Your Pre-Screening Interview

As mentioned in Chapter 7, pre-group interviews are vital for the success of any group but are especially important with adolescents. The individual time allows for the counselor to begin building rapport with the client, provides an orientation to the group process, and screens out people not suitable for the group. As a part of the rapport-building, group leaders are encouraged to expect resistance and work through it by helping the client find their own reason for being in the group. The following excerpt shows one way of doing this:

CLIENT: Well, I'm just here because my mom is making me come. She's pissed because she thinks I don't respect her. It's so stupid.

COUNSELOR: So, you think she wants you to come to group and learn some respect.

CLIENT: [*Laughs.*] Yeah, I guess so, but I don't think I have anything to learn. Maybe she should come to the group and learn something.

COUNSELOR: Well, groups can be helpful for all types of people. If you don't think you need to learn respect, what could you get out of the group?

CLIENT: I have no idea.

COUNSELOR: I can tell you are having a hard time figuring out how this group will be useful to you. I guess what I'm trying to say is that group isn't about what your mom wants to change about you, it's about what you want to change.

CLIENT: What if I don't want to change anything?

COUNSELOR: Then I suppose you won't be a good fit for the group. I really don't want people who think they are perfect in the group [*smiles*].

CLIENT: [*Laughs.*] I didn't say I was perfect.

COUNSELOR: I know. What I meant is that to get into the group, you need to find a reason to be in there. It may be difficult. You may not even want to admit there is something because then your mom might say, "I told you so!" but it's still important to find something. You know, one thing you already mentioned is that you and your mom argue a lot. You might want to change the dynamics of that relationship. You know, look at your part.

CLIENT: So, it would be easier on her?

COUNSELOR: No, it would be easier on you . . . and her probably, if it improves the overall relationship. The focus would be on how you interact in the relationship and then on what you could change about that.

CLIENT: And I get to pick?

COUNSELOR: Sure. The group will help you explore, and you'll find things of interest along the way. You will also hear about other people's lives and how they struggle and succeed in relationships with parents, friends, teachers, etc. You'll find some interesting things in their stories too.

CLIENT: Hmm . . . I'll give it a shot.

COUNSELOR: Great. If it's not working, be sure to let me know and we'll talk.

When Exploring Issues Don't Try to Be Cool and Go Slow!

When supervising beginning group leaders or consulting with seasoned professionals on working with adolescents in group, two main issues arise that complicate dealing with resistance. First is when the group leader tries to be "cool." This usually occurs because the group leader is attempting to get the adolescent members to see him or her as different from the other adults they experience. As a result, the leader tries to demonstrate allegiance and similarity by adopting the mannerisms, likes, or language of the teens. This does not work for several reasons. Mainly, the adolescents will see right through the attempt because the leader is *not* an adolescent. The group will see you as a fraud or as someone who is trying to trick them. It is helpful to remember that you are trying to be different from other adults in the way you *treat and interact* with the members. This has nothing to do with talking like them or liking the things they like. As Eaves and Sheperis (2011: 267) noted, "Adolescents respond best to leaders who are caring, enthusiastic, open and direct . . . congruent and genuine." Face it, you will not be cool. The good news is that being cool is not what will produce change in the group.

The second issue that complicates resistance is moving too fast. This occurs when the group leader experiences silence or short answers, believes the group is just too uncomfortable with the issue, and so moves on to the next topic. If the leader moves fast enough, the group will blow through everything in fifteen minutes. Group leaders must understand that all groups start off anxious and adolescent groups are no different. Give them time to explore and don't move off a topic area until you feel the group has a very deep understanding of the perspectives of each group member. Speed up and the group will norm around superficial discussion. Take your time and the group will gradually learn how to process at a deep level.

Activities Are Great, but Trust the Processing Too

It is well documented that adolescents respond well to activities within group settings (Ashby et al. 2008; Attaway 2010; Belmont 2006; Lowenstein 2010). However, activities should be chosen carefully with an eye on process and goal impact. With an overreliance on activities, group leaders may believe that the activity is a panacea for resistance concerns while finding that the resistance returns as soon as the activity is over. Ideally, group leaders will use the activity as a method for connecting and exploring in a way that is appealing to the group members. As the activity unfolds, competent group leaders will make sure there is plenty of time to process the exercise, which will get the group used to doing something with the connection that was facilitated by the activity. Keep in mind: the activity is not the goal. The activity is a tool to get the group to a deeper level.

Psycho-Educational Groups and Adolescents

Topic- or theme-oriented groups fit naturally into the developmental concerns of adolescents and have been shown to be quite effective with those adolescents typically labeled as difficult or hard to reach. These are the adolescents who do not feel they fit in and thus do not identify with or feel they are a part of the school setting. They lack motivation in the direction desired by most adults in schools but nevertheless are motivated in the direction of what seems to them to be important in their lives. We believe all adolescents are motivated. *The counselor's task, therefore, becomes one of developing the kind of setting and atmosphere that builds upon this motivation rather than trying to develop motivation.* Peer identification among "hard-to-reach" adolescents is one of the most powerful sources of motivation they experience and can be utilized in the group-counseling setting to help such adolescents to examine and change their attitudes, goals, and self-defeating behaviors. Beginning group counselors are often amazed at the constructive suggestions and creative problem-solving ideas generated by adolescents who have been labeled as problem students by other adults. This inherent group move or push toward positive, constructive behavior has been noted in a wide variety of special high-risk groups focusing on topics such as school truancy, classroom-management problems, repeated discipline violations, drug abuse, and runaways. In a caring, supportive environment such as that which develops in a counseling group, adolescents can move toward accepting greater self-responsibility and in turn encourage other members to do the same.

Example of a Psycho-Educational Group

One of the most exciting topic- or theme-oriented groups I (KAF) experienced was structured around adolescent male aggression that was occurring in one sixth-grade class. The project is described here as an example of how such groups can be organized. More detail of this group can be found in Fall and McMahon (2001).

Identified Group

Sixth-grade males struggling with aggression issues.

Rationale

Adolescent males face a wide range of social and psychological pressures, and, unfortunately, many do not take advantage of the counseling resources available in the school or community. The intersection between normal life stressors and a societal norm that forms an obstacle to boys discussing their problems creates a pressure-cooker effect on many boys. For some, the internal pressure is relieved through acts of aggression toward others. Garbarino (1999) concluded that accumulated risk factors combine to create a very real and frightening foundation for adolescent male violence and suicide. In light of these growing problems, ways to address these issues are desperately needed.

Group Membership

The group was a twelve-session group and met for an hour once a week during school hours. The facilitators experimented with several times over the course of two years with different groups. The first hour of the day (homeroom time) or lunch periods seemed to work best.

The largest challenge was balancing the intense nature of the group and creating an attraction to the group itself. The facilitators wanted to get the members who needed the group most into the group but did not want to make the group a punishment. To meet these goals, the leaders advertised the group through a one-page information and consent form. Boys who were referred by teachers were contacted on an individual basis and encouraged to participate. In each manifestation of group, the facilitators aimed for a heterogeneous group with regard to personality and current aggression level. The rationale was that boys who were struggling behaviorally and emotionally could learn from those who were not and vice versa.

Written consent was obtained from parents for permission to participate in the group. Each member also filled out a questionnaire that asked for responses to "What would you contribute to the group?" and "What do you envision group being like?" These questions were designed to give the members a sense that they had some responsibility in the group and were used in the screening process.

Topics for Discussion

The topics of this group were drawn from the literature on the issues related to adolescent male stress. The rationale was that aggression was just one way to deal with universal concerns. By dealing with the universal issues, all members in the group could be helped. The group was divided into four stages with each stage consisting of approximately three groups:

1. introduction and identity (orientation, who am I, and how others see me);
2. examining parental relationships;
3. skill building (accountability, trust, emotions, and communication); and
4. skill generalization/closure.

Although each stage had its own unique goals, the stages were sequenced so that the skills built as the group progressed.

Structure of Sessions

Each session began with a discussion of the homework and any questions that arose from the work outside of group. The homework discussion provided the segue into the day's topic, which was introduced through information presented by the leader, followed by group processing of the topic. Leaders facilitated personal application of the given topic through the group members sharing personal examples and experiencing the topic in the group (e.g., how trust develops in our group). Deeper aspects of the topic were explored through participation in an experiential activity, followed by processing and the introduction of the following week's homework.

Fall and McMahon (2001) emphasized that although the group had a structure designed to keep it on task, it was also important to keep the group flexible enough to honor the needs of the group on any given day. Flexibility helped build trust between members and leaders and group leaders could use spontaneous issues that were presented by group members and respectfully process and tie them into past, present, and future topics of the group.

Counseling Groups with Adolescents

Although most adolescent groups are psycho-educational in format, it is possible to conduct successful counseling groups for teens. Counseling groups focus on the interpersonal relationships formed as the group progresses and are less structured than psycho-educational groups. This requires that the group leader trust not only the group process but also the adolescents' ability to talk and process without the safety of activities or other learning aids. As with all counseling groups, the group leader will need to listen to the superficial connection of the group members and try to discern themes that will connect the members. The following is a "cheat sheet" list of common themes that appear in adolescent groups:

Trust

Trust is a universal theme that impacts all people. In the world of the adolescent, trust issues create anxiety in friendships and intimate relationships and with authority figures such as parents and teachers. Trust will also be a central issue of any group, so it is a natural connecting theme. Consider the following interchange:

ERIC: I guess I am losing the connection I used to have with my parents. I just have a hard time believing anything they say.

LEADER: It sounds like you are struggling with trusting them. I wonder if anyone else can relate to what Eric is saying about trust?

LINDSEY: Oh yeah! I mean, I don't trust anybody. It's just not worth it.

LEADER: Tell us more about "it's not worth it." What does trusting cost you?

LINDSEY: Everything! You trust and you get hurt. I have been in counseling forever. My last counselor, I saw for, like, two years, and then one day he was gone. No good-bye, just moved or something.

LEADER: So, someone that you thought was there for you just left you. That must have been confusing and painful.

LINDSEY: Yeah, but whatever. I don't really care.

LEADER: I think you do care, and it makes sense why you would. I am guessing you are wondering about this experience and whether or not you want to risk caring in this group.

LINDSEY: [*crying*] I am trying but it's scary and weird.

BOBBY: Yeah, it is scary. I am trying to figure out the same thing, but it seems we are all doing the same thing . . . trying to work it out, while being scared and careful.

Independence vs. Dependence

For most adolescents, life feels like existing with one foot in adulthood and the other foot in childhood. This tug of war is exacerbated by other relationships (parents, etc.) that pull and push the adolescent to one side or the other. The key with this theme is to get the adolescent to understand how the relationships are impacting them and their current goals. For example, it is common to find that several group members are behaving to counterbalance an external demand but find themselves in a place of discomfort. For example, consider the story of Gary:

GARY: There are things that I can do and my parents just don't think I can do them. It's like they want me to be eight again, so they treat me like a little kid. That pisses me off so much! I just want to prove to them that I can do it, but I struggle sometimes. The weird thing is that I can't ask for help. I'm afraid if I do, my mom will think I can't do anything and she'll be all over me. So, I just suffer alone. I will ask my friends for help, but sorry, y'all don't know any more than I do sometimes. So, I'm just stuck. Then I fail, or don't do as good as I could have and my parents are all over me anyway! It's like I can't win!

Identity Issues

Adolescence is a time when one's identity is coalescing, but is also impacted by a wide range of external influences. The teen's need to belong and connect creates a conflict between the desire to be accepted and the want to be oneself, especially when being oneself leads to social rejection. When a person feels they cannot be accepted by others by being oneself, many negative outcomes can result. This inter- and intrapersonal theme will often occur in the group as the group members confront the task of acceptance versus rejection very early in the group process. The following case dialogue illustrates some aspects of this theme.

LISA: I feel like sometimes I have to play dumb in order for certain guys to like me.

MARY: Well, maybe those guys aren't worth liking! [*Laughs.*]

LEADER: Perhaps, but I wonder what that's like . . . wanting to connect with someone, but feeling like you have to be something you are not?

SIDNEY: I think we all do that some of the time. To fit in, so you won't get made fun of.

BLAKE: Yeah, I sometimes wonder if some of my friends would like me if they knew the real me.

LEADER: Well, that's a great question. I guess part of it has to do with how much we risk to show people the real us. Do we really give them a chance?

MARY: Well, it can be dangerous to show too much. I think it just takes time.

LEADER: How is that happening right now? Look around the room and ask yourself, "Do these people really know the real me?" What are you doing in group to take that risk to let people know the real you?

Summary

Because of the developmental issue of peer pressure, perhaps no other age group needs group counseling more than adolescents. Socialization issues and self-awareness are key areas of focus and exploration by adolescents and, unlike children's groups, are dealt with primarily through verbal interaction. Insight and self-discovery are exciting adventures for adolescents, especially those adolescents who have poor self-concepts, unsatisfying social relationships, and poor impulse control. The group affords an excellent opportunity for adolescents to learn appropriate ways to express feelings, to accept responsibility for self, to discover they are not alone, to experience acceptance, and to discover they can give as well as receive help.

For many adolescents, this is a time of isolation and introversion, and a struggle for independence and a need for dependence. How confusing! There are pressures to conform on the one hand and admonishments on the other to be different, and accompanying this bewildering confusion is an overpowering need for approval. The setting is ripe for stress, and the inner process of struggle often bubbles over or just simply explodes. Counselors must be sensitive to this process and should be actively involved in providing group-counseling experiences for adolescents that will match the inner dynamics of their struggles with an equally dynamic process of therapeutic interaction.

References

Aronson, S., & Scheidlinger, S. (1996). Group therapy for adolescents. In *The Hatherleigh guide to child and adolescent therapy* (pp. 175–189). London and New York: Hatherleigh.

Ashby, J. S., Kottman, T., & DeGraaf, D. (2008). *Active interventions for kids and teens: Adding adventured and fun to counseling.* Alexandria, VA: American Counseling Association.

Attaway, K. (2010). *Potholes in my yard.* New York: AuthorHouse.

Belmont, J. A. (2006). *103 group activities and TIPS.* New York: Premiere Publishing.

Corder, B., Whiteside, L., & Haizlip, T. (1981). A study of the curative factors in group psychotherapy with adolescents. *International Journal of Group Psychotherapy, 31,* 345–354.

Eaves, S. H., & Sheperis, C. J. (2011). Special issues in group work with children and adolescents. In B. T. Erford (Ed.), *Group work: Process and applications* (pp. 263–276). New York: Pearson.

Garbarino, J. (1999). *Lost boys: Why our sons turn violent and how we can save them.* New York: Free Press.

Lowenstein, L. (2010). *Assessment and treatment activities for children, adolescents and families,* vol. II. New York: Champion Press.

Malott, K. M., Paone, T. R., Humphreys, K., & Martinez, T. (2010). Use of group counseling to address ethnic identity development: Application with adolescents of Mexican descent. *Professional School Counseling, 13,* 257–267.

Sanci, L. (2011). Clinical preventive services: Facing the challenge of proving "an ounce of prevention is worth a pound of cure." *Journal of Adolescent Health, 49,* 450–452.

Schectman, Z., & Mor, M. (2011). Groups for children and adolescents with trauma-related symptoms: Outcomes and processes. *International Journal of Group Psychotherapy, 60,* 221–244.

APPENDIX A

A PRIMER OF GROUP COUNSELING TERMINOLOGY

action exploration: Provides children in play therapy with materials and situations that demand exploration of others as well as themselves. Planned opportunities for children to test themselves in relation to social reality.

adjourning: Closing skills that can bring unity to the group and consolidate learning. Summary and evaluation.

adolescent groups: Help adolescents deal with age-related developmental issues such as status, sexual adjustment, fear of intimacy, and search for identity.

aging groups: Help older adults feel more in control of their lives. Typical issues include loneliness, social isolation, poverty, and feelings of loss, rejection, uselessness, helplessness, and hopelessness.

AIDS groups: Support for those impacted by the disease, including persons with AIDS (PWAs), their parents, and spouses or partners. Issues include the threat of early death, the unpredictability of the course of the disease, and stigmas related to the illness.

altruism: Behaviors that benefit others at some expense to the individual with no apparent personal gain as the primary intent of the action.

antitherapeutic defenses: Group collaborative avoidance resulting from group members constructing standards of behavior that dictate avoidance of real intimacy and closeness.

Association for Specialists in Group Work (ASGW): A division of the American Counseling Association. Provides leadership in training, credentialing, ethics, continuing education, and professionalization of group leaders.

authoritarian leadership style: Autocratic style of behavior with emphasis on leader power and authority. Decision making and goal setting by leader.

authority cycle: Conflict and issues of dominance and power. A dependency stage where the group's organizational roles emerge. How the group resolves this issue is related to leader personality.

autonomy: Self-determination or self-governance. Involves authenticity, independence, and freedom of action and motives that are one's own.

bridging: Techniques that may be used in group counseling to strengthen emotional connections between members.

charismatic leadership style: Characterized by self-confidence, active helping, directive interventions, a sense of moral righteousness, and an unquestioning willingness for followership from group members. Can be either a leadership asset or liability, and must be used judiciously by those who score high on personal charisma.

closed group: Membership that remains consistent throughout the life of the group and whose life span or termination date has most often been decided upon at the beginning of the group.

closure stage: Final stage of group development in which consolidation of learning and perspective are primary issues. Termination may also facilitate exploration of feelings about separation and loss.

coercion and pressure: Vaguely felt and sometimes unconscious influence causing members to discount their own beliefs and expectations in order to adapt to group circumstances or goals.

cognitive-restructuring groups: A rational behavior therapy based on the assumption that clinical disorders are the result of faulty thought patterns. The task of therapy is to identify these patterns and replace them with more adaptive cognitions.

cohesiveness: Emotional bonds based upon mutual attractiveness that bind a group together and govern a group's capacity to resist dissolution and outside threat.

coming-out groups: Groups for gay and lesbian individuals to assist them in dealing with issues arising from the process of acknowledging their sexual orientation to themselves or others.

commitment: An initial resolution of willingness to participate in the group experience, which later in the process may be enhanced by the promise of exploration, affiliation, and intimacy.

confidentiality: An administrative and emotional condition of privacy considered an essential prerequisite for the development of group trust, safety, cohesion, and productive closure.

conflict resolution: The ability to systematically deal with the emotional and behavioral turbulence that often accompanies differences in thoughts, feelings, or actions in the group.

confrontation: The process of identifying discrepancies in behavior without conveying disapproval or judgment. Often used to influence a member's avoidant processes.

congruence: Matching external behaviors and expressions with internal thoughts and feelings.

coping and skill-training groups: Teach step-by-step processes that develop skills to manage stressful situations effectively.

counterdependence: Active resistance to feelings of dependency often exhibited by members who perceive arbitrary authority and rigid rules within the group.

couples' groups: Groups of couples who may have similar relationship problems. Format may be an intensive weekend encounter or more traditional weekly meetings.

curative factors: Yalom posited twelve factors that operate in each therapy group. They are altruism, group cohesiveness, guidance, interpersonal learning, intrapersonal learning, universality, catharsis, family reenactment, self-understanding, identification, instillation of hope, and existential factors.

cutting off: Blocking or stopping damaging or nonproductive interaction using a direct approach in a manner that allows members not to feel discounted.

democratic leadership style: The leader reflects an egalitarian orientation and serves as a knowledgeable resource while helping to create a safe atmosphere for members to include themselves in the process of the group. Members share responsibility for setting goals and maintaining direction in the group.

development of belonging: A comfortable sense of personal ownership through a safe, close, and secure relationship with the group as a whole.

development of inclusion: Defines a person's group membership identity through the degree to which he or she becomes an active group member while maintaining personal autonomy and uniqueness.

drug and alcohol abuse groups: Persons who are addicted to a substance interact around themes of recovery including abstinence, relapse prevention, and other related topics.

ego states: According to transactional analysis, internalized sources of instinctual behavior distinguished by emotional childlike wanting, harsh parental demands, and an adult rational sense of purpose and logic. They reflect an internal pattern of experience consistent with a corresponding external pattern of behavior.

empowerment: A personal sense of right and place. Self-enablement of one's own authority and personhood.

encounter group: Associated with Carl Rogers, the therapy focuses on establishing intimate interactions in a present time orientation. Member feelings are valued, and intellectualization is discouraged.

enhancement stage: Members actively pursue change in their lives outside the group while continuing to utilize the support, pressure, and motivation of the group.

equitable treatment: Leadership characterized by justice, fairness, and impartiality. Leaders avoid favoritism, treat members equally and with respect, and allot time equitably.

Ethical Guidelines for Group Counselors: ASGW provides guidance for minimal standards of practice in the general areas of leader competence, informed consent, screening and orientation of members, preparation of members, voluntary participation, psychological risks, confidentiality, experimentation, research and recordings, member rights, leader values and expectations, time distribution and equal treatment, personal relationships, member independence and goal development, use of alcohol and drugs, and follow-up.

ethnic group: Members belonging to specific national, racial, or religious groups with the concomitant influence of the prevailing cultural beliefs, values, and mores.

fidelity: Involves faithfulness to obligations, duties, and responsibilities. Keeping promises.

follow-up: Generally involves keeping track of the progress of and providing needed services for former members. Special follow-up sessions might be planned to provide support, reinforcement, and closure.

forming: An initial or first developmental stage where members are dependent on each other and the leader while trying to define a personal place in the group. Individuals begin to come together and clarify the task of the group.

functional leadership: Helper who may not have a formal degree or credential but who possesses certain skills of a practical nature.

grief: An acute sense of despair over a loss. Survivors of loss who are allowed to undergo the social experience of grief often can receive external validation for their feelings.

group composition: Describes the makeup of people who belong to the group. They may be similar in some respect (homogeneous) or different (heterogeneous).

group counseling: Designed for individuals with normal developmental coping concerns. The group provides a safe structure for modifying attitudes and behaviors.

group guidance: An educational-informational, preventive, and growth-oriented emphasis that takes a proactive teaching and skill acquisition approach to the group.

group involvement stage: Typically the first stage of group development, where the issue of mutual trust is explored. Early content tends to be social and superficial. Power and group member influence are assigned, often unconsciously, whereas roles and norms emerge that eventually become the guiding ground rules for the group.

group maintenance behaviors: Actions aimed at preserving or strengthening the group.

group membership: Composition characteristics of the group that include age, gender, commonality of issues, and other personality and demographic features.

group methods: Procedures and processes emphasized in groups that provide support, caring, and confrontation through an interactive environment not available in individual counseling.

group norms: Implicit or explicit agreed-upon standards that govern behavior in the group.

group psychotherapy: Concerned with the treatment of severe psychological disorders, often with hospitalized inpatients. Leaders are trained to intervene with abnormal populations and focus upon correcting psychological problems that interfere with an individual's life functioning and with restructuring the personality.

group rules and limitations: Generally agreed-upon standards and rules that provide a minimal level of operating structure and enhance group process.

group screening: Process of selecting appropriate members into the group.

group therapy: Similar to group counseling in methods and procedures but tends to provide treatment that is more reconstructive and long term in dealing with more severe emotional problems.

here and now: To focus on the immediate experience of the moment by being aware of and genuine with one's relationship with self and the group.

heterogeneous groups: Relative dissimilarity in various demographic or characterological traits among group members that typically results in diversity in the membership.

hidden agendas: Private, covert, unconscious, or unacknowledged itineraries that are a routine expectation in group process but nevertheless interfere with stated tasks.

holism: A preventative, wellness approach to health that incorporates social, psychological, physical, and spiritual domains.

homogeneous groups: Membership based upon some commonality of issue, characterological traits, or any number of other similarities. Homogeneity often results in quicker cohesion and higher rates of attendance and commitment to the group.

human development and training groups: Frequently used in education and industry to increase productivity and efficiency. Early training models later expanded to include awareness, encounter, sensitivity, marathon, and other physical tactile groups. Gazda more recently structured training groups to deal with seven developmental life skills.

humanism: A set of beliefs, based upon Maslow's growth model and Rogers' person-centered principles, designed to achieve full human potential or self-actualization.

human potential movement: Stimulated by the work of Maslow, Rogers, Gibb, and others in the 1960s, group encounter was the keystone for what became somewhat of a cultural phenomenon. With a focus on authenticity and body contact, it engendered ethical concerns regarding leadership and other issues.

informed consent: A written document that provides the informational framework for counseling and seeks to protect the rights of clients to make fully apprised choices.

interdependence: A stage in group development where various subgroups, such as dependent and counterpersonal personalities, form a work alliance based upon the expectation of mutual benefit.

interpersonal therapy: Leader focus is on interactions and relationships that form in the group. Attention is paid primarily to the group as a whole, here-and-now ongoing group dynamics, and potential obstacles to effective group development.

irrational beliefs: Ideas that are perpetuated by a self-defeating belief system. According to Ellis, the founder of rational emotive theory, these faulty beliefs constitute the origin of emotional disturbances.

laissez-faire leadership style: Leader participates minimally while placing responsibility directly on the group itself. Although typically very passive, the leader may serve as a technical consultant offering process interpretations and assistance if requested.

leadership styles: The three major group leadership styles are authoritarian, democratic, and laissez-faire.

loss support groups: Specific issue groups originally organized for cancer or chronic disease patients but more recently expanded to include support for persons experiencing many different forms of abandonment and loss.

marathon group: A group that meets continuously for twenty-four hours or more, offering unremitting contact and fatigue that often produce lowered inhibitions and defense systems. Members are encouraged to risk going beyond masks and social façades to discover genuine aspects of self and to develop open, authentic, self-responsible behavior.

member roles: Behavioral positions that group members take for themselves in the group. They often resemble the characterizations either appropriated or assigned in the members' family of origin.

multicultural counseling: Groups with members from diverse ethnocultural backgrounds and orientations where the focus is upon understanding and accepting differences.

National Training Laboratories (NTL): Headquartered in Bethel, Maine. Sensitivity training (t-groups), which emphasized group process and interpersonal relations in promoting constructive social change, originated at the NTL in the 1940s.

norming: Process by which group members agree upon group rules that structure the operation of the group, protect the members, and promote individual and group growth.

open group: A group without a fixed or predetermined concluding date, which permits membership to vary during the course of the group.

parenting groups: Parents who meet to share insights into common concerns for the express purpose of helping children grow and thrive.

peer-help groups: A group of people of similar rank or ability with a peer or counterpart facilitator. These groups are most often found in school settings or among adolescents.

performing: A working stage of group development characterized by functional role relationships, goal directedness, and shared responsibility. The group is concerned with both task completion and process, honesty, and meeting individual emotional needs.

personal growth groups: Small groups of people interested in increasing self-knowledge through giving and receiving honest and empathic feedback in a safe and permissive group setting that tends to place emphasis upon feelings and direct experience rather than cognitions and intellect.

persons with AIDS (PWAs): People who have the human immunodeficiency virus (HIV) and have had opportunistic infection or a T cell count below 200.

phenomenological: How a person believes life to be from a purely personal point of view or perspective. An individual's subjective reality.

polarization: Group members representing sharply contradictory attitudes who coalesce at opposite extremes.

precommitment stage: Includes the early sequences of group development when the major tasks include resolution of purpose and boundary issues. Testing of group limits, avoidance, power alliances, and group roles are process issues that typically surface during this stage.

pre-group screening: Procedures used to select members of a group. Depending upon the type of group, screening can be used for inclusion/exclusion, balance, or determining the best mix of people to help create conditions for maximal functioning of the group.

problem-solving groups: Task groups organized to alleviate relevant problems. The process focuses upon goal attainment through strategic and rational interaction and plans.

process therapy: The primary approach to therapy is to study the mechanisms or dynamics of interactions in the group.

Professional Standards for Training of Group Workers: Training requirements adopted by the Council for Accreditation of Counseling and Related Education Programs (CACREP). A minimum core of cognitive and applied group leader competencies identified by the Association for Specialists in Group Work (ASGW) that serve as guidelines in graduate-level counselor-training programs.

psychodrama: A series of dramatic and expressive techniques developed by J. L. Moreno. With the use of a director (therapist), participants enact life situations that have emotional significance to them. Group members serve as fellow actors in the drama and as the audience. The protagonist is encouraged to freely express and discover a spontaneous self coupled with the courage to attempt new approaches to living.

psychotherapeutic groups: Membership usually is hospitalized psychiatric patients or outpatients with severe emotional difficulties. Leader focus is upon correcting psychological problems that interfere with an individual's life functioning and with restructuring the personality.

resistance: Reluctance of a member, or sometimes a coalition of members, to commit themselves fully to the therapeutic process. Resistances may be active or passive (avoidance, silence, or talking too much).

self-actualization: A humanistic principle that posits that individuals strive to grow and develop their talents and abilities to the fullest and to enhance the basic or true self.

self-disclosure: An unrehearsed sharing of a person's present experience. Usually a feeling, it may involve unexpected personal data (vertical) or a reaction to another member of the group (horizontal).

self-help groups: Individuals sharing similar issues who come together to provide mutual assistance and support, most often without a trained professional leader. Group leaders typically are persons who have "been there," and each member of the group is a potential future leader.

self-monitoring group: A group in which the members take personal responsibility for the depth of their own involvement in the process and also assume joint custodianship for the level of commitment from all other members.

sensitivity group: Brief, intensive structured programs designed to improve human relations skills, raise consciousness, and impact awareness of targeted issues. A humanistic form of group involvement that emphasizes improving relations with other people or groups.

short-term group therapy goals: Has an immediate objective to restore a functional level of behavior and to modify self-defeating actions.

silence: A potentially therapeutic period of time in the group process when no one is talking. Silences may be reflective and solution seeking or resistant and counterproductive.

social interest: A feeling of being part of a group's social identity; a need or willingness to contribute to the group's cultural advancement.

social support groups: Groups that attempt to offer a safe environment to practice new interpersonal strategies and behaviors and to enhance a person's ability to live a socially satisfying life.

solidarity: A sense of cohesiveness that develops among members with a common interest while developing a consistency of behavior for the purpose of attaining a mutual goal.

standardization: Norms that result from the various influences that the group exerts over its members.

storming: Stage in group therapy when anger and hostility, issues with authority, and group identity emerge.

strength bombardment: Group method of reinforcing the positive self-image of an individual by having a member list personal strengths followed by a recitation of the person's strong points as viewed by other group members. Negative feedback is discouraged during this activity.

survivors' groups: Groups composed of survivors of similar traumatic events that can provide mutual aid and social support networks.

task group: A group in which the primary goal is the completion of a specific behavior or task.

termination: The ending stage of a group. Major concerns involve summarizing, dealing with unfinished business, consolidating learning, and making sense of the group process.

t-groups: A specialized process approach to group work that focuses upon member transactions and behavior in the group as it struggles to create a productive organization.

therapeutic factors in groups: Dynamic forces in groups that permit insight to develop constructive changes in behavior. Some of the factors operating are empathy, trust and respect, hope, personal power, commitment to change, intimacy, self-disclosure, and freedom to experiment.

therapeutic groups: Groups whose major aim is to change behavior and/or attitudes of the members in an ongoing process.

transitions: Periods of time in the group process when a majority of the members are shifting from one developmental group stage to another.

unfinished business: May relate to incomplete issues between members or to general group process. It may represent unexpressed feelings such as resentment, rage, hurt, pain, anxiety, or guilt and grief that may persist and seek completion in the group.

universality: A mechanism that reduces interpersonal distance and loneliness as a person realizes that others share similar problems and life situations.

voluntary/involuntary: Refers to whether participation in the group is compulsory or mandated in some way as opposed to elective or freely chosen for some or all of the members.

APPENDIX B

ASGW BEST PRACTICE GUIDELINES

The Association for Specialists in Group Work (ASGW) is a division of the American Counseling Association whose members are interested in and specialize in group work. Group workers are defined as mental health professionals who use a group modality as an intervention when working with diverse populations. We value the creation of community while recognizing diverse perspectives; service to our members, clients, and the profession; and value leadership as a process to facilitate the growth and development of individuals and groups within their social and cultural contexts.

Preamble

The Association for Specialists in Group Work recognizes the commitment of its members to the Code of Ethics (as revised in 2005) of its parent organization, the American Counseling Association, and nothing in this document shall be construed to supplant that code.

These Best Practice Guidelines are intended to clarify the application of the ACA Code of Ethics to the field of group work by defining Group

Approved by the ASGW Executive Board, March 29, 1998. Prepared by: Lynn Rapin and Linda Keel; ASGW Ethics Committee Co-Chairs. Revised by: R. Valorie Thomas and Debra A. Pender; ASGW Ethics Committee Co-Chairs. Revisions Approved by the ASGW.

Executive Board, March 23, 2007.

Workers' responsibility and scope of practice involving those activities, strategies and interventions that are consistent and current with effective and appropriate professional ethical and community standards. ASGW views ethical process as being integral to group work and views Group Workers as ethical agents. Group Workers, by their very nature in being responsible and responsive to their group members, necessarily embrace a certain potential for ethical vulnerability.

It is incumbent upon Group Workers to give considerable attention to the intent and context of their actions because the attempts of Group Workers to influence human behavior through group work always have ethical implications. These Best Practice Guidelines address Group Workers' responsibilities in planning, performing and processing groups.

Section A: Best Practice in Planning

A.1. Professional Context and Regulatory Requirements

Group Workers actively know, understand and apply the ACA Code of Ethics (2005), the ASGW Professional Standards for the Training of Group Workers, these ASGW Best

Practice Guidelines, the ASGW diversity competencies, and the AMCD Multicultural Counseling

Competencies and Standards, relevant state laws, accreditation requirements, relevant National Board for Certified Counselors Codes and Standards, their organization's standards, and insurance requirements impacting the practice of group work.

A.2. Scope of Practice and Conceptual Framework

Group Workers define the scope of practice related to the core and specialization competencies defined in the ASGW Training Standards. Group Workers are aware of personal strengths and weaknesses in leading groups. Group Workers develop and are able to articulate a general conceptual framework to guide practice and a rationale for use of techniques that are to be used. Group Workers limit their practice to those areas for which they meet the training criteria established by the ASGW Training Standards.

A.3. Assessment

a. Assessment of self. Group Workers actively assess their knowledge and skills related to the specific group(s) offered. Group Workers assess their values, beliefs and theoretical orientation and how these impact upon the group, particularly when working with a diverse and multicultural population.

b. Ecological assessment. Group Workers assess community needs, agency or organization resources, sponsoring organization mission, staff competency, attitudes regarding group work, professional training levels of potential group leaders regarding group work; client attitudes regarding group work, and multicultural and diversity considerations.

Group Workers use this information as the basis for making decisions related to their group practice, or to the implementation of groups for which they have supervisory, evaluation, or oversight responsibilities.

A.4. Program Development and Evaluation

a. Group Workers identify the type(s) of group(s) to be offered and how they relate to community needs.

b. Group Workers concisely state in writing the purpose and goals of the group. Group Workers also identify the role of the group members in influencing or determining the group goals.

c. Group Workers set fees consistent with the organization's fee schedule, taking into consideration the financial status and locality of prospective group members.

d. Group Workers choose techniques and a leadership style appropriate to the type(s) of group(s) being offered.

e. Group Workers have an evaluation plan consistent with regulatory, organization and insurance requirements, where appropriate.

f. Group Workers take into consideration current professional guidelines when using technology, including but not limited to Internet communication.

A.5. Resources

Group Workers coordinate resources related to the kind of group(s) and group activities to be provided, such as: adequate funding; the appropriateness and availability of a trained co-leader; space and privacy requirements for the type(s) of group(s) being offered;

marketing and recruiting; and appropriate collaboration with other community agencies and organizations.

A.6. Professional Disclosure Statement

Group Workers maintain awareness and sensitivity regarding cultural meaning of confidentiality and privacy. Group Workers respect differing views towards disclosure of information. They have a professional disclosure statement which includes information on confidentiality and exceptions to confidentiality, theoretical orientation, information on the nature, purpose(s) and goals of the group, the group services that can be provided, the role and responsibility of group members and leaders, Group Workers qualifications to conduct the specific group(s), specific licenses, certifications and professional affiliations, and address of licensing/credentialing body.

A.7. Group and Member Preparation

a. Group Workers screen prospective group members if appropriate to the type of group being offered. When selection of group members is appropriate, Group Workers identify group members whose needs and goals are compatible with the goals of the group.

b. Group Workers facilitate informed consent. They communicate information in ways that are both developmentally and culturally appropriate. Group Workers provide in oral and written form to prospective members (when appropriate to group type): the professional disclosure statement; group purpose and goals; group participation expectations including voluntary and involuntary membership; role expectations of members and leader(s); policies related to entering and exiting the group; policies governing substance use; policies and procedures governing mandated groups (where relevant); documentation requirements; disclosure of information to others; implications of out-of-group contact or involvement among members; procedures for consultation between group leader(s) and group member(s); fees and time parameters; and potential impacts of group participation.

c. Group Workers obtain the appropriate consent/assent forms for work with minors and other dependent group members.

d. Group Workers define confidentiality and its limits (for example, legal and ethical exceptions and expectations; waivers implicit with treatment plans, documentation and insurance usage). Group Workers have the responsibility to inform all group participants of the need for confidentiality, potential consequences of breaching confidentiality and that legal privilege does not apply to group discussions (unless provided by state statute).

A.8. Professional Development

Group Workers recognize that professional growth is a continuous, ongoing, developmental process throughout their career.

a. Group Workers remain current and increase knowledge and skill competencies through activities such as continuing education, professional supervision, and participation in personal and professional development activities.

b. Group Workers seek consultation and/or supervision regarding ethical concerns that interfere with effective functioning as a group leader.

Supervisors have the responsibility to keep abreast of consultation, group theory, process, and adhere to related ethical guidelines.

c. Group Workers seek appropriate professional assistance for their own personal problems or conflicts that are likely to impair their professional judgment or work performance.

d. Group Workers seek consultation and supervision to ensure appropriate practice whenever working with a group for which all knowledge and skill competencies have not been achieved.

e. Group Workers keep abreast of group research and development.

A.9. Trends and Technological Changes

Group Workers are aware of and responsive to technological changes as they affect society, and the profession. These include but are not limited to changes in mental health delivery systems; legislative and insurance industry reforms; shifting population demographics and client needs; and technological advances in Internet and other communication devices and delivery systems. Group Workers adhere to ethical guidelines related to the use of developing technologies.

Section B: Best Practice in Performing

B.1. Self Knowledge

Group Workers are aware of and monitor their strengths and weaknesses and the effects these have on group members. They explore their own cultural identities and how these affect their values and beliefs about group work.

B.2. Group Competencies

Group Workers have a basic knowledge of groups and the principles of group dynamics, and are able to perform the core group competencies, as described in the ASGW Professional Standards for the Training of Group Workers (ASGW 2000). They gain knowledge, personal, personal awareness, sensitivity, and skills pertinent to working with a diverse client population. Additionally, Group Workers have adequate understanding and skill in any group specialty area chosen for practice (psychotherapy, counseling, task, psychoeducation, as described in the ASGW Training Standards).

B.3. Group Plan Adaptation

a. Group Workers apply and modify knowledge, skills and techniques appropriate to group type and stage, and to the unique needs of various cultural and ethnic groups.

b. Group Workers monitor the group's progress toward the group goals and plan.

c. Group Workers clearly define and maintain ethical, professional, and social relationship boundaries with group members as appropriate to their role in the organization and the type of group being offered.

B.4. Therapeutic Conditions and Dynamics

Group Workers understand and are able to implement appropriate models of group development, process observation and therapeutic conditions. Group Workers manage the flow of communication, addressing safety and pacing of disclosures to protect group members from physical, emotional, or psychological trauma.

B.5. Meaning

Group Workers assist members in generating meaning from the group experience.

B.6. Collaboration

Group Workers assist members in developing individual goals and respect group members as co-equal partners in the group experience.

B.7. Evaluation

Group Workers include evaluation (both formal and informal) between sessions and at the conclusion of the group.

B.8. Diversity

Group Workers practice with broad sensitivity to client differences including but not limited to ethnic, gender, religious, sexual, psychological maturity, economic class, family history, physical characteristics or limitations, and geographic location. Group Workers continuously seek information regarding the cultural issues of the diverse population with whom they are working both by interaction with participants and from using outside resources.

B.9. Ethical Surveillance

Group Workers employ an appropriate ethical decision making model in responding to ethical challenges and issues and in determining courses of action and behavior for self and group members. In addition, Group Workers employ applicable standards as promulgated by ACA, ASGW, or other appropriate professional organizations.

Section C: Best Practice in Group Processing

C.1. Processing Schedule

Group Workers process the workings of the group with themselves, group members, supervisors or other colleagues, as appropriate. This may include assessing progress on group and member goals, leader behaviors and techniques, group dynamics and interventions; developing understanding and acceptance of meaning. Processing may occur both within sessions and before and after each session, at time of termination, and later follow up, as appropriate.

C.2. Reflective Practice

Group Workers attend to opportunities to synthesize theory and practice and to incorporate learning outcomes into ongoing groups. Group Workers attend to session dynamics of members and their interactions and also attend to the relationship between session dynamics and leader values, cognition and affect.

C.3. Evaluation and Follow-Up

a. Group Workers evaluate process and outcomes. Results are used for ongoing program planning, improvement and revisions of current group and/or to contribute to professional research literature. Group Workers follow all applicable policies and standards in using group material for research and reports.

b. Group Workers conduct follow-up contact with group members, as appropriate, to assess outcomes or when requested by a group member(s).

C.4. Consultation and Training with Other Organizations

Group Workers provide consultation and training to organizations in and out of their setting, when appropriate. Group Workers seek out consultation as needed with competent professional persons knowledgeable about group work.

References

American Counseling Association (ACA). (2005). *ACA code of ethics.* Alexandria, VA: ACA.
Association for Specialists in Group Work (ASGW). (1998). ASGW best practice guidelines. *Journal for Specialists in Group Work, 23,* 237–244.
—— (2000). ASGW professional standards for the training of group workers. *Journal for Specialists in Group Work, 25,* 327–342.

APPENDIX C

ASGW PROFESSIONAL STANDARDS FOR THE TRAINING OF GROUP WORKERS

Revision Approved by the Executive Board, January 22, 2000
Prepared by F. Robert Wilson and Lynn S. Rapin, Co-Chairs, and Lynn Haley-Banez, Member, ASGW Standards Committee
Consultants: Robert K. Conyne and Donald E. Ward

Preamble

For nearly two decades, the Association for Specialists in Group Work (herein referred to as ASGW or as the Association) has promulgated professional standards for the training of group workers. In the early 1980s, the Association published the ASGW Training Standards for Group Counselors (1983) which established nine knowledge competencies, seventeen skill competencies, and clock-hour baselines for various aspects of supervised clinical experience in group counseling. The focus on group counseling embodied in these standards mirrored the general conception of the time that whatever counselors did with groups of individuals should properly be referred to as group counseling.

New ground was broken in the 1990 revision of the ASGW Professional Standards for the Training of Group Workers with (a) the articulation of the term, *group work*, to capture the variety of ways in which counselors work with groups, (b) differentiation of core training, deemed essential for all counselors, from specialization training required of those intending to engage in group work as part of their professional practice, and (c) the differentiation among four distinct group work specializations: task and work group facilitation, group psychoeducation, group counseling, and group psychotherapy. Over the ten years in which these standards have been in force, commentary and criticism has been elicited through discussion groups at various regional and national conferences and through published analyses in the Association's journal, the *Journal for Specialists in Group Work*.

In this Year-2000 revision of the ASGW Professional Standards for the Training of Group Workers, the foundation established by the 1990 training standards has been preserved and refined by application of feedback received through public discussion and scholarly debate. The Year-2000 revision maintains and strengthens the distinction between core and specialization training with requirements for core training and aspirational guidelines for specialization training. Further, the definitions of group work specializations have been expanded and clarified. Evenness of application of training standards across the specializations has been assured by creating a single set of guidelines for all four specializations with specialization specific detail being supplied where necessary. Consistent with both the pattern for training standards established by the Council for Accreditation of Counseling and Related Educational Programs accreditation standards and past editions of the ASGW training standards, the Year-2000 revision addresses both content and clinical instruction. Content instruction is described in terms of both course work requirements and knowledge objectives while clinical instruction is articulated in terms of experiential requirements and skill objectives. This revision of the training standards was informed by and profits from the seminal ASGW Best Practice Guidelines (1998) and the ASGW Principles for Diversity-Competent Group Workers (1999). Although each of these documents have their own form of organization, all address the group work elements of planning, performing, and processing and the ethical and diversity-competent treatment of participants in group activities.

Purpose

The purpose of the Professional Standards for the Training of Group Workers is to provide guidance to counselor training programs in the construction of their curricula for graduate programs in counseling (e.g., masters, specialist, and doctoral degrees and other forms of advanced graduate study). Specifically, core standards express the Association's view on the minimum training in group work all programs in counseling should provide for all graduates of their entry level, master's degree programs in counseling, and specialization standards provide a framework for documenting the training philosophy, objectives, curriculum, and outcomes for each declared specialization program.

Core Training in Group Work

All counselors should possess a set of core competencies in general group work. The Association for Specialists in Group Work advocates for the incorporation of core group work competencies as part of required entry level training in all counselor preparation programs. The Association's standards for core training are consistent with and provide further elaboration of the standards for accreditation of entry level counseling programs identified by the Council for Accreditation of Counseling and Related Educational Programs (CACREP 1994). Mastery of the core competencies detailed in the ASGW training standards will prepare the counselor to understand group process phenomena and to function more effectively in groups in which the counselor is a member. Mastery of basic knowledge and skill in group work provides a foundation which specialty training can extend but does not qualify one to independently practice any group work specialty.

Specialist Training in Group Work

The independent practice of group work requires training beyond core competencies. ASGW advocates that independent practitioners of group work must possess advanced competencies relevant to the particular kind of group work practice in which the group work student wants to specialize (e.g., facilitation of task groups, group psychoeducation, group counseling, or group psychotherapy). To encourage program creativity in development of specialization training, the specialization guidelines do not prescribe minimum trainee competencies. Rather, the guidelines establish a framework within which programs can develop unique training experiences utilizing scientific foundations and best practices to achieve their training objectives. In providing these guidelines for specialized training, ASGW makes no presumption that a graduate program in counseling must provide training in a group work specialization nor that adequate training in a specialization can be accomplished solely within a well-rounded master's degree program in counseling. To provide adequate specialization training, completion of post-master's options such as certificates of post-master's study or doctoral degrees may be required. Further, there is no presumption that an individual who may have received adequate training in a given declared specialization will be prepared to function effectively with all group situations in which the graduate may want to or be required to work. It is recognized that the characteristics of specific client populations and employment settings vary widely. Additional training beyond that which was acquired in a specific graduate program may be necessary for optimal, diversity-competent, group work practice with a given population in a given setting.

Definitions

Group Work: is a broad professional practice involving the application of knowledge and skill in group facilitation to assist an interdependent collection of people to reach their mutual goals which may be intrapersonal, interpersonal, or work-related. The goals of the group may include the accomplishment of tasks related to work, education, personal development, personal and interpersonal problem solving, or remediation of mental and emotional disorders.

Core Training in Group Work: includes knowledge, skills, and experiences deemed necessary for general competency for all master's degree prepared counselors. ASGW advocates for all counselor preparation programs to provide core training in group work regardless of whether the program intends to prepare trainees for independent practice in a group work specialization. Core training in group work is considered a necessary prerequisite for advanced practice in group work.

Specialization Training in Group Work: includes knowledge, skills, and experiences deemed necessary for counselors to engage in independent practice of group work. Four areas of advanced practice, referred to as specializations, are identified: Task Group Facilitation, Group Psychoeducation, Group Counseling, and Group Psychotherapy. This list is not presumed to be exhaustive and while there may be no sharp boundaries between the specializations, each has recognizable characteristics that have professional utility. The definitions for these group work specializations have been built upon the American Counseling Association's model definition of counseling (adopted by the ACA Governing Council in 1997), describing the methods typical of the working stage of the group being defined and the typical purposes to which those methods are put and the typical populations served by those methods. Specialized training presumes mastery of prerequisite core knowledge, skills, and experiences.

Specialization in Task and Work Group Facilitation: The application of principles of normal human development and functioning through group based educational, developmental, and systemic strategies applied in the context of here-and-now interaction that promote efficient and effective accomplishment of group tasks among people who are gathered to accomplish group task goals.

Specialization in Psychoeducation Group Leadership: The application of principles of normal human development and functioning through group based educational and developmental strategies applied in the context of here-and-now interaction that promote personal and interpersonal growth and development and the prevention of future difficulties among people who may be at risk for the development of personal or interpersonal problems or who seek enhancement of personal qualities and abilities.

Specialization in Group Counseling: The application of principles of normal human development and functioning through group based cognitive, affective, behavioral, or systemic intervention strategies applied in the context of here-and-now interaction that address personal and interpersonal problems of living and promote personal and interpersonal growth and development among people who may be experiencing transitory maladjustment, who are at risk for the development of personal or interpersonal problems, or who seek enhancement of personal qualities and abilities.

Specialization in Group Psychotherapy: The application of principles of normal and abnormal human development and functioning through group based cognitive, affective, behavioral, or systemic intervention strategies applied in the context of negative emotional arousal that address personal and interpersonal problems of living, remediate perceptual and cognitive distortions or repetitive patterns of dysfunctional behavior, and promote personal and interpersonal growth and development among people who may be experiencing severe and/or chronic maladjustment.

Core Training Standards

I. Coursework and Experiential Requirements

Coursework Requirements

Core training shall include at least one graduate course in group work that addresses such as but not limited to scope of practice, types of group work, group development, group process and dynamics, group leadership, and standards of training and practice for group workers.

Experiential Requirements

Core training shall include a minimum of ten clock hours (twenty clock hours recommended) observation of and participation in a group experience as a group member and/or as a group leader.

II. Knowledge and Skill Objectives

A. Nature and Scope of Practice

1. *Knowledge Objectives.* Identify and describe:

a.   the nature of group work and the various specializations within group work
b.   theories of group work including commonalties and distinguishing characteristics among the various specializations within group work
c.   research literature pertinent to group work and its specializations

2. *Skill Objectives.* Demonstrate skill in:

a.   preparing a professional disclosure statement for practice in a chosen area of specialization
b.   applying theoretical concepts and scientific findings to the design of a group and the interpretation of personal experiences in a group

B. Assessment of Group Members and the Social Systems in which they Live and Work

1. *Knowledge Objectives.* Identify and describe:

a.   principles of assessment of group functioning in group work
b.   use of personal contextual factors (e.g., family-of-origin, neighborhood-of-residence, organizational membership, cultural membership) in interpreting behavior of members in a group

2. *Skill Objectives.* Demonstrate skill in:

a. observing and identifying group process
b. observing the personal characteristics of individual members in a group
c. developing hypotheses about the behavior of group members
d. employing contextual factors (e.g., family of origin, neighborhood of residence, organizational membership, cultural membership) in interpretation of individual and group data

C. Planning Group Interventions

1. *Knowledge Objectives.* Identify and describe:

a. environmental contexts, which affect planning for, group interventions
b. the impact of group member diversity (e.g., gender, culture, learning style, group climate preference) on group member behavior and group process and dynamics in group work
c. principles of planning for group work

2. *Skill Objectives.* Demonstrate skill in:

a. collaborative consultation with targeted populations to enhance ecological validity of planned group interventions
b. planning for a group work activity including such aspects as developing overarching purpose, establishing goals and objectives, detailing methods to be used in achieving goals and objectives, determining methods for outcome assessment, and verifying ecological validity of plan

D. Implementation of Group Interventions

1. *Knowledge Objectives.* Identify and describe:

a. principles of group formation including recruiting, screening, and selecting group members
b. principles for effective performance of group leadership functions
c. therapeutic factors within group work and when group work approaches are indicated and contraindicated
d. principles of group dynamics including group process components, developmental stage theories, group member roles, group member behaviors

2. *Skill Objectives.* Demonstrate skill in:

a. encouraging participation of group members
b. attending to, describing, acknowledging, confronting, understanding, and responding empathically to group member behavior
c. attending to, acknowledging, clarifying, summarizing, confronting, and responding empathically to group member statements
d. attending to, acknowledging, clarifying, summarizing, confronting, and responding empathically to group themes
e. eliciting information from and imparting information to group members

f.   providing appropriate self-disclosure
g.   maintaining group focus; keeping a group on task
h.   giving and receiving feedback in a group setting

E. Leadership and Co-Leadership

1. *Knowledge Objectives.* Identify and describe:

a.   group leadership styles and approaches
b.   group work methods including group worker orientations and specialized group leadership behaviors
c.   principles of collaborative group processing

2. *Skill Objectives.* To the extent opportunities for leadership or co-leadership are provided, demonstrate skill in:

a.   engaging in reflective evaluation of one's personal leadership style and approach
b.   working cooperatively with a co-leader and/or group members
c.   engaging in collaborative group processing.

F. Evaluation

1. *Knowledge Objectives.* Identify and describe:

a.   methods for evaluating group process in group work
b.   methods for evaluating outcomes in group work

2. *Skill Objectives.* Demonstrate skill in:

a.   contributing to evaluation activities during group participation
b.   engaging in self-evaluation of personally selected performance goals

G. Ethical Practice, Best Practice, Diversity-Competent Practice

1. *Knowledge Objectives.* Identify and describe:

a.   ethical considerations unique to group work
b.   best practices in group work
c.   diversity competent group work

2. *Skill Objectives.* Demonstrate skill in:

a.   evidencing ethical practice in planning, observing, and participating in group activities
b.   evidencing best practice in planning, observing, and participating in group activities
c.   evidencing diversity-competent practice in planning, observing, and participating in group activities

Specialization Guidelines

I. Overarching Program Characteristics

A. The program has a clearly specified philosophy of training for the preparation of specialists for independent practice of group work in one of the forms of group work recognized by the Association (i.e. task and work group facilitation, group psychoeducation, group counseling, or group psychotherapy).

1. The program states an explicit intent to train group workers in one or more of the group work specializations.
2. The program states an explicit philosophy of training, based on the science of group work, by which it intends to prepare students for independent practice in the declared specialization(s).

B. For each declared specialization, the program specifies education and training objectives in terms of the competencies expected of students completing the specialization training. These competencies are consistent with

1. the program's philosophy and training model,
2. the substantive area(s) relevant for best practice of the declared specialization area, and
3. standards for competent, ethical, and diversity sensitive practice of group work

C. For each declared specialization, the program specifies a sequential, cumulative curriculum, expanding in breadth and depth, and designed to prepare students for independent practice of the specialization and relevant credentialing.

D. For each declared specialization, the program documents achievement of training objectives in terms of student competencies.

II. Recommended Coursework and Experience

A. *Coursework.* Specialization training may include coursework which provide the student with a broad foundation in the group work domain in which the student seeks specialized training:

1. *Task/Work Group Facilitation:* coursework includes but is not limited to organizational development, management, and consultation, theory and practice of task/work group facilitation
2. *Group Psychoeducation:* coursework includes but is not limited to organizational development, school and community counseling/psychology, health promotion, marketing, program development and evaluation, organizational consultation, theory and practice of group psychoeducation
3. *Group Counseling:* coursework includes but is not limited to normal human development, health promotion, theory and practice of group counseling
4. *Group Psychotherapy:* coursework includes but is not be limited to normal and abnormal human development, assessment and diagnosis of mental and emotional disorders, treatment of psychopathology, theory and practice of group psychotherapy

B. *Experience.* **Specialization training includes**

1. *Task/Work Group Facilitation:* a minimum of thirty clock hours (forty-five clock hours recommended) supervised practice facilitating or conducting an intervention with a task or work group appropriate to the age and clientele of the group leader's specialty area (e.g., school counseling, student development counseling, community counseling, mental health counseling)
2. *Group Psychoeducation:* a minimum of thirty clock hours (forty-five clock hours recommended) supervised practice conducting a psychoeducation group appropriate to the age and clientele of the group leader's specialty area (e.g., school counseling, student development counseling, community counseling, mental health counseling)
3. *Group Counseling:* a minimum of forty-five clock hours (sixty clock hours recommended) supervised practice conducting a counseling group appropriate to the age and clientele of the group leader's specialty area (e.g., school counseling, student development counseling, community counseling, mental health counseling)
4. *Group Psychotherapy:* a minimum of forty-five clock hours (sixty clock hours recommended) supervised practice conducting a psychotherapy group appropriate to the age and clientele of the group leader's specialty area (e.g., mental health counseling)

III. Knowledge and Skill Elements

In achieving its objectives, the program has and implements a clear and coherent curriculum plan that provides the means whereby all students can acquire and demonstrate substantial understanding of and competence in the following areas:

A. Nature and Scope of Practice

The program states a clear expectation that its students will limit their independent practice of group work to those specialization areas for which they have been appropriately trained and supervised.

B. Assessment of Group Members and the Social Systems in Which they Live and Work

All graduates of specialization training will understand and demonstrate competence in the use of assessment instruments and methodologies for assessing individual group member characteristics and group development, group dynamics, and process phenomena relevant for the program's declared specialization area(s). Studies should include but are not limited to:

1. methods of screening and assessment of populations, groups, and individual members who are or may be targeted for intervention
2. methods for observation of group member behavior during group interventions
3. methods of assessment of group development, process, and outcomes

C. Planning Group Interventions

All graduates of specialization training will understand and demonstrate competence in planning group interventions consistent with the program's declared specialization area(s). Studies should include but are not limited to:

1. establishing the overarching purpose for the intervention
2. identifying goals and objectives for the intervention
3. detailing methods to be employed in achieving goals and objectives during the intervention
4. selecting methods for examining group process during group meetings, between group sessions, and at the completion of the group intervention
5. preparing methods for helping members derive meaning from their within-group experiences and transfer within-group learning to real-world circumstances
6. determining methods for measuring outcomes during and following the intervention
7. verifying ecological validity of plans for the intervention

D. Implementation of Group Interventions

All graduates of specialization training will understand and demonstrate competence in implementing group interventions consistent with the program's declared specialization area(s). Studies should include but are not limited to:

1. principles of group formation including recruiting, screening, selection, and orientation of group members
2. standard methods and procedures for group facilitation
3. selection and use of referral sources appropriate to the declared specialization
4. identifying and responding constructively to extra-group factors which may influence the success of interventions
5. applying the major strategies, techniques, and procedures
6. adjusting group pacing relative to the stage of group development
7. identifying and responding constructively to critical incidents
8. identifying and responding constructively to disruptive members
9. helping group members attribute meaning to and integrate and apply learning
10. responding constructively to psychological emergencies
11. involving group members in group session processing and on-going planning

E. Leadership and Co-Leadership

All graduates of specialization training will understand and demonstrate competence in pursuing personal competence as a leader and in selecting and managing the interpersonal relationship with a co-leader for group interventions consistent with the program's declared specialization area(s). Studies should include but are not limited to:

1. characteristics and skills of effective leaders
2. relationship skills required of effective co-leaders
3. processing skills required of effective co-leaders.

F. Evaluation

All graduates of specialization training will understand and demonstrate competence in evaluating group interventions consistent with the program's declared specialization area(s). Studies should include but are not limited to methods for evaluating participant outcomes and participant satisfaction.

G. Ethical Practice, Best Practice, Diversity-Competent Practice

All graduates of specialization training will understand and demonstrate consistent effort to comply with principles of ethical, best practice, and diversity-competent practice of group work consistent with the program's declared specialization area(s). Studies should include but are not limited to:

1. ethical considerations unique to the program's declared specialization area
2. best practices for group work within the program's declared specialization area
3. diversity issues unique to the program's declared specialization area

Implementation Guidelines

Implementation of the Professional Standards for the Training of Group Workers requires a commitment by a program's faculty and a dedication of program resources to achieve excellence in preparing all counselors at core competency level and in preparing counselors for independent practice of group work. To facilitate implementation of the training standards, the Association offers the following guidelines.

Core Training in Group Work

Core training in group work can be provided through a single, basic course in group theory and process. This course should include the elements of content instruction detailed below and may also include the required clinical instruction component.

Content Instruction

Consistent with accreditation standards (CACREP 1994; Standard II. J.4), study in the area of group work should provide an understanding of the types of group work (e.g., facilitation of task groups, psychoeducation groups, counseling groups, psychotherapy groups); group development, group dynamics, and group leadership styles; and group leadership methods and skills. More explicitly, studies should include, but not be limited to the following:

*   principles of group dynamics including group process components, developmental stage theories, and group member's roles and behaviors;
*   group leadership styles and approaches including characteristics of various types of group leaders and leadership styles;
*   theories of group counseling including commonalties, distinguishing characteristics, and pertinent research and literature;
*   group work methods including group leader orientations and behaviors, ethical standards, appropriate selection criteria and methods, and methods of evaluating effectiveness;
*   approaches used for other types of group work, including task groups, prevention groups, support groups, and therapy groups; and,
*   skills in observing member behavior and group process, empathic responding, confronting, self-disclosing, focusing, protecting, recruiting and selecting members, opening and closing sessions, managing, explicit and implicit teaching, modeling, giving and receiving feedback.

Clinical Instruction

Core group work training requires a minimum of ten clock hours of supervised practice (20 clock hours of supervised practice is recommended). Consistent with CACREP standards for accreditation, the supervised experience provides the student with direct experiences as a participant in a small group, and may be met either in the basic course in group theory and practice or in a specially conducted small group designed for the purpose of meeting this standard. (CACREP 1994; Standard II. D). In arranging for and conducting this group experience, care must be taken by program faculty to assure that the ACA ethical standard for dual relationships and ASGW standards for best practice are observed.

Specialist Training in Group Work

Though ASGW advocates that all counselor training programs provide all counseling students with core group work training, specialization training is elective. If a counselor training program chooses to offer specialization training (e.g., task group facilitation, group psychoeducation, group counseling, group psychotherapy), ASGW urges institutions to develop their curricula consistent with the ASGW standards for that specialization.

Content Instruction

Each area of specialization has its literature. In addition to basic course work in group theory and process, each specialization requires additional coursework providing specialized knowledge necessary for professional application of the specialization:

- **Task Group Facilitation**: course work in such areas as organization development, consultation, management, or sociology so students gain a basic understanding of organizations and how task groups function within them.
- **Group Psychoeducation**: course work in community psychology, consultation, health promotion, marketing, curriculum design to prepare students to conduct structured consciousness raising and skill training groups in such areas as stress management, wellness, anger control and assertiveness training, problem solving.
- **Group Counseling**: course work in normal human development, family development and family counseling, assessment and problem identification of problems in living, individual counseling, and group counseling, including training experiences in personal growth or counseling group.
- **Group Psychotherapy**: coursework in abnormal human development, family pathology and family therapy, assessment and diagnosis of mental and emotional disorders, individual therapy, and group therapy, including training experiences in a therapy group.

Clinical Instruction

For Task Group Facilitation and Group Psychoeducation, group specialization training recommends a minimum of thirty clock hours of supervised practice (45 clock hours of supervised practice is strongly suggested). Because of the additional difficulties presented by Group Counseling and Group Psychotherapy, a minimum of forty-five clock hours of supervised practice is recommended (60 clock hours of supervised practice is strongly suggested). Consistent with CACREP standards for accreditation, supervised experience should provide an opportunity for the student to perform under supervision a variety of activities that a professional counselor would perform in conducting group work consistent with a given specialization (i.e. assessment of group members and the social systems in which they live and work, planning group interventions, implementing group interventions, leadership and co-leadership, and within-group, between-group, and end-of-group processing and evaluation).

In addition to courses offering content and experience related to a given specialization, supervised clinical experience should be obtained in practica and internship experiences. Following the model provided by CACREP for master's practica, we recommend that one quarter of all required supervised clinical experience be devoted to group work:

- **Master's Practicum**: At least ten clock hours of the required forty clock hours of direct service should be spent in supervised leadership or co-leadership experience in group work, typically in Task Group Facilitation, Group Psychoeducation, or Group Counseling (at the master's practicum level, experience in Group Psychotherapy would be unusual) (CACREP 1994; Standard III. H.1).
- **Master's Internship**: At least sixty clock hours of the required 240 clock hours of direct services should be spent in supervised leadership or co-leadership in group work consistent with the program's specialization offering(s) (i.e. in Task Group Facilitation, Group Psychoeducation, Group Counseling, or Group Psychotherapy).
- **Doctoral Internship**: At least 150 clock hours of the required 600 clock hours of direct service should be spent in supervised leadership or co-leadership in group work consistent with the program's specialization offering(s) (i.e. in Task Group Facilitation, Group Psychoeducation, Group Counseling, or Group Psychotherapy).

References

Association for Specialists in Group Work (1983). *ASGW professional standards for group counseling.* Alexandria, VA: Association for Specialists in Group Work.

—— (1990). *Professional standards for the training of group workers.* Alexandria, VA: Association for Specialists in Group Work.

—— (1998). ASGW best practice guidelines. *Journal for Specialists in Group Work,* 23, 237–244.

—— (1999). ASGW principles for diversity-competent group workers. *Journal for Specialists in Group Work,* 24, 7–14.

Council for Accreditation of Counseling and Related Educational Programs (CACREP) (1994). *CACREP accreditation standards and procedures.*

APPENDIX D

ASSESSMENT OF GROUP COUNSELORS' COMPETENCIES

Goal Statement

The professional counselor possesses the personality characteristics, knowledge, and skills required of the effective helper; complies with ethical standards; as appropriate to his or her credentials, is able to discern when individual or group counseling would be most helpful; understands basic principles of group dynamics; and is familiar with major group theories, stages of group development, group member roles, and research related to group counseling.

Group Counseling Competencies	Performance Guidelines		Assessment				
The Counselor Is a Skilled Professional Who Is Able to Do the Following:	The Professional Counselor Provides Evidence of Competence by Demonstrating the Ability to Do the Following:		*Low* 1	2	*Average* 3	4	*High* 5
Discern when individual or group counseling would be most helpful for the problem presented and for the client. (This implies recognition of referral responsibility when appropriate.)	1.1	Specify the types of problems that are particularly suited to group or individual counseling.					
	1.2	Structure specialized groups as to topic and purpose as well as membership.					
	1.3	Specify the effectiveness of both peer and traditional models on individual behavior.					
	1.4	Coordinate and sequence a client's participation in both individual and group counseling sessions.					
	1.5	Explain how the power of groups can be both advantageous and disadvantageous to members.					
Use principles of group dynamics and group therapeutic conditions in various group activities that facilitate attitude and behavior change appropriate to the age level of the client.	2.1	Display a working knowledge of group dynamics, such as					
	2.1a	content and process variables,					
	2.1b	various leadership styles, and					
	2.1c	the conditions under which groups promote healthy growth.					
	2.2	Display a working knowledge of developmental tasks and coping behaviors of different age levels and the skill to use various group techniques appropriate for client level, including					
	2.2a	play and activity groups,					

Group Counseling Competencies	*Performance Guidelines*	*Assessment*				
		Low 1	2	*Average* 3	4	*High* 5

	2.2b	modeling–social learning techniques, and
	2.2c	role playing and psychodrama.
	2.3	Observe and record verbal and nonverbal interaction in groups, following predetermined cues and procedures for making such observations.
	2.3a	Use the anecdotal method of observation and recording to report the significant components of individual and group interaction.
	2.3b	Chart group interaction through the use of an appropriate interaction tool.
	2.3c	Rate the initiative and responsive dimensions of group interaction.
	2.3d	Record the operant level, and chart baseline data on selected behaviors as they emerge in the group (various physical phenomena, hostile statements, etc.).
Demonstrate a familiarity with the unique characteristics of at least three of the major group theories and the persons associated with their development.	3.1	Communicate and use appropriate and consistent methodologies included in at least three of the following group theories:
	3.1a	Adlerian psychology,
	3.1b	behavioral group counseling,
	3.1c	Gestalt group therapy,
	3.1d	group psychodrama,
	3.1e	human resource development training,
	3.1f	person-centered group therapy,
	3.1g	rational-emotive therapy,
	3.1h	reality therapy,
	3.1i	transactional analysis,
	3.1j	family therapy groups, and
	3.1k	addiction or recovery groups.
Demonstrate a familiarity with the history of group work and the important individuals and organizations who have contributed to its growth, such as	4.1a	J. H. Pratt,
	4.1b	Alfred Adler,
	4.1c	J. L. Moreno,
	4.1d	S. R. Slavson,
	4.1e	C. R. Rogers,
	4.1f	National Training Laboratory,
	4.1g	the human potential movement,
	4.1h	Fritz Perls,
	4.1i	Merle M. Ohlsen,
	4.1j	G. G. Kemp,
	4.1k	G. M. Gazda, and
	4.11	I. D. Yalom.
Demonstrate competence in dealing with terms specific to discriminating among the various kinds of group activities.	5.1	Adequately define and explain the differences in orientation, methodology, procedures, leadership qualifications, and client population associated with
	5.1a	group guidance,

Group Counseling Competencies	Performance Guidelines	Assessment				
		Low		*Average*		*High*
		1	2	3	4	5

	5.1b	group counseling,
	5.1c	group psychotherapy, and
	5.1d	human relations training.
	5.2	Display a functional knowledge of the following terms and concepts and their application to groups:
	5.2a	Group dynamics
	5.2b	T-groups
	5.2c	Psychodrama
	5.2d	Open and closed groups
	5.2e	Self-help and support groups
	5.2f	Specific issue groups
	5.2g	Procedural rules for groups
	5.2h	Process analysis
Communicate familiarity with a number of group growth and intervention systems, and advise as to the appropriate group activity.	6.1	Function as a member or leader in the following kinds of group experiences:
	6.1a	An encounter group
	6.1b	A family therapy group
	6.1c	A play therapy or an activity therapy group
	6.2	Co-lead ongoing group sessions in conjunction with an instructor, supervisor, or selected colleague.
	6.3	Describe and/or experience various specialized methods and techniques in group counseling, such as
	6.3a	critique of group tapes by self or others,
	6.3b	focused feedback,
	6.3c	observation of group counseling (live or taped),
	6.3d	systematic desensitization,
	6.3e	psychodrama,
	6.3f	modeling,
	6.3g	role playing,
	6.3h	extended sessions or marathon groups, and
	6.3i	issue group specific to the counselor's expertise such as stress management groups, assertiveness groups, and team-building groups.
Demonstrate a familiarity with the typical stages of groups and appropriate intervention strategies and leader behaviors.	7.1	Organize and prepare for a group, and get the initial group started.
	7.2	Explain the beginning stages of a group.
	7.3	Explain the working stages.
	7.4	Explain the ending stages and termination procedures.
Indicate an awareness of the most frequently observed facilitative and debilitative roles that group members may	8.1	Describe and work with
	8.1a	the compulsive talker or monopolizing member,
	8.1b	the silent member,
	8.1c	the group clown,

Group Counseling Competencies	*Performance Guidelines*	*Assessment*				
		Low 1	2	*Average* 3	4	*High* 5

Group Counseling Competencies	*Performance Guidelines*
take, along with relevant management strategies.	8.1d the intellectualizer, 8.1e the rescuer, 8.1f the attacker, 8.1g the alienated member, 8.1h the withdrawn member, 8.1i the overly dependent member, and 8.1j the member who gives inappropriate advice.
Be conversant with the body of research related to group counseling, both landmark and current, particularly as it relates to one's area of specialty.	9.1 Stay current with professional literature in areas such as 9.1a school counseling, 9.1b student development work, 9.1c community agencies, 9.1d mental health facilities, and 9.1e specific issue groups such as groups for depression, AIDS, eating disorders, and chemical abuse and other addictions.
Demonstrate personal behaviors and a sensitivity to issues that indicate an appreciation of ethical practices in group work.	10.1 This is related critically to specific professional guidelines that address ethics in group work, such as 10.1a providing information and orienting new group members; 10.1b screening potential group members; 10.1c maintaining confidentiality; 10.1d working with voluntary or involuntary participants; 10.1e having procedures for leaving the group; 10.1f protecting group members against undue coercion and pressure, intimidation, and physical threats; 10.1g imposing counselor values on group members; 10.1h treating each group member equitably and equally; 10.1i avoiding dual relationships; 10.1j using group techniques in which the leader is not trained; 10.1k consulting with members and other professionals between group meetings; 10.1l terminating the group; 10.1m conducting evaluation and follow-up procedures; 10.1n managing referral to other appropriate professionals; and 10.1o continuing the leader's professional development.

APPENDIX E

TYPICAL ISSUES IN GROUP COUNSELING

Questions and Answers about Common Group Issues

The following edited protocol involves us sharing our personal, clinical insights into a number of group issues with a group of graduate students in group counseling.

Question: Dr. Landreth, what differences do you see between the role of the counselor in a group setting and a counselor in an individual setting?

Landreth: That's a good question to start with. It is basic to what we do in group counseling and one that I have pondered for myself. First, let me focus on myself. I see myself being different in a group. I am not sure just why I am. Some of the same basic skills are necessary in both settings, but I feel more personally free in the group, free to express myself, free to risk in some areas that I would never risk in or have not in individual counseling. Take touching, for instance. I cannot recall having touched a client in the middle of an individual counseling session. Although I have felt an inclination to do that, I'm not sure just why I haven't. But in group counseling, I do feel more comfortable in getting up and going across the circle and hugging a group member and have done that. Not that I do that in every session, but I have done that in some.

Berg: In addition to the personal freedom that Garry is talking about, the group leader needs to be aware of several more dimensions than is required of an individual counselor. The group leader takes some responsibility for the entire group as well as the individual of focus. That requires a special kind of attending and a certain knowledge about groups of people and how they respond to one another. The leader should be aware of the impact of an individual's disclosure on other members of the group and how they might respond. The group leader can't be completely responsible for all of those things, but being aware of them is important. In a group, there's always a lot going on at any specific time.

Fall: The biggest difference I notice is the way I process information and connect with the client. In individual [counseling], the connection is between me and the client. For example, if you are spinning plates, in individual counseling, there is only one plate to spin and the only one facilitating the spinning is the counselor. In group, there are many plates [members], and I have to focus on the speed and balance of each plate in order to maintain the process. In group [counseling], another dynamic takes place, that being the influence of the members on one another's growth. In individual, the counselor is the primary change agent. In group, the leader must be skilled at incorporating all the members into the push for change.

Landreth: One of the things I have noticed that's different about me in group counseling is that in individual counseling, I'm very conscious of the member's feelings right off and have a tendency to respond most to these feelings, whereas in the first session of group counseling, my tendency is to react more to the interactions that are occurring, helping members to get in, and linking members together. So, as a result of that, I'm sure I spend less of my time in the first session focusing on individual feelings, although I have a natural inclination to do that. I have noticed as we have worked together, Bob, you spend more time initially focusing on the individual, and I spend more time helping the members to engage in the interaction process.

Berg: That may not be a function of individual style as much as it may be you and I working together. I think that over the twenty-some years that you and I have been leading groups together, we have come to know each other, what to expect from each other, and the result is a natural balance.

Question: Why do so many successful, well-trained individual counselors find it difficult to make the transition to group work?

Berg: My speculation is that many good individual therapists do not always feel comfortable in a group setting, and one of the reasons for that may be that they haven't had enough experience in a group. Group settings are more difficult to control than individual settings, and whether we like it or not, therapists like to be in control. Also, therapists who chose to do group work tend to be slightly more expressive, risk-taking personalities.

Fall: I was "well trained" in group and had difficulty getting motivated to set up groups in my practice setting. The primary obstacle for me was that groups seem to be more difficult to create than making individual client appointments. With group, there is more planning, marketing, and finding a good time and enough clients to make the group. The logistical barrier was huge for me. However, once I got started, I found groups to be much easier to maintain than individual clients.

Landreth: Some counselors are just not comfortable in a group setting. That's also true of members. Not everyone should be in group. Some people work better as a client in individual counseling. The same holds true for counselors. Some counselors work better with individuals than with groups. I think one possible reason for this has to do with the dimension of risk. If the counselor has very little need for control, that person is probably more tolerant of ambiguity and will have less need to know exactly where the group is going and how the experience is going to end. That kind of person will probably be more comfortable in the group.

Question: What do I do if there is a long silence in the group and I'm the group leader?

Landreth: That experience probably plagues the beginning group leader more than anything else that can happen in a group because most group leaders want something to be happening. The tendency is to assume that not much is going on if there is no verbal communication. If there is anything I have learned from working in groups, it's to be comfortable with silence. Just because there are no words being used doesn't mean there's no work. I think one of the things a skilled group counselor needs to do is to be able to distinguish between the working silence and a silence that is not really productive. I don't know how to describe that. When I sense or feel a silence is being productive, I am just comfortable with it. Then there are other silences where I feel not much is going on, and I feel comfortable to break that silence. I think one of the worst things that can happen to beginning group counselors is to get caught in the game of "Who's going to break the silence first?" That can be deadly because the group leader is sitting there determined not to break the silence, and there is a point where the group will not break the silence either and the leader may need to intervene. So the group leader needs to be sensitive to the group, sensitive to whether there is work going on, and then to be patient with silences that do occur.

Berg: There are different kinds of silences. One might be a resistant silence. If in the life of the group the group leader senses, and I use that word "sense" because we do so much of that, if the leader senses a resistance in a silence, I think the best thing the leader can do is to go back to the group as a whole and ask them to examine the silence, to take a look at themselves and their own behavior and what might be underlying the resistance.

Fall: Silence is often more disturbing to the leader than it is for the members. I often time the silence and ask the leader how long they thought it lasted. Invariably, the leader overestimates the duration. It is a real skill to learn to be comfortable with silence. If you can't develop a general level of comfort, then it will be much more difficult to tell the difference between productive and unproductive silences.

Landreth: Also, I think there is a tendency on the part of group leaders to think, "Whatever happens here is up to me," and so if there is a silence, it is up to the leader to do something. I feel comfortable in letting the group decide what to do with the silence. It's not always up to me. They can decide what to do next and maybe learn something in the process about their responsibility in this group.

Question: How structured or active do you think the group counselor should be in the group?

Berg: In a group with relatively little experience, I find myself busier, more active verbally, more structured in the initial phases. My involvement tends to decrease as time goes by and members assume more responsibility for themselves and the direction of the group. I don't favor a lot of prepackaged structure, other than ice-breakers at the beginning when people are anxious. Typically, I don't use a lot of structured activities in the group. My reason is that there is *always* something going on in the group. An important thing I have learned about myself is to trust my ability to read or sense what is going on in the group at any given time. A good permission giver for that trust is to forgive myself when I'm wrong. I don't mind making mistakes nearly as much as I might have at one time. If I can risk being wrong, it is a process that the group members can relate to. So I'm busier in the initial stages, modeling, and demonstrating to group members the types of responses I think are constructive and helpful. As I hear those words coming back to me from the group, I feel much more comfortable in sitting back and letting the group members help each other. Part of the learning, part of the group process, is for the members to learn not only to help themselves, but also to help others.

Landreth: Bob, one of the reasons we work so well together is that you focus on the modeling and helping members learn how to make helpful responses, while my initial tendency is to help the member get into the group and interact, thus to shift the responsibility to the group. In this process, members are really getting both sides, both ends of the continuum.

Fall: I think different types of groups call for different levels of structure. Psychoeducational and task groups naturally need more structure than counseling or psychotherapy groups. In counseling groups, I think structure is more appropriate in the beginning stages of group as a way to get the group started, but should taper off as the need [for] activity-based interaction is replaced with spontaneous connection and sharing.

Question: What do you feel is the optimal number of members per group?

Berg: Primarily, the groups I have in mind are process-oriented groups, and such groups function on the basis of several assumptions. One assumption is that the members are able to function in their lives and roles relatively well. They may run the range of normal to neurotic personality difficulties. Individuals who have personality problems or relationship difficulties serious enough to keep them from profiting from the group should be excluded. When group members are functioning interpersonally, at least minimally, the group leader can rely on group members helping each other, getting involved in the group process itself, learning from the process, and being a part of it. Interpersonal process groups tend to function best with seven to nine people in a group. If the group is much larger than that, people are not going to have the opportunity to get verbally involved in the process. If the group is smaller than that, there can be great pressure on people to contribute verbally. I don't like that.

Landreth: Groups for children in primary grades should have four or five members. For Grades 4, 5, and 6, probably about six members would be optimum for that age group.

Question: How do you get a cohesive group?

Landreth: My first reaction is that I don't know how to "get" a group to be cohesive. There are some things that I can do to contribute to a group becoming cohesive, but whether or not the group becomes cohesive is up to the group. A group leader may work as hard as he or she can, and the group may never become cohesive even though the leader is doing the same sort of things that he or she did in a group that became cohesive. I think the way I present myself initially contributes to the cohesiveness of a group. One of the things I have found about myself is that I can help people to feel safe with me or comfortable with me. I think that's because I feel comfortable with myself in that setting. Then, feeling safe and comfortable, they feel safe enough to risk saying something to me or other members or to reveal some part of their inner person. That's the beginning stage of moving toward cohesiveness. The crucial element, in addition to the sharing of self, is there must be interaction among the members. In groups where there is a focus on individual counseling in the group setting, it is almost impossible to develop cohesiveness because there is not interaction among group members. Members feel good about being there, but they don't have any sharing or interaction among themselves to make them a part of another person's life. I think interaction and sharing are crucial to the development of cohesion. When there is a feeling that I have been able to contribute in some way to your life, and you also have been able to contribute to my life, then a feeling of closeness develops and that is cohesion.

Berg: Cohesiveness is also related to the chemistry or makeup of the group. Some groups may never achieve true cohesiveness. Verbal participation is very important to the development of cohesion. There are some indicators that a group is becoming cohesive. Cohesiveness is a togetherness, a glue that keeps the group together. A cohesive group is one in which members assign priority to the life of the group itself. Attendance can indicate the level of cohesiveness of a group. In a cohesive group, people will attend and [will] miss other things to get there and be on time. Verbal interaction also tells you something about cohesiveness. How people begin to link themselves to other members' statements will tell you about cohesiveness. In a cohesive group, members tend to call each other and provide a support system during the week and will check on each other at the beginning of group session to see how things went during the week in relation to some person's problem. Also, some groups can become too cohesive; therefore, cohesiveness is not something you strive for and maintain at all costs. If a group becomes too cohesive, the members may begin to protect and rescue each other. This is something the group leader must be sensitive to and guard against.

Question: What factors would you want to consider as a group leader when screening potential group members?

Berg: One of my primary screening criteria is that a person have some other satisfactory interpersonal relationship outside and exclusive of the group. That can be any kind of relationship—spousal, romantic, friendship, family—but the kind that is chosen and satisfactory to both people. I check that out rather carefully. Groups are so interpersonal that if a member doesn't have a historical base of minimal social skills, this has to be achieved in some way in the group. That can get pretty neurotic and not very helpful for other group members.

I prefer heterogeneous groups. I have never preferred groups focused around a single problem. I enjoy personality differences and diversity. I like to have some assertive members and some members who are more passive. There's much that can be learned from differences in people. An exception would be if there is a person whose problem area is so profound at any given point that they would demand or need a large amount of group time; I would probably suggest that person get individual or concurrent counseling rather than relying totally on the group.

Fall: For me, the pre-group interview is a great way to see how the person interacts with people. You are getting insight into how the person will be in your group. I also assess the person's expectations and goals for group to see if they match with the group's intent. I agree with Bob: I am not looking for a group of one type of person, or even "great group members." I want different combinations of people in my group. For group to work best, it really needs to reflect the real world as much as possible in terms of backgrounds and personality styles. Unless the group is designed specifically for one particular disorder, I will screen out severe psychopathology (personality disorders, psychotic disorders, untreated mood or anxiety disorders) based on the level of care that would be appropriate.

Landreth: Typically, more attention is focused on screening group members as we go up the age scale. Perhaps that is because children have fewer problems interacting than adults. I know they experience their world just as intensely as we do. Or it could be that they are more resilient and more adjustable and capable in interacting with their peers despite their problems. Another possibility is that they are more accepting of the differences that occur in people. I also prefer a heterogeneous group. I like the challenge of "Now that we are together, what can we create?" For that reason, I'm not as cautious about putting a certain type of group together. I think we should screen because there are certain members who don't work out well in a group. I prefer not to work in a group focused on one particular problem. However, one of the most exciting groups I've led was a group of teenage chronic traffic violators. Other than that initial similarity, though, they were a very diverse group, and we seldom focused on their driving habits.

Question: What type of training do you think is necessary to become a group counselor?

Fall: The Association for Specialists in Group Work and CACREP [Council for Accreditation of Counseling and Related Educational Programs, counseling's accrediting body] have developed a very detailed description of group-work training standards. One class in group does not constitute complete training in my mind. I tend to rely on the triad of competency. The three elements include formal education, supervised clinical work, and continuing education.

Landreth: There are two experiences that are absolutely essential. One is that the group counselor be well read in the area of group counseling and have some formal training. However, the typical group-counseling course is not enough. It is essential that the group facilitator learn as much as can possibly be learned about himself or herself. In training, the group leader can learn skills to apply and certain things to do in specific situations, but when there is a real crisis in the group the ultimate tool the group leader has is his or her personality at that moment and the accompanying creativity and courage. How well these dimensions are utilized will depend on the group leader's acceptance of self. Therefore, I would recommend some personal group counseling. Perhaps from ten to fifteen group sessions that provide the potential group leader an opportunity to find out not only what it's like to be a member but also how other people react to him or her. If the group leader is not aware of how other people react to him, he will not be sensitive to how the group members see him. Most of all, the group leader must be open to learning about self from the group he leads. That does not mean I go into the group to work on my issues or focus on myself a lot, but secondarily in the learning experience to be open to learning about myself. Out of that comes a general presentation of self that others find helpful. One of the things that has been most helpful for me is to turn loose of the need to be helpful to everyone. There are some people who react to Bob in a positive way that would not react to me in that way.

Berg: Theory, techniques, and all the cognitive information we carry around [are] less important than who we are as persons. We need to understand human development, and we need to understand groups and how they work. We need to understand how people relate to each other, but the main thing we have going for us is how we utilize ourselves. So, in addition to experiencing group therapy, self-inspection must become an attitude, a way of life. I'm constantly amazed and sometimes scared about what I continue to learn about me, as far as how I relate to other people, how I see myself. The more I do that, the more I keep in touch with myself, and the more doors open for me. The payoff is that it's easier to be empathetic with others. To be more responsible for my own behavior helps me get outside of me and to be fully present with the group or with another person, wherever I am. This is not being self-obsessed. It's possible to be introspective without being self-obsessed.

Landreth: That process of introspection is one of happenings and learnings that aren't being looked for. It's like a discovery in the process of interacting in the group: "Look at that. Why am I feeling this? I wasn't aware of this in me," and then some self-awareness coming on the spot, maybe in the group.

Question: At what particular point would you terminate a participant in a group if the personality conflict gets to be really strong?

Landreth: There are basic guidelines. The individual is important. I will be sensitive to the individual. I do care about this person. I care about the individual more perhaps than the total group in terms of personal feeling. The individual is important, but not more important than the group, and the group is important, but not more than the individual. So it depends on whether the group is able to react in an appropriate way to that individual. If it seemed to me that the group, in terms of their reactions, was not handling a member very well, I feel very comfortable in removing a member.

I do it very gently and not abruptly in the middle of the session, but to talk with a member after the session about individual counseling, not continuing with the group at this time or perhaps individual counseling now and joining with another group at some point. I would never allow one member, I know that sounds like I'm in control and it's not all up to me, but I would not want to allow a member to destroy the group because I believe that the group is important too.

Berg: The bottom line is a clinical judgment. There are a few things that pop into my mind. One is when a person is so needy that they need to dominate group time or they just can't connect with other members of the group because everything in the group seems to remind them of their own problem. At that point, we need to ask the question "Is the group the best intervention system available for this particular person?" I don't have any qualms about saying to a person, "We may have made a mistake with regards to placement. Let's look at some other alternatives." If someone is very angry, whether they are aware of it or not, and that keeps popping out in the group, the group may not be the best place for that person. Oftentimes, it can be helpful to a group to learn to deal with conflict. But if it's a pervasive kind of thing and it goes on and on, that can become a problem. One of the problems with a person who is very different, by that I mean personality-wise quite different from the group norm, is that they can set themselves up as the scapegoat in the group. It's not helpful for the group members to find someone they can pick on and dump hostilities on. What typically happens is that it forces that person into a defensive posture that just perpetuates the problem. I don't view group as a panacea for the world's ills. In fact, in terms of intervention systems, I view groups as an adjunct, something people can profit from after they have done phase 1 individual work where they have taken care of their own intrapersonal dynamics. My preference would be that members of an adult group have had some individual counseling where they have looked at their primary relationships, examined their roots, looked at their history, and have a reasonably good handle on where they come from and why they behave in certain ways and are wanting to test out new ways of behaving in a social context.

Landreth: I'm less restrictive about who can join a group. In high school, junior high, and elementary school, where there may not be an opportunity for individual counseling, I would go ahead and put a group of children together without any concern about individual counseling unless there was a major emotional problem. Most children in public schools aren't going to be functioning in that setting very well if there is a major emotional problem. They will have already been removed and placed in a private school or diagnostic setting. Also, with adults, I feel free to take a group of people without delving too much into their background, other than some initial screening. If they have an eagerness to be in the group and to have that experience, I'll see how that works out and they can see how the group works out. As to the question about removing someone from the group, sometimes it is helpful to just call the person aside and discuss with them their own perception of how they are doing in the group or how the group is reacting to them. This may give them a chance to reveal their own apprehension about the group. They may reveal, without you even bringing it up, some other experience or a desire to not continue in the group. Or, if you're working with a long-term group, you may have the opportunity for a member to exit the group for three to four sessions, get some individual work, and be ready to come back into the group. I experienced that with a group of fifth-grade students. One little boy in the group, Erik, was the general of the school. He would strong-arm kids in the bathroom to get their lunch money. In the group, he was a physically active youngster, so much so that there were times when I had to physically restrain him. He was just so physically aggressive the group members kept a physical distance. There just wasn't much cohesiveness evolving because he kept people separated. After five sessions, he was removed from the group and placed in individual counseling. His removal came as a result of his own decision. The group had established a rule that in the group, members had to sit in the circle if they wanted to stay in the group. Failure to do so meant the member could not stay in the group and would have to go back to the classroom. Erik chose not to sit in the circle, so he chose to go back to his classroom. When I left to escort him to the classroom, the group came together physically just like a group of quail huddling up. It was a dramatic portrayal of how they felt separated because of him. Three weeks later, after individual counseling twice a week, he was able to come back into the group and function.

Question: If the group was involuntary, what would you do to minimize this impact on the group? I work with juvenile delinquents, and there are four to five strong-armers in the group. How do you minimize these four to five for the remaining members?

Landreth: My inclination is to go the other way, to help the group members react rather than my reacting to the disruptive member. I want to help the group members to become strong enough, perhaps with my support, and I think that would be a very indirect form of support, for them to discover that they could cope with that person. I think there is always the potential that they can be just as strong as that person is in reacting to him. They can really discover that they don't have to give in.

Berg: I would agree. Part of the frustration in dealing with involuntary issues is that it will slow the process down. Working with juvenile delinquents can be very taxing. Part of the problem in working with groups that are involuntary, such as groups of offenders, is that they have similar skills available to them. That's typically what's gotten them in trouble in the first place. They don't perceive a lot of options, in terms of behavior. In a group like that, you would have to be patient and do more teaching, modeling, pointing out, confronting of behaviors that have not worked in the past. If such behaviors had worked, these members wouldn't be where they are now. Even in involuntary groups, the leader has the right to exit a person if that person is being totally disruptive in the group. Again, that's a decision the leader has to make about the welfare of this person, the welfare of the group, and the welfare of the entire system. Even in a prison setting, the leader can exit a person.

Landreth: One thing that bothers me about the question is the indication there is nothing that can be done, that the individuals must be in the group. My preference would be that there is some opportunity for the member to not be present if the member chooses by his behavior not to be here. The other individuals in the group are important also, as is the person causing so much trouble. Sometimes, there is a decision that needs to be made for the welfare of the group. Do we allow this one member to destroy the whole group week after week? I would like some opportunity to have the member sit one or more sessions out for a while if possible.

Fall: Those are good points. I have worked for over ten years with court-mandated group members. The first thing I try to do is make sure they know they have a choice in whether or not they attend group. This is vital. If they cannot find their choice in the process, then group becomes a power struggle, a consequence. What is their choice? Well, they can choose to come see me or they can go to jail, or whatever else the court wants to do with them. That's not much of a choice, but it's a start. If I can help them see that choice from the beginning, then the foundation is laid to help them find other choices in the process. For example, the court says you have to be here, but you get to decide what you get out of the group. Also, if they can see the choice between group and jail, then when they do not abide by the rules of the group, it helps me frame their disruption as a choice to leave group (which means they are choosing jail).

Question: What would you consider a nonproductive session?

Berg: I could say there's no such thing. However, I have been bored in sessions. I have left groups feeling like I did not do as well as I would have liked to. I've left groups thinking that the group members did not do what I had hoped for them to do. My first answer is probably best. The second two probably have to do with my own need to be productive, my need to get somewhere. The more I can convince myself that individuals in groups will do what they need to do, the more I can let the river flow and certainly not try to push the river, then the more at peace and off the hook I'll feel. There is a theory in groups that if very little is going on, let the members sit that way until they get bored enough to go to work. I don't have a lot of that in me, though. At the same time, I do think the leader can take too much responsibility, and I believe that's a mistake. If a group decides to work, a group will come in one week and just work, work, work, and the leader will think, "That's terrific!" If they work like that every week, we're really going to get someplace. The next week, the group members go on vacation, and the leader may wonder if it's the same group. Those kinds of groups are OK with me.

Fall: *Productive* is a loaded word. Group is a process that flows, so it is very difficult to take one session and assess it without the whole. I have experiences [with] unproductive groups (as a whole), but even those have moments of movement. I have often found that my definition of *productive* is very different from my group members." I have also gotten great results from processing "bad" sessions. When I share my perceptions, I am amazed at the issues that emerge within the group. I actually look forward to slow parts of the process because it tends to act as a catalyst for the group.

Landreth: I have mixed reactions to that question because I have had some experiences where I went away from a session feeling, "This was a real bummer. Nothing happened," only to come back the next week and someone comes in, sits down, and says, "Last week was the most terrific session we've had. I learned so much about myself." I've had that happen many times, and I have concluded, for myself, that I can't evaluate whether it was a productive session for anyone else. Maybe it wasn't productive for me, but perhaps it was for someone else in the group. The reason I have mixed reactions is that there are typically some things that indicate the group is being productive. If there is sharing within the group, at a feeling level, and if individuals talk about themselves as opposed to activities, that does seem to be more productive. If the experience is one in which members personally react to each other and give feedback, we know that can be productive. We also know there are other experiences that perhaps we are not wise enough to discern that can be productive— as in a silence. There is a lot of work that can go on within a silence, and people can experience that as being a very productive time. I may sit there and not learn anything about myself during the silence and thus evaluate it as not very productive, but for someone else it may be a very productive time. My inclination is to try not to evaluate what is going on. And yet there is still a part of me that sometimes comes away from a group session saying, "This was a better session," or, "This was a session that seemed to be productive," or, "This was a session where we were struggling and I don't think very much happened here." So I still find myself making those kinds of evaluations in spite of the fact that I have learned otherwise.

Question: What special suggestions do you have for persons leading a group of people from multiracial backgrounds?

Berg: That is one thing I caution against for an inexperienced leader. Diversity groups can have tremendous potential benefit, but [are] not something recommended for a relatively inexperienced group leader. The group leader must first have general group counseling experience and a good acquaintance with the culture from which the members come. Cultural and ethnic differences make an enormous difference interpersonally.

Landreth: One of the reasons for this caution is such a group can be so volatile emotionally because of the members' lack of understanding of each other's cultural background. The members' own experiences may trigger some emotional reaction, and it's because of that potential volatile expression that the leader must be experienced.

Fall: ASGW has done a very nice job of developing the "Principles for Diversity-Competent Group Workers." This set of guidelines helps new and seasoned group workers explore some important aspects of leading groups in a pluralistic society. I enjoy considering how one's culture impacts the group's cohesion. Every group is a multicultural group, and each member's uniqueness has an opportunity to help the group grow and learn, or it can be an obstacle to growth. Honoring differences has long been a hallmark of group work, and so I try to get these issues out in the open as soon as possible.

Question: You briefly talked about resistance. Can you talk a little more about it: what you do, how you recognize it?

Berg: Silence is one of the primary and direct ways a group will exhibit resistance. Other ways are to ignore the deeper level of transactions and stay on surface topics, not directly deal with each other, and a reluctance to disclose oneself. I have a feeling, when I'm seeing those behaviors, that there is something wrong with the way in which we have dealt with the issues of purpose, commitment, and boundaries in the initial stages of the group. There are different ways to commit oneself to a group, but unless those issues are dealt with pretty specifically in the initial stages, at some time the group is going to hit bumps in the road. When the leader senses resistance, one of the best interventions is that the leader shares his feeling and/or reaction with the group. The leader could say, "Look, we don't seem to be doing what we agreed on initially. Let's look at why we're here, what it is we want to accomplish, and why it seems so hard for us as a group to trust one another." This will open up those issues for reexamination. I have found that the most resistances are related to safety and trust concerns at some level—either vague or specific. This is always a topic for examination.

Landreth: Resistance is not necessarily a negative thing. It may mean that the group is experiencing and exhibiting resistance because the members are aware that they are about to move into a deeper emotional period in the group. There may be some "getting ready" time that is necessary, and that time can be short-lived or long-lived depending on the group or how the leader reacts. So we don't always view resistance as something negative. There are times when I have experienced a group doing what I call *working at not working*, which is resistance. It appears on the surface that things are going great in the group. There may be a lot of interaction, a lot of talk, a lot of sharing. But the interaction is talk about why the group is not doing what they would like to do, why they aren't working, and what they need to do. Members go on and on and on about what the group needs to do, and everyone has a clear idea about what the group needs to do, but they continue to talk about what the group needs to do and why the group isn't doing it. Sometimes, it helps for the leader to identify that. Perhaps the leader could say, "As I listen, it seems to me that, as a group, we are working real hard at not working." Just mentioning that may be enough for the members to shift. I think sometimes groups get caught up in the process of analyzing the group's behavior, or they get caught up in the topic of the moment, and even though it's not what they really want to do, it's as if they are going downhill, and they don't know how to stop or aren't aware they're going downhill, and someone needs to say, "Hold it. Are you aware of what's happening?" As Bob said, "Is this what you want to discuss or spend your time doing at the moment?" You have to be ready for an answer either way. If the leader opens that up and the group says, "Yes," then what does the leader do? That may be a real test of the leader's acceptance. The leader must allow the group to set their own direction and to struggle with the process of accomplishing what they want.

Summary

Some of the significant issues in group counseling have been dealt with in this chapter. A strong recommendation has been presented for the scheduling of some group-counseling sessions more frequently than once a week. The issue of structuring has been discussed as a potential means for contributing to the development of interaction in groups. In all groups, some degree of structuring is present. Silences in group counseling are especially perplexing to inexperienced group facilitators who often feel that something observable must be going on in the group at all times. We have presented silence as a natural and dynamic part of the interactional process in groups. Contracting for behavioral change has been presented as a possible procedure for enhancing group activity, productivity, and cohesiveness.

An edited protocol discussed some frequently asked questions concerning group process and possible problem areas. Specific answers focused on possible solutions and areas for consideration for the developing group counselor.

References

Carrell, S., & Keenan, T. (2000). *Group exercises for adolescents*. Thousand Oaks, CA: Sage.

Carroll, M. R. (1970). Silence is the heart's size. *Personnel and Guidance Journal*, 48, 536–551.

Corder, B. F. (1994). *Structured adolescent psychotherapy groups*. Sarasota, FL: Professional Resource Press.

Crutchfield, L., & Garrett, M. T. (2001). Unity circle: A model of group work with children. In K. A. Fall and J. E. Levitov (Eds.), *Modern application to group work* (pp. 3–18). Huntington, NY: Nova Science.

Devencenzi, J., & Pendergast, S. (1988). *Belonging: Self and social discovery for children of all ages*. San Luis Obispo, CA: Belonging.

Donigian, J., & Molnati, R. (1997). *Systemic group therapy: A triadic model*. Pacific Grove, CA: Brooks/Cole.

Drucker, C. (2003). Group counseling in the middle and junior high school. In K. R. Greenberg (Ed.), *Group counseling in K–12 schools*. New York: Allyn & Bacon.

Fall, K. A., & MacMahon, H. G. (2001). Engaging adolescent males: A group approach. In K. A. Fall and J. E. Levitov (Eds.), *Modern application to group work* (pp. 43–68). Huntington, NY: Nova Science.

Huss, S. (2001). Groups for bereaved children. In K. A. Fall and J. E. Levitov (Eds.), *Modern application to group work* pp. 19–42). Huntington, NY: Nova Science.

Jacobs, E. E., Harvill, R. L., & Masson, R. L. (2006). *Group counseling: Strategies and skills* (5th ed.). Pacific Grove, CA: Brooks/Cole.

Khalsa, S. S. (1996). *Group exercises for enhancing social skills and self esteem*. Sarasota, FL: Professional Resource.

Kottler, J. E. (2001). *Learning group leadership: An experiential approach*. Boston, MA: Allyn & Bacon.

Landy, L. (1992). *Child support through small group counseling*. Charlotte, NC: Kidsrights.

Lane, K. (1991). *Feelings are real: Group activities for children*. Muncie, IN: Accelerated Development.

Walker, E. (2000). *Helping at-risk students: A group counseling approach for grades 6–9*. New York: Guilford.

APPENDIX F

ASGW PRINCIPLES FOR DIVERSITY-COMPETENT GROUP WORKERS

Note: From Haley-Banez, L. et al. (1999). Association for specialists in group work principles for diversity-competent group workers. *Journal for Specialists in Group Work 24* (1). Taylor & Francis Group, LLC. No further reproduction is permitted without written permission of Taylor & Francis Group, LLC.
Approved by the ASGW Executive Board, August 1, 1998
Prepared by Lynn Haley-Bañez, Sherlon Brown, and Bogusia Molina
Consultants: Michael D'Andrea, Patricia Arrendondo, Niloufer Merchant, and Sandra Wathen

Preamble

The Association for Specialists in Group Work (ASGW) is committed to understanding how issues of diversity affect all aspects of group work. This includes but is not limited to training diversity-competent group workers; conducting research that will add to the literature on group work with diverse populations; understanding how diversity affects group process and dynamics; and assisting group facilitators in various settings to increase their awareness, knowledge, and skills as they relate to facilitating groups with diverse memberships.

As an organization, ASGW has endorsed this document with the recognition that issues of diversity affect group process and dynamics, group facilitation, training, and research. As an organization, we recognize that racism, classism, sexism, heterosexism, ableism, and so forth affect everyone. As individual members of this organization, it is our personal responsibility to address these issues through awareness, knowledge, and skills. As members of ASGW, we need to increase our awareness of our own biases, values, and beliefs and how they impact the groups we run. We need to increase our awareness of our group members' biases, values, and beliefs and how they also impact and influence group process and dynamics. Finally, we need to increase our knowledge in facilitating, with confidence, competence, and integrity, groups that are diverse on many dimensions.

Definitions

For the purposes of this document, it is important that the language used is understood. Terms such as *dominant*, *nondominant*, and *target* persons and/or populations are used to define a person or groups of persons who historically, in the USA, do not have equal access to power, money, certain privileges (such as access to mental health services because of financial constraints, or the legal right to marry in the case of a gay or lesbian couple), and/or the ability to influence or initiate social policy because of unequal representation in government and politics. These terms are not used to denote a lack of numbers in terms of representation in the overall US population. Nor are these terms used to continue to perpetuate the very biases and forms of oppression, both overt and covert, that this document attempts to address.

For the purposes of this document, the term *disabilities* refers to differences in physical, mental, emotional, and learning abilities and styles among people. It is not meant as a term to define a person, such as a learning disabled person, but rather in the context of a person with a learning disability.

Given the history and current cultural, social, and political context in which this document is written, the authors of this document are limited to the language of this era. With this in mind, we have attempted to construct a "living document" that can and will change as the sociopolitical and cultural context changes.

The Principles

- awareness of self;
- attitudes and beliefs.

Diversity-competent group workers demonstrate movement from being unaware to being increasingly aware and sensitive to their own race, ethnic and cultural heritage, gender, socioeconomic status (SES), sexual orientation, abilities, and religion and spiritual beliefs, and to valuing and respecting differences.

Diversity-competent group workers demonstrate increased awareness of how their own race, ethnicity, culture, gender, SES, sexual orientation, abilities, and religion and spiritual beliefs are impacted by their own experiences and histories, which in turn influence group process and dynamics.

Diversity-competent group workers can recognize the limits of their competencies and expertise with regard to working with group members who are different from them in terms of race, ethnicity, culture (including language), SES, gender, sexual orientation, abilities, religion, and spirituality and their beliefs, values, and biases. (For further clarification on limitations, expertise, and type of group work, refer to the training standards and best practice guidelines, Association for Specialists in Group Work, 1998; and the ethical guidelines, American Counseling Association, 1995.)

Diversity-competent group workers demonstrate comfort, tolerance, and sensitivity with differences that exist between themselves and group members in terms of race, ethnicity, culture, SES, gender, sexual orientation, abilities, religion, and spirituality and their beliefs, values, and biases.

Knowledge

Diversity-competent group workers can identify specific knowledge about their own race, ethnicity, SES, gender, sexual orientation, abilities, religion, and spirituality, and how they personally and professionally affect their definitions of "normality" and the group process.

Diversity-skilled group workers demonstrate knowledge and understanding regarding how oppression in any form—such as racism, classism, sexism, heterosexism, ableism, discrimination, and stereotyping—affects them personally and professionally.

Diversity-skilled group workers demonstrate knowledge about their social impact on others. They are knowledgeable about communication style differences, how their style may inhibit or foster the group process with members who are different from themselves along the different dimensions of diversity, and how to anticipate the impact they may have on others.

Skills

Diversity-competent group workers seek out educational, consultative, and training experiences to improve their understanding and effectiveness in working with group members who self-identify as Indigenous Peoples, African Americans, Asian Americans, Hispanics, Latinos/Latinas, gays, lesbians, bisexuals, transgendered persons, and/or persons with physical, mental/emotional, and/or learning disabilities, particularly with regard to race and ethnicity. Within this context, group workers are able to recognize the limits of their competencies and (a) seek consultation, (b) seek further training or education, (c) refer members to more qualified group workers, or (d) engage in a combination of these.

Group workers who exhibit diversity competence are constantly seeking to understand themselves within their multiple identities (apparent and unapparent differences), for example, gay, Latina, Christian, working class and female, and are constantly and actively striving to unlearn the various behaviors and processes they covertly and overtly communicate that perpetuate oppression, particularly racism.

Group Worker's Awareness of Group Member's Worldview

Attitudes and Beliefs

Diversity-skilled group workers exhibit awareness of any possible negative emotional reactions toward Indigenous Peoples, African Americans, Asian Americans, Hispanics, Latinos/Latinas, gays, lesbians, bisexuals, transgendered persons, and/or persons with physical, mental/emotional, and/or learning disabilities that they may hold. They are willing to contrast in a nonjudgmental manner their own beliefs and attitudes with those of Indigenous Peoples, African Americans, Asian Americans, Hispanics, Latinos/Latinas, gays, lesbians, bisexuals, transgendered persons, and persons with physical, mental/emotional, and/or learning disabilities who are group members.

Diversity-competent group workers demonstrate awareness of the stereotypes and preconceived notions that they may hold toward Indigenous Peoples, African Americans, Asian Americans, Hispanics, Latinos/Latinas, gays, lesbians, bisexuals, transgendered persons, and persons with physical, mental/emotional, and/or learning disabilities.

Knowledge

Diversity-skilled group workers possess specific knowledge and information about Indigenous Peoples, African Americans, Asian Americans, Hispanics, Latinos/Latinas, gays, lesbians, bisexuals, transgendered people, and group members who have mental/emotional, physical, and/or learning disabilities with whom they are working. They are aware of the life experiences, cultural heritage, and sociopolitical background of Indigenous Peoples, African Americans, Asian Americans, Hispanics, Latinos/Latinas, gays, lesbians, bisexuals, transgendered persons, and group members with physical, mental/emotional, and/or learning disabilities. This particular knowledge-based competency is strongly linked to the various racial/minority and sexual identity development models available in the literature (Atkinson, Morten, & Sue 1993; Cass 1979; Cross 1995; D'Augelli & Patterson 1995; Helms 1992).

Diversity-competent group workers exhibit an understanding of how race, ethnicity, culture, gender, sexual identity, different abilities, SES, and other immutable personal characteristics may affect personality formation, vocational choices, manifestation of psychological disorders, physical "dis-ease" or somatic symptoms, help-seeking behavior(s), and the appropriateness or inappropriateness of the various types of and theoretical approaches to group work.

Group workers who demonstrate competency in diversity in groups understand and have the knowledge about sociopolitical influences that impinge upon the lives of Indigenous Peoples, African Americans, Asian Americans, Hispanics, Latinos/Latinas, gays, lesbians, bisexuals, transgendered persons, and persons with physical, mental/emotional, and/or learning disabilities. Immigration issues, poverty, racism, oppression, stereotyping, and/or powerlessness adversely impact many of these individuals and therefore impact group process or dynamics.

Skills

Diversity-skilled group workers familiarize themselves with relevant research and the latest findings regarding mental health issues of Indigenous Peoples, African Americans, Asian Americans, Hispanics, Latinos/Latinas, gays, lesbians, bisexuals, transgendered persons, and persons with physical, mental/emotional, and/or learning disabilities. They actively seek out educational experiences that foster their knowledge and understanding of skills for facilitating groups across differences.

Diversity-competent group workers become actively involved with Indigenous Peoples, African Americans, Asian Americans, Hispanics, Latinos/Latinas, gays, lesbians, bisexuals, transgendered persons, and persons with physical, mental/emotional, and/or learning disabilities outside of their group work/counseling setting (community events, social and political functions, celebrations, friendships, neighborhood groups, etc.) so that their perspective of minorities is more than academic or experienced through a third party.

Diversity-Appropriate Intervention Strategies

Attitudes and Beliefs

Diversity-competent group workers respect clients' religious and/or spiritual beliefs and values, because they affect worldview, psychosocial functioning, and expressions of distress.

Diversity-competent group workers respect indigenous helping practices; respect Indigenous Peoples, African Americans, Asian Americans, Hispanics, Latinos/Latinas, gays, lesbians, bisexuals, transgendered persons, and persons with physical, mental/emotional, and/or learning disabilities; and can identify and utilize community intrinsic help-giving networks.

Diversity-competent group workers value bilingualism and sign language and do not view another language as an impediment to group work.

Knowledge

Diversity-competent group workers demonstrate a clear and explicit knowledge and understanding of generic characteristics of group work and theory and how they may clash with the beliefs, values, and traditions of Indigenous Peoples, African Americans, Asian Americans, Hispanics, Latinos/Latinas, gays, lesbians, bisexuals, transgendered persons, and persons with physical, mental/emotional, and/or learning disabilities.

Diversity-competent group workers exhibit an awareness of institutional barriers that prevent Indigenous Peoples, African Americans, Asian Americans, Hispanics, Latinos/Latinas, gays, lesbians, bisexuals, transgendered members, and members with physical, mental/emotional, and/or learning disabilities from actively participating in or using various types of groups (that is, task groups, psychoeducational groups, counseling groups, and psychotherapy groups) or the settings in which the services are offered.

Diversity-competent group workers demonstrate knowledge of the potential bias in assessment instruments and use procedures and interpret findings, or actively participate in various types of evaluations of group outcome or success, keeping in mind the linguistic, cultural, and other self-identified characteristics of the group member.

Diversity-competent group workers exhibit knowledge of the family structures, hierarchies, values, and beliefs of Indigenous Peoples, African Americans, Asian Americans, Hispanics, Latinos/Latinas, gays, lesbians, bisexuals, transgendered persons, and persons with physical, mental/emotional, and/or learning disabilities. They are knowledgeable about the community characteristics, the resources in the community, and the family.

Diversity-competent group workers demonstrate an awareness of relevant discriminatory practices at the social and community level that may be affecting the psychological welfare of persons and access to services of the population being served.

Skills

Diversity-competent group workers are able to engage in a variety of verbal and nonverbal group-facilitating functions, dependent upon the type of group (task, counseling, psychoeducational, or psychotherapy) and the multiple, self-identified statuses of various group members (such as Indigenous Peoples, African Americans, Asian Americans, Hispanics, Latinos/Latinas, gays, lesbians, bisexuals, transgendered persons, and persons with physical, mental/emotional, and/or learning disabilities). They demonstrate the ability to send and receive both verbal and nonverbal messages accurately, appropriately, and across or between the differences represented in the group. They are not tied down to one method or approach to group facilitation and recognize that helping styles and approaches may be culture bound. When they sense that their group facilitation style is limited and potentially inappropriate, they can anticipate and ameliorate its negative impact by drawing upon other culturally relevant skill sets.

Diversity-competent group workers have the ability to exercise institutional intervention skills on behalf of their group members. They can help a member determine whether a "problem" with the institution stems from the oppression of Indigenous Peoples, African Americans, Asian Americans, Hispanics, Latinos/Latinas, gays, lesbians, bisexuals, trans-gendered persons, and persons with physical, mental/emotional, and/or learning disabilities, such as in the case of developing or having a "healthy" paranoia, so that group members do not inappropriately personalize problems.

Diversity-competent group workers do not exhibit a reluctance to seek consultation with traditional healers and religious and spiritual healers and practitioners, when appropriate, in the treatment of members who are self-identified Indigenous Peoples, African Americans, Asian Americans, Hispanics, Latinos/Latinas, gays, lesbians, bisexuals, transgendered persons, and/or group members with mental/emotional, physical, and/or learning disabilities.

Diversity-competent group workers take responsibility for interacting in the language requested by the group member(s) and, if not feasible, make an appropriate referral. A serious problem arises when the linguistic skills of a group worker and a group member or members, including sign language, do not match. The same problem occurs when the linguistic skills of one member or several members do not match. This being the case, the group worker should (a) seek a translator with cultural knowledge and appropriate professional background, and (b) refer to a knowledgeable, competent, bilingual group worker or a group worker competent or certified in sign language. In some cases, it may be necessary to have a group for group members of similar languages or to refer the group member for individual counseling.

Diversity-competent group workers are trained and have expertise in the use of traditional assessment and testing instruments related to group work, such as in screening potential members, and they also are aware of the cultural biases and limitations of these tools and processes. This allows them to use the tools for the welfare of diverse group members following culturally appropriate procedures.

Diversity-competent group workers attend to as well as work to eliminating biases, prejudices, oppression, and discriminatory practices. They are cognizant of how socio-political contexts may affect evaluation and provision of group work and should develop sensitivity to issues of oppression, racism, sexism, heterosexism, classism, and so forth.

Diversity-competent group workers take responsibility in educating their group members to the processes of group work, such as goals, expectations, legal rights, sound ethical practice, and the group worker's theoretical orientation with regard to facilitating groups with diverse membership.

Conclusion

This document is the "starting point" for group workers as we become increasingly aware, knowledgeable, and skillful in facilitating groups whose memberships represent the diversity of our society. It is not intended to be a "how-to" document. It is written as a call to action and/or a guideline and represents ASGW's commitment to moving forward with an agenda for addressing and understanding the needs of the populations we serve. Using this as a "living document," the ASGW acknowledges the changing world in which we live and work and therefore recognizes that this is the first step in working with diverse group members with competence, compassion, respect, and integrity. As our awareness, knowledge, and skills develop, so too will this document evolve. As our knowledge as a profession grows in this area and as the sociopolitical context in which this document was written changes, new editions of these "Principles for Diversity-Competent Group Workers" will arise. The operationalization of this document (article in process) will begin to define appropriate group leadership skills and interventions as well as make recommendations for research in understanding how diversity in group membership affects group process and dynamics.

References

American Counseling Association. (1995). *Code of ethics and standards.* Alexandria, VA: ACA.

Association for Specialists in Group Work. (1998). Best practice guidelines. *Journal for Specialists in Group Work, 23,* 237–244.

Atkinson, D. R., Morten, G., & Sue, D. W. (Eds.). (1993). *Counseling American minorities* (4th ed.). Madison, WI: Brown & Benchmark.

Cass, V. C. (1979). Homosexual identity formation: A theoretical model. *Journal of Homosexuality, 4,* 219–236.

Cross, W. E. (1995). The psychology of Nigrescence: Revising the Cross model. In J. G. Ponterotto, J. M. Casas, L. A. Suzuki, & C. M. Alexander (Eds.), *Handbook of multicultural counseling* (pp. 93–122). Thousand Oaks, CA: Sage.

D'Augelli, A. R., & Patterson, C. J. (Eds.). (1995). *Lesbian, gay and bisexual identities over the lifespan.* New York: Oxford University Press.

Helms, J. E. (1992). *A race is a nice thing to have.* Topeka, KS: Context Communications.

APPENDIX G

ASGW ETHICAL GUIDELINES FOR GROUP COUNSELORS

Preamble

One characteristic of any professional group is the possession of a body of knowledge, skills, and voluntarily self-professed standards for ethical practice. A Code of Ethics consists of those standards that have been formally and publicly acknowledged by the members of a profession to serve as the guidelines for professional conduct, discharge of duties, and the resolution of more moral dilemmas. By this document, the Association for Specialists in Group Work (ASGW) has identified the standards of conduct appropriate for ethical behavior among its members.

ASGW recognizes the basic commitment of its members to the Ethical Standards of its parent organization, the American Association for Counseling and Development (AACD) and nothing in this document shall be construed to supplant that code. These standards are intended to complement AACD standards in the area of group work by clarifying the nature of ethical responsibility of the counselor in the group setting and by stimulating a greater concern for competent group leadership.

The group counselor is expected to be a professional agent and to take the processes of ethical responsibility seriously. ASGW views "ethical process" as being integral to group work and views group counselors as "ethical agents." Group counselors, by their very nature in being responsible and responsive to their group members, necessarily embrace a certain potential for ethical vulnerability. It is incumbent upon group counselors to give considerable attention to the intent and context of their actions because the attempts of counselors to influence human behavior through group work always have ethical implications.

The following ethical guidelines have been developed to encourage ethical behavior of group counselors. These guidelines are written for students and practitioners, and are meant to stimulate reflection, self-examination, and discussion of issues and practices. They address the group counselor's responsibility for providing information about group work to clients and the group counselor's responsibility for providing group counseling services to clients. A final section discusses the group counselor's responsibility for safeguarding ethical practice and procedures for reporting unethical behavior. Group counselors are expected to make these standards known to group members.

Ethical Guidelines

Orientation and Providing Information

Group counselors adequately prepare prospective or new group member[s] by providing as much information about the existing or proposed group as necessary. Minimally, information related to each of the following areas should be provided.

Entrance procedures, time parameters of the group experience, group participation expectations, methods of payment (where appropriate), and termination procedures are explained by the group counselor as appropriate to the level of maturity of group.

Group counselors have available for distribution a professional disclosure statement that includes information on the group counselor's qualifications and group services that can be provided, particularly as related to the nature and purpose(s) of the specific group.

Group counselors communicate the role expectations, rights, [and] responsibilities of group members and group counselors(s).

The group goals are stated as concisely as possible by the group counselor, including "whose" goal it is (the group counselor's, the institution's, the parent's, the law's, society's, etc.) and the role of group members in influencing or determining the group's goal(s).

Group counselors explore with group members the risks of potential life changes that may occur because of the group experience and help members explore their readiness to face these possibilities.

Group members are informed by the group counselor of unusual or experimental procedures that might be expected in their group experience.

Group counselors explain, as realistically as possible, what services can and cannot be provide[d] within the particular group structure offered.

Group counselors emphasize the need to promote full psychological functioning and presence among group members. They inquire from prospective group members whether they are using any kind of drug or medication that may affect functioning in the group. They do not permit any use of alcohol and/or illegal drugs during group sessions and they discourage the use of alcohol and/or drugs (legal or illegal) prior to group meetings which may affect the physical or emotional presence of the member or other group members.

Group counselors inquire from prospective group members whether they have ever been a client in counseling or psychotherapy. If a prospective group member is already in a counseling relationship with another professional person, the group counselor advises the prospective group member to notify the other professional of his or her participation in the group.

Group counselors clearly inform group members about the policies pertaining to the group counselor's willingness to consult with them between group sessions.

In establishing fees for group counseling services, group counselors consider the financial status and the locality of prospective group members. Group members are not charged fees for group sessions where the group counselor is not present and the policy of charging for sessions missed by a group member is clearly communicated. Fees for participating as a group member are contracted between group counselor and group member for a specified period of time. Group counselors do not increase fees for group counseling services until the existing contracted fee structure has expired. In the event that the established fee structure is inappropriate for a prospective member, group counselors assist in finding comparable services of acceptable cost.

Screening of Members

The group counselor screens prospective group members (when appropriate to their theoretical orientation). Insofar as possible, the counselor selects group members whose needs and goals are compatible with the goals of the group, who will not impede the group process, and whose well-being will not be jeopardized by the group experience. An orientation to the group (i.e. ASGW Ethical Guideline #1) is included during the screening process.

Screening may be accomplished in one or more ways, such as the following:

- individual interview;
- group interview of prospective group members;
- interview as part of a team staffing; and
- completion of a written questionnaire by prospective group members.

Confidentiality

- Group counselors protect members by defining clearly what confidentiality means, why it is important, and the difficulties involved in enforcement.
- Group counselors take steps to protect members by defining confidentiality and the limits of confidentiality (i.e. when a group member's condition indicates that there is clear and imminent danger to the member, others, or physical property, the group counselor takes reasonable personal action and/or informs responsible authorities).
- Group counselors stress the importance of confidentiality and set a norm of confidentiality regarding all group participants' disclosures. The importance of maintaining confidentiality is emphasized before the group begins and various times in the group. The fact that confidentiality cannot be guaranteed is clearly stated.
- Members are made aware of difficulties involved in enforcing and ensuring confidentiality in a group setting. The counselor provides examples of how confidentiality can nonmaliciously be broken to increase members' awareness, and helps to lessen the likelihood that this breach of confidence will occur. Group counselors inform group members about the potential consequences of intentionally breaching confidentiality.
- Group counselors can only ensure confidentiality on their part and not on the part of the members.
- Group counselors video or audio tape a group session only with the prior consent and the members' knowledge of how the tape will be used.
- When working with minors, the group counselor specifies the limits of confidentiality.
- Participants in a mandatory group are made aware of any reporting procedures required of the group counselor.
- Group counselors store or dispose of group members' record[s] (written, audio, video, etc.) in ways that maintain confidentiality.
- Instructors of group counseling courses maintain the anonymity of group members whenever discussing group counseling cases.

Voluntary/Involuntary Participation

- Group counselors inform members whether participation is voluntary or involuntary.
- Group counselors take steps to ensure informed consent procedures in both voluntary and involuntary groups.
- When working with minors in a group, counselors are expected to follow the procedures specified by the institution in which they are practicing.

- With involuntary groups, every attempt is made to enlist the cooperation of the members and their continuance in the group on a voluntary basis.
- Group counselors do not certify that group treatment has been received by members who merely attend sessions, but did not meet the defined group expectations. Group members are informed about the consequences for failing to participate in a group.

Leaving a Group

- Provisions are made to assist a group member to terminate in an effective way.
- Procedures to be followed for a group member who chooses to exit a group prematurely are discussed by the counselor with all group members either before the group begins, during a prescreening interview, or during the initial group session.
- In the case of legally mandated group counseling, group counselors inform members of the possible consequences for premature self-termination.
- Ideally, both the group counselor and the member can work cooperatively to determine the degree to which a group experience is productive or counterproductive for that individual.
- Members ultimately have a right to discontinue membership in the group, at a designated time, if the predetermined trial period proves to be unsatisfactory.
- Members have the right to exit a group, but it is important that they be made aware of the importance of informing the counselor and the group members prior to deciding to leave. The counselor discusses the possible risks of leaving the group prematurely with a member who is considering this option.
- Before leaving a group, the group counselor encourages members (if appropriate) to discuss their reasons for wanting to discontinue membership in the group. Counselors intervene if other members use undue pressure to force a member to remain in the group.

Coercion and Pressure

- Group counselors protect member rights against physical threats, intimidation, coercion, and undue peer pressure insofar as is reasonably possible.
- It is essential to differentiate between "therapeutic pressure" that is part of any group and "undue pressure," which is not therapeutic.
- The purpose of a group is to help participants find their own answer, not to pressure them into doing what the group thinks is appropriate.
- Counselors exert care not to coerce participants to change in directions which they clearly state they do not choose.
- Counselors have a responsibility to intervene when other[s] use undue pressure or attempt to persuade member[s] against they [sic] will.
- Counselors intervene when any member attempts to act out aggression in a physical way that might harm another member or themselves.
- Counselors intervene when a member is verbally abusive or inappropriately confrontive to another member.

Imposing Counselor Values

- Group counselors develop an awareness of their own values and needs and the potential impact they have on the intervention likely to be made.

- Although group counselors take care to avoid imposing their values on members, it is appropriate that they expose their own beliefs, decisions, needs, and values, when concealing them would create problems for the members.
- There are value[s] implicit in any group, and these are made clear to potential members before they join the group. (Examples of certain values include; expressing feelings, being direct and honest, sharing personal material with others, learning how to trust, improving interpersonal communication, and deciding for oneself.)
- Personal and professional needs of group counselors are not met at the members' expense.
- Group counselors avoid using the group for their own therapy.
- Group counselors are aware of their own values and assumptions, and how these apply in a multicultural context.
- Group counselors take steps to increase their awareness of ways that their personal reactions to members might inhibit the group process and they monitor their counter transference. Through an awareness of the impact of stereotyping and discrimination (i.e. biases based on age, disability, ethnicity, gender, race, religion, or sexual preference), group counselors guard the individual rights and personal dignity of all group members.

Equitable Treatment

- Group counselors make every reasonable effort to treat each member individually and equally.
- Group counselors recognize and respect differences (e.g., cultural, racial, religious, lifestyle, age, disability, gender) among group members.
- Group counselors maintain an awareness of their behavior toward individual group members and are alert to the potential detrimental effects of favoritism or partiality toward any particular group member to the exclusion or detriment of any other member(s). It is likely that group counselors will favor some members over others, yet all group members deserve to be treated equally.
- Group counselors ensure equitable use of group time for each member by inviting silent members to become involved, acknowledging nonverbal attempts to communicate, and discouraging rambling and monopolizing of time by members.
- If a large group is planned, counselors consider enlisting another qualified professional to serve as a co-leader for the group sessions.

Dual Relationships

- Group counselors avoid dual relationships with group members that might impair their objectivity and professional judgment, as well as those which are likely to compromise a group member's ability to participate fully in the group.
- Group counselors do not misuse their professional role and power as group leader to advance personal or social contacts with members throughout the duration of the group.
- Group counselors do not use their professional relationship with group members to further their own interest either during the group or after the termination of the group.
- Sexual intimacies between group counselors and members are unethical.
- Group counselors do not barter (exchange) professional services with group members for services.
- Group counselors do not admit their own family member[s], relatives, employees, or personal friends as member[s] to their groups.

- Group counselors discuss with group members the potential detrimental effects of group members engaging in intimate intermember relationships outside of the group.
- Students who participate in a group as a partial course requirement for a group course are not evaluated for an academic grade based upon their degree of participation as a member in a group. Instructors of group counseling courses take steps to minimize the possible negative impact on students when they participate in a group course by separating course grades from participation in the group and by allowing students to decide what issues to explore and when to stop.
- It is inappropriate to solicit members from a class (or institutional affiliation) for one's private counseling or therapeutic group.

Use of Techniques

- Group counselors do not attempt any technique unless trained in its use or under supervision by a counselor familiar with the intervention.
- Group counselors are able to articulate a theoretical orientation that guides their practice, and they are able to provide a rationale for their interventions.
- Depending upon the type of an intervention, group counselors have training commensurate with the potential impact of a technique.
- Group counselors are aware of the necessity to modify their techniques to fit the unique needs of various cultural and ethnic groups.
- Group counselors assist members in translating in-group learning to daily life.

Goal Development

- Group counselors make every effort to assist members in developing their personal goals.
- Group counselors use their skills to assist members in making their goals specific so that others present in the group will understand the nature of the goal.
- Throughout the course of a group, group counselors assist members in assessing the degree to which personal goals are being met, and assist in revising any goals when it is appropriate.
- Group counselors help members clarify the degree to which the goals can be met within the context of a particular group.

Consultation

- Group counselors develop and explain policies about between-session consultation to group members.
- Group counselors take care to make certain that members do not use between-session consultation to avoid dealing with issues pertaining to the group that would be dealt with best in the group.
- Group counselors urge member[s] to bring the issues discussed during between-session consultations into the group if they pertain to the group.
- Group counselors seek out consultation and/or supervision regarding ethical concerns or when encountering difficulties which interfere with their effective functioning as group leaders.
- Group counselors seek appropriate professional assistance for their own personal problems or conflicts that are likely to impair their professional judgment and work performance.

- Group counselors discuss their group cases only for professional consultation and educational purposes.
- Group counselors inform members about policies regarding whether consultations will be held confidential.

Termination from the Group

- Depending upon the purpose of participation in the group, counselors promote termination of members from the group in the most efficient period of time.
- Group counselors maintain a constant awareness of the progress made by each group member and periodically invite the group members to explore and reevaluate their experiences in the group. It is the responsibility of group counselors to help promote the independence of members from the group in a timely manner.

Evaluation and Follow-up

- Group counselors make every attempt to engage in ongoing assessment and to design follow-up procedures for their groups.
- Group counselors recognize the importance of ongoing assessment of a group, and they assist members in evaluating their own progress.
- Group counselors conduct evaluation of the total group experience at the final meeting (or before termination), as well as ongoing evaluation.
- Group counselors monitor their own behavior and become aware of what they are modeling in the group.
- Follow-up procedures might take the form of personal contact, telephone contact, or written contact.
- Follow-up meetings might be with individuals, or groups, or both to determine the degree to which; (i) members have reached their goals, (ii) the group had a positive or negative effect on the participants, (iii) members could profit from some type of referral, and (iv) information could be used for possible modification of future groups. If there is no follow-up meeting, provisions are made available for individual follow-up meetings to any member who needs or requests such a contact.

Referrals

- If the needs of a particular member cannot be met within the type of group being offered, the group counselor suggests other appropriate professional referrals.
- Group counselors are knowledgeable of local community resources for assisting group members regarding professional referrals.
- Group counselors help members seek further professional assistance, if needed.

Professional Development

- Group counselors recognize that professional growth is a continuous, ongoing, developmental process throughout their career.
- Group counselors maintain and upgrade their knowledge and skill competencies through educational activities, clinical experiences, and participation in professional development activities.
- Group counselors keep abreast of research findings and new developments as applied to groups.

Safeguarding Ethical Practice and Procedures for Reporting Unethical Behavior

The preceding remarks have been advanced as guidelines which are generally representative of ethical and professional group practice. They have not been proposed as rigidly defined prescriptions. However, practitioners who are thought to be grossly unresponsive to the ethical concerns addressed in this document may be subject to review of their practices by ACA Ethics Committee and ASGW peers.

For consultation and/or questions regarding these ASGW Ethical Guidelines or group ethical dilemmas, you may contact the Chairperson of the ASGW Ethics Committee. The name, address, and telephone number of the current ASGW Ethics Committee Chairperson may be acquired by telephoning the ACA office in Alexandria, Virginia, at (703) 823–9800.

If group counselors' behavior is suspected as being unethical, the following procedures are to be followed.

Collect more information and investigate further to confirm the unethical practice as determined by the ASGW Ethical Guidelines.

Confront the individual with the apparent violation of ethical guidelines for the purposes of protecting the safety of any clients and to help the group counselor correct any inappropriate behaviors. If satisfactory resolution is not reached through this contact, then:

A complaint should be made in writing, including the specific facts and dates of the alleged violation and all relevant supporting data. The complaint should be included in an envelope marked "CONFIDENTIAL" to ensure confidentiality for both the accuser(s) and the alleged violator(s) and forwarded to all of the following sources:

- The name and address of the Chairperson of the State Counselor Licensure Board for the respective state, if in existence.
- The Ethics Committee, c/o The President, American Counseling Association, 5999 Stevenson Avenue, Alexandria, Virginia 22304
- The name and address of all private credentialing agencies in which the alleged violator maintains credentials or holds professional membership.

INDEX

Please note that references to Figures/Tables are in *italic* print